UNDER ORDERS

The Diary of a Racehorse Owner's Husband

JOHN TIMPSON

IN ASSOCIATION WITH

The Social Side of Racing

ECLIPSEMAGAZINE.CO.UK

ICON

Published in the UK in 2016
by Icon Books Ltd, Omnibus Business Centre,
39–41 North Road, London N7 9DP
email: info@iconbooks.com
www.iconbooks.com

Sold in the UK, Europe and Asia
by Faber & Faber Ltd, Bloomsbury House,
74–77 Great Russell Street,
London WC1B 3DA or their agents

Distributed in the UK, Europe and Asia
by Grantham Book Services,
Trent Road, Grantham NG31 7XQ

Distributed in the USA
by Publishers Group West,
1700 Fourth Street, Berkeley, CA 94710

Distributed in Australia and New Zealand
by Allen & Unwin Pty Ltd,
PO Box 8500, 83 Alexander Street,
Crows Nest, NSW 2065

Distributed in South Africa
by Jonathan Ball, Office B4, The District,
41 Sir Lowry Road, Woodstock 7925

Distributed in India by Penguin Books India,
7th Floor, Infinity Tower – C, DLF Cyber City,
Gurgaon 122002, Haryana

Distributed in Canada
by Publishers Group Canada,
76 Stafford Street, Unit 300,
Toronto, Ontario M6J 2S1

ISBN: 978-1-78578-145-2

Typeset in Agmena Pro by Marie Doherty

Printed and bound in the UK
by Clays Ltd, St Ives plc

CONTENTS

GRATEFUL THANKS

I would like to say a mammoth thank you to the four people who have made my involvement with racing such an unexpected pleasure.

If I hadn't been married to Alex I probably never would have been near a racecourse. This book describes how I was given the opportunity to turn her big dream into reality and share her pleasure in planning and participating in life as a National Hunt owner. Alex loved people, and people-watching, and found plenty to see and enjoy during thirteen years as an owner. Sharing that experience introduced me to the rich pageantry of the racing world and provided the contents for this book.

My heartfelt thanks also go to Henry Daly, Paul Webber and Venetia Williams who patiently taught us all we know about racing. This book persistently points out the cost of being an owner, an investment that is seldom rewarded with prize money but Alex gained enormous pleasure from having a string of horses in training.

We might have lost money, but statistically our trainers have helped us perform better than most owners. As well as providing plenty of winners they also became close friends.

I hope they will forgive me for invading their world by talking about trainers from an owner's perspective. I make it quite clear that horse ownership is likely to lose you money but I hope the reader will sense the pleasure that it brings and that I can tempt some new owners to join the sport.

This book is dedicated to Alex, who brought so much fun and adventure into my life, but she would have been the first to acknowledge how lucky we were to find the perfect three trainers to give us an above average amount of success and an awful lot of pleasure.

AN EXPENSIVE HOBBY

It's amazing how many astute businessmen abandon common sense and invest in a football club. I would never fall for such a foolish trap. My football investment has been limited to three season tickets and the 1,000 Manchester City shares I gave Alex for Christmas in 1998. She liked the shares, but really wanted the racehorse she had coveted for twenty years.

In 1978 I bought her a greyhound called 'Pepper Hill'. It did well, a first and a couple of seconds in six outings. To advertise shoe repairs, I changed its name to 'While You Wait', two weeks later it went lame. We had fun while it lasted but I always knew the dog was a poor substitute for the horse Alex really wanted.

For the next two decades horses never crossed Alex's mind: she was too preoccupied with children – not just cooking meals and attending school plays, speech days and sports days for Victoria, James and Edward but also doing exactly the same for 90 foster children and our adopted sons Oliver and Henry. With so many distractions I was confident that the desire to own a racehorse had disappeared to the very back of her mind. But the more I got to know Alex the more she surprised me.

In 2001 Alex's interest in racing was rekindled at Uttoxeter during a 'personal experience package' bought in a charity auction. She went behind the scenes, sat in the commentary box, spent time in the weighing room, observed a stewards' enquiry and saw scantily dressed jockeys changing between races.

I weakened and promised Alex her racehorse. First we needed a trainer. Following a tip, Alex spoke to longtime friend and past racehorse owner Mike Coghlan to ask: 'Can you find me a good-looking racehorse trainer within an hour's drive of our home?' Mike put the same question to a trainer he knew well, Paul Webber, who didn't have to think for long. 'There can be only one man,' said Paul, 'Henry Daly at Downton Stables near Ludlow.' So the next day I rang Henry Daly and asked a silly question: 'I want to buy a horse, can you help?'

Within a week, we visited Henry's yard. The stables are in wonderful countryside, near to Ludlow's prodigious choice of restaurants. Alex didn't notice the scenery, her eyes were on Henry, whose charm has recruited plenty of women owners. Before we left, he had the job of finding our winner. 'Must be a grey,' insisted Alex. 'Greys are more expensive,' said Henry, as he handed over his schedule of training fees.

Henry went to Newmarket and bought a grey. It was expensive, at £17,500 a lot more than I'd expected. Transatlantic, successful on the Flat, was about to become our National Hunt star. I knew I was committed when Alex chose her racing colours. 'City blue and white will look pretty on a grey.'

Three weeks later we returned to Ludlow. I expected Transatlantic would be put through his paces, chasing across the gallops and jumping a few fences, but he simply walked round the yard. Alex was delighted until she faced a difficult decision. To ensure jumping success, Transatlantic must be gelded, and I had to pay our first vets' fee.

After two months' schooling, we watched him on the gallops. 'He is doing well,' said Henry, 'just a bit keen.' I nodded knowingly. We were keen too, we desperately wanted to see him on a racecourse, but Henry was in no rush.

We waited three months for Transatlantic's first race, Henry kept saying the going was too soft. We prayed for sun and at last he announced Transatlantic was running at Ludlow next Thursday.

The *Racing Post* quoted Transatlantic as 3/1 favourite. Seeing my excitement several colleagues at the office visited the bookies. At Ludlow, I raced to the Tote to place £20 each way.

In the parade ring Henry looked pretty pleased. 'He's a bit keen,' he said to leading jockey Richard Johnson. 'Keep him at the back, settle down and let him go five from home.' Transatlantic ran sideways down to the start and the odds went out to 8/1.

As soon as the race started I understood what Henry meant by 'a bit keen'. Transatlantic's head pulled in every direction while Richard Johnson held him back. The crowd started giggling and within 2 furlongs Transatlantic was a laughing stock. With five fences left, he was shattered, finishing 72 lengths behind the winner. As I left the racecourse, an unhappy punter discarded his betting slip muttering, 'bloody grey'.

His next race was little better, 7th out of nine at Worcester. At Huntingdon, Transatlantic wasn't quite as keen and finished 5th.

His last race of the season, at Hereford, clashed with a family funeral. We watched in the bookies at Castle Cary. I placed £10 each way, and Alex revealed her ownership to our three fellow customers. He faded with three hurdles to go, and the room went quiet, a man with sideburns, swayed by our enthusiasm, had £40 on the nose.

Henry decided it was time for a summer break. Transatlantic went out to grass and my training fees halved.

At Henry's Open Day, Alex proudly watched Transatlantic parade before a large crowd. 'New here this year,' said Henry. 'Transatlantic performs well on the gallops but has a distinct dislike of racecourses.' For the first time I began to wonder whether he had any chance of being a future champion.

His next appearance was at Leicester, a racecourse without charm or atmosphere. He was still pretty keen, but instead of fading on the second circuit, ran on strongly to finish 2nd, winning £378.00. Alex was ecstatic. I did a quick calculation.

'Those winnings give you a 1 per cent return on my investment.' 'That's good,' she said.

Our attention turned to Bangor-on-Dee, where I sponsored the fifth race as a surprise for our second son, 'The Edward Timpson 30th Birthday Hurdle'. To add to the occasion, we persuaded Henry Daly to enter Transatlantic, who started second favourite in the first race.

Bangor is our local course and the crowd included twelve members of my golf club. They all backed Transatlantic. He was keener than ever and faded with six fences left. A jaded jockey met us after the race. 'Problem there,' he said, with an Irish accent. 'Veers right, can't take left-handed courses.' That eliminated half of Britain's tracks and shattered Alex's dream of Cheltenham and Aintree.

When Henry rang a fortnight later, it wasn't good news. 'Something happened in the loose box last weekend,' he said. 'It may be a bruise but it could be a tendon. I've called the vet.' Three vets' fees later, the news was no better. Transatlantic was confined to quarters and Henry declared the end to another season.

That night, I gave Alex some financial facts. 'Transatlantic has only cost us £44,000, Manchester City pay Robbie Fowler that much in a week. Investing in football clubs is like pouring money down a drain, at least with horses you lose money at a somewhat slower rate.' Alex wasn't listening. 'I spoke to Henry today,' she said. 'We are visiting the Doncaster Sales. One horse is great fun, but to really enjoy racing, you need at least five.'

It was foolish to think that Alex's horseracing ambition would stop at the first fence, if I'd really thought it through, one horse was bound to lead to another. I was, however, lucky that the next step was somewhat cheaper. Following a casual conversation with long-time friend Mike Coghlan we took a quarter share in a syndicate by buying a leg of a horse called Pressgang, trained by Paul Webber at Cropredy near Banbury. But this smart move didn't stop Alex taking me to the Doncaster Sales where Henry Daly successfully bid for Thievery. Instead of one horse we now had two-and-a-quarter.

Pressgang was a winner. Despite the difficulty of finding the right race in a hard winter, when several meetings were cancelled, we easily got a place in the Weatherbys Bumper at the Cheltenham Festival. Alex's goal was a runner at The Festival and within three years of becoming an owner she was there – albeit only owning a leg, but at least she was 25 per cent there.

We had been to Cheltenham before – corporately entertained and fighting the crowds between every race. Life in the Owners' and Trainers' wasn't any more comfortable but with a runner, and an enthusiastic mention in that day's *Racing Post*, we felt pretty high up The Festival pecking order.

All four legs were well represented at lunch, we chatted in the bar, watched Pressgang being saddled up and posed in the parade ring. We watched the race in silence as Pressgang, always handy, put his nose in front as the field went up the hill towards the finish.

Despite the temptation to dream of a win I had an uncharacteristically pessimistic view of our prospects. All that changed when Pressgang was in the lead with 2 furlongs to go. Despite Pressgang producing an inexperienced wobble from side to side on the hill towards the finish, Paul Webber was so convinced we'd won he gave me an enormous hug. It was a premature celebration, we lost by a head.

In retrospect our taste of Cheltenham Festival prize money came too soon. We didn't realise how rare it is to own a horse that is good enough to enter, never mind finding one that can stride proudly into the Winners' enclosure.

Encouraged by our syndicate success Alex was happy for

us to buy another leg – this time it was Presence of Mind trained by Emma Lavelle based between Andover and Newbury. We were the northern cousins of the syndicate and quickly found that 'our' horse never ran at a nearby racecourse. Bangor, Aintree and Haydock are a long way from Andover. Presence of Mind did us a favour by failing to make any progress through the handicaps and we decided our personality is more suited to sole ownership. A correct (but expensive) decision.

We quickly bought two more horses: Ordre de Bataille with Henry Daly (the French breeders wouldn't let us change the name) and our first wholly owned horse with Paul Webber, which I was allowed to call Key Cutter.

Ordre de Bataille made history when he gave Alex her first win – a hurdle race at Warwick which we were awarded after the true winner was disqualified. The *Racing Post* reported 'Killard Point, ridden by Joe Tizzard was demoted following a stewards' enquiry for causing interference to Ordre de Bataille in a head to head struggle after the final flight.' At the finish they were separated by a short head. 'I feel sorry for trainer Caroline Bailey, who was denied her first winner,' said winning trainer Henry Daly, 'but it means a first winner for owner Alex Stimpson.' Alex subsequently became much better known on the racing scene and most pundits now know how to spell her name.

Flushed with success it wasn't long before we went beyond the suggested target of five horses in training with the addition of Timpo and Cobbler's Queen. I hoped that we had now invested enough to make Alex's new hobby really interesting. Some might think that by owning a number of horses we would benefit from economies of scale, but the simple rule is 'The more horses you own the more you pay out'.

Racehorse ownership came at the perfect time for Alex. For 25 years foster caring had filled her life. It wasn't just the 80 children who spent between two weeks and two years in our home; Alex kept a close eye on many who went back to mum or dad and became a long term family mentor in her role as foster granny.

In 2003 we decided it was time to retire from fostering. With a growing number of grandchildren of our own, a wish to spend more time on holiday and James, our eldest son, now running the family business, it seemed the right time to be a bit more selfish and give Alex her long held wish to be a racehorse owner.

I should have known that Alex wouldn't stick to the plan. We continued fostering for another four years and looked after seven more children before Alex decided that we would continue for just a few more months to look after a family of three children. They stayed for over two years.

Alex has always been interested in children. She was trained as a nursery nurse and before we were married worked as a nanny for families in London and Cheshire. When our youngest child went to school Alex looked for something to do to fill her time. She loved people watching and got to know lots of other mums at the school gate but preferred inviting their children round for tea to going out clothes shopping or meeting the other mothers for lunch. She can remember the names of most of those children, proof that your memory retains the details that interest you most.

When looking to find a way to fill the time while our children were at school Alex saw an advert appealing for foster carers and found the interest that filled a big chunk of her life.

Alex finally gave up fostering after 31 years but still found a way to look after more children by becoming a Home Start volunteer.

I have no doubt that racing helped to take a bit of Alex's attention away from her vastly extended family, but I wasn't surprised to discover that she quickly started to show the same unselfish care and attention to the world of racing. The welfare of her horses, the stable lads, the jockeys, our trainers and, of course, their children is far more important than winning a race.

Alex always gave her trainers the freedom to make the major decisions, but they eventually realised that she had become very knowledgeable about racing and knew a lot about her horses. They became another part of her extended family.

Towards the end of 2007, Alex decided to alter our kitchen. She only wanted to move the Aga, but it got a bit out of hand and led to a redesign of half our house. To fill a large expanse of wall by our refectory table Alex commissioned a painting by horse artist Alex Charles Jones. The picture was of Cheltenham during The Festival, with Transatlantic, our first racehorse, at the centre of a group of runners waiting at the start. Transatlantic was a promising 2nd on a miserable Monday at Leicester, but he never went to Cheltenham for any meeting and certainly hasn't appeared at The Festival. We were still waiting for his first win when I was sent to watch him run at Stratford. Alex couldn't get a baby sitter for our foster children so I went to the course on my own, with strict instructions to give £20 to the stable lad and listen carefully to what our jockey, Richard Johnson, said after the race.

I did as I was told, handing the money over as Transatlantic was saddled up and even made careful note of the pre-race conversation in the paddock: 'Settle him down in the middle of the field, keep him handy and hope we are in with a shout with 2 furlongs to go.'

From the start 'Tranny', as Alex affectionately called her horse, followed the plan. Richard Johnson settled him into the middle of the field and I felt the tingle of excitement that most owners experience whenever they watch one of their horses contesting a race. With half a mile to go I felt that tingle turn to disappointment as Tranny failed to get handy and lost touch with the leading pack. We finished 11th out of thirteen.

To complete my brief I rushed over to the area where the unplaced horses were unsaddled and hosed down while their jockeys explained why things hadn't gone according to plan. 'Nice horse,' Richard told me, trying to soften the bad news, 'but there simply isn't enough pace there. Mind you,' he continued, 'if we look hard enough over the next two or three years we will eventually find a race he can win, but if I were you I wouldn't bother.' That was enough for me, Transatlantic had run his last race, he was retired and came to the fields behind our house in Cheshire where he was cared for by Jan who rents and runs the riding stables at the end of our garden.

Jan's clients thought Transatlantic (now renamed 'Tricky') was very pretty but no one could ride him. 'Too highly strung,' they said. 'A thoroughbred trained for racing – hardly the sort to take for a hack.' Jan was the only person who could ride Tricky and once she built his confidence she started to teach him a few new tricks. One day Jan came down to our house carrying a rosette. Tricky had won a junior dressage class. We proudly pinned the rosette on a framed copy of a picture, taken of Transatlantic after his best run at Leicester, that was hanging in the kitchen next to the painting of his make believe appearance at Cheltenham.

This was the first of many rosettes. Every week Jan took Tricky to another level and one week she even won £6. After three years of training and vets' fees I was at last seeing some income in return for my expenditure, but it didn't last long. Tricky was getting so good at dressage, Jan said he needed a trainer, who, for a fairly modest fee, accelerated their progress. But the extra exercises took their toll and Tricky 'got a leg'. I paid off the trainer and started paying the vet.

At first Tricky responded to treatment and there were even hints that if all went well he could have the talent to challenge for the Olympics. Unfortunately we never got the chance to commission a picture of Tricky in the London 2012 dressage arena. A repetition of the leg injury ended his career before he was able to catch the GB selectors' eyes and just before his dressage prize money reached the £378 he had won while racing in Alex's colours.

He now lives a life of leisure, eating our grass, in the fields behind our house, rent free. He hardly ever troubles the vet and has cost me a lot less since he stopped trying to win any prize money.

Cobbler's Queen ran her first race in a big money, mares-only bumper at Sandown on 8 March 2008 and finished 7th.

'A bit green,' said Richard Johnson, as he returned to the paddock. 'She shied away from the starter and travelled 1½ miles at the back of the field before she started to race. But coming 7th in a quality field shows some promise.'

The owners next to us in the paddock looked depressed. They expected their mare to win – it didn't. 'But,' said their jockey, 'it's a nice horse and should do well over hurdles next season.'

Two weeks later Henry Daly telephoned to tell us Cobbler's Queen was entered for the Friday of the Grand National meeting at Aintree, which, he added, is one of the five best days on the racing calendar. The race was at 5.30pm, giving me time to spend the morning at our office. Without my approval, son James introduced Dress-Down Friday so many colleagues turn up in jeans and a t-shirt. Being a rebel, I put on a pinstripe suit and a particularly loud shirt that Alex gave me for my birthday. It brought some cutting comments at our pensions meeting.

We got to Aintree for the second race. It was very busy. Forty-eight thousand racegoers were taking Friday off to have a party. It was Ladies' Day, the sun was shining and the girls must have seen the weather forecast. They were scantily dressed, prepared for a heat wave.

On the way to the Owners' and Trainers' we passed groups of girls in wedding gear and others fit for a nightclub. Evening gowns, puff ball dresses, stilettos, garish colours, sequins and lots of orange sun tan. In the safety of the Owners' and Trainers', mixing with rather less bare flesh but plenty of silly hats, we claimed our free sandwich and our son Edward went to the bar. I gave him a £10 note, but Alex wanted champagne so I swapped it for £20. Edward returned with two glasses of champagne and a lager. I held my hand out for the change – there wasn't any. 'I had to put in another £1.50,' said Edward.

The third race was the big one. Master Minded was odds-on favourite, but Edward backed Voy Por Ustedes. We watched the race with difficulty. Why do some people stand within two feet of the television screen, obscuring the view for the twenty decent folk who keep a sensible distance? The favourite faltered at the second from home and Edward won enough money to fund his betting for the rest of the day. I should have been pleased for him, but felt a feeling of jealous irritation as I tore up my betting slip.

For the next three races I went from paddock to Tote to grandstand and only once returned to the Tote to collect a very modest return for a horse that came 3rd. I didn't see much of the horses but understood why Henry Daly thinks this is such an important day on the racing calendar. We were part of an amazing fashion parade and I was glad I was wearing my fancy shirt.

Alcohol gradually eliminated any inhibitions, but the sexes remained separated. Boys stuck together with their big ties and open-necked shirts and the girls spent all afternoon showing off to other girls – and they had plenty to show. With gravity-defying dresses and powerful bras putting plenty of orange flesh on view to reveal the results of cosmetic surgery – we even saw a few boobs popping up in the Owners' and Trainers' bar.

Henry Daly concentrated on the horses. He had a good

day. Palarshan finished 5th over the Grand National fences and in the next race Alderburn came 3rd. Henry had a big smile as he put the saddle on Cobbler's Queen, '5th, 3rd, what next?'

In the paddock I looked up at the big video screen and there we all were. Alex was centre stage talking to Henry and our jockey, Mark Bradburne. But our picture didn't stay on screen for long, it quickly flicked to show more of the girls, this time tottering home – most didn't stay for the last race.

Cobbler's Queen was pretty keen and stopped suddenly on the way to the start, but Mark continued and was unceremoniously dumped on the ground. Reunited for the start they settled in the middle of the field and that's where they stayed – finishing 13th. Mark came towards us and jumped off Cobbler's Queen. 'Bit green,' he said, 'but a lovely horse. She'll be good over hurdles next season.'

Slightly disappointed we made our way back to the car. We will give Ladies' Day another go next season.

Five years after we bought our first horse, Transatlantic, I got a call from Karen. Karen's father, who had died suddenly a year earlier, was a long-time member of the snooker club that plays at my house. Karen was starting a website about racing, and asked me to write a short article through the eyes of an owner. I've written something every few weeks ever since for eclipsemagazine.co.uk. This book is based on those notes which chart the ups and downs of an owner's phlegmatic husband who has managed to find plenty of pleasure among a catalogue of failures and joy from the occasional success.

Karen not only prompted me to keep more careful notes but also persuaded me to reveal a few financial facts. 'I know you realise you are losing money but how much?' she said.

It took some time to face up to reality so before I reveal the extent of our financial folly I think the casual racegoer should learn some of the basic facts before I turn them into figures.

My notes could provide helpful research for anyone with thoughts of following Alex and becoming an owner. If you have the courage to follow in her footsteps you are about to enter a new world where you will have a lot of fun mixed with a fair slice of disappointment. You will need a lot of luck and never know quite what is going to happen next, but I can almost 100 per cent guarantee that your investment in racing will lose you money.

A BEGINNER'S GUIDE TO HORSERACING

A LOT TO LEARN

When I went with Alex to Downton Stables and asked Henry Daly to buy our first racehorse, I was totally naïve. I knew next to nothing about the world of racing. To help readers of this book avoid the same level of ignorance, I'm starting with some useful facts, discovered through experience, during the fourteen years I've given Alex's hobby the financial encouragement it required. This knowhow probably cost me about £1 million, but I'm happy to hand it on for free. The facts that follow are unlikely to make you a profit, but they should help you understand my story and spot where I could have saved more money, and lost a little bit less.

FLAT OR NATIONAL HUNT

Some fixtures are on the Flat, at others the horses jump fences (National Hunt). There's a big difference between the two – at least as big as the gap between rugby union and rugby league and probably as far apart as rugby and Association football. The meetings are usually held at different courses with different horses involving a completely different set of people. Different trainers, jockeys, owners and racegoers, but you see the same bookies.

I'm lucky that Alex only wanted to follow National Hunt racing. The leading Flat owners are multi-billionaire Sheikhs from Dubai while we only have to compete with multi-millionaires from Ireland. Flat horses have to be quick, speed that is nearly always inherited from their parents, so you will probably have to pay at least £300,000 for a horse with the credentials to run in The Derby with a late entry fee costing up to £60,000. Six-figure sums are also paid for jump horses but it is possible to pick up a future Grand National winner for £20,000.

You won't find many National Hunt jockeys riding on the Flat because most of them are too tall and have enough trouble keeping their weight down to ten stone, the minimum weight a horse has to carry over the jumps. Flat jockeys need to be two stone lighter but you won't persuade them to go over fences, which involve a far greater chance of falling off and finishing the race in an ambulance.

It's not just the jockeys that look different, Flat horses are built for speed over a short distance (usually no more than a mile) while jump horses are made of sterner stuff, some with the stamina to go over 4 miles on muddy ground. A National Hunt horse usually doesn't make its debut until it has reached four years and can still be competing at the age of thirteen. Flat horses start racing when they are two and may be retired to stud before they are four.

Flat races use starting stalls with the draw for position giving some runners a substantial advantage. National Hunt jockeys walk their horses gently towards a tape that is casually released by the starter. With a race of at least 4 miles the starting position doesn't make much difference. A Flat race of 5 furlongs seems to be over in a blink of an eye while a jumping drama can go on for five minutes or more.

Although there are National Hunt meetings all year round the serious stuff happens in the winter (from November until just after the Grand National in April). Flat racing starts with the Lincoln Handicap at the end of March until the November Handicap, but to please the bookies Flat races take place on all-weather tracks nearly every day of the year.

A few horses, some jockeys and a lot of racegoers have their first experience at a Point-to-Point. This is jump racing for amateur riders over some farmers' fields watched by a crowd wearing tweeds and Hunter wellies, eating smoked salmon sandwiches and drinking champagne by the boots of their Range Rovers.

These Point-to-Point followers will almost certainly take their tweeds to Cheltenham but if they have to go to Epsom, Chester and York (reluctantly accepting corporate entertainment) they will look as if they are guests at a fairly posh family wedding.

Some courses only do Jump racing, including Towcester, Uttoxeter, Bangor-on-Dee, Warwick, Wetherby and Wincanton, and it is Flat only at others, such as Redcar, Ripon, Windsor and Wolverhampton, but there are plenty of courses that do both, including Carlisle, Catterick, Leicester and Lingfield.

This book follows the fortunes of our string of National Hunt horses – I suspect it is just as easy to lose money on the Flat.

SIGNS OF A GOOD HORSE

If you go to the races you'll find a lot of the crowd crammed into the bar, but some dedicated spectators spend time studying form by watching runners in the parade ring. Look out for the knowledgeable punters leaning on the rail making meaningful notes in their race card. You may wonder what they are looking for, why they pick one horse ahead of another and what's behind their authoritative remarks: 'you have to like the look of that grey', or 'he's much more composed than last time out' and 'that mare's built for chasing'.

There are some obvious warning signs to make you think twice about placing a bet. Keep clear if a horse is sweating before even seeing a hurdle or so keen the head is being jerked in all directions. Horses in the paddock should look calm and content. The experts on the rails will also look at bone structure, leg movement and body shape – 'notice a strong line through the withers' – but the first-time racegoer doesn't need to be an expert to pick a winner.

It's reassuring to discover that the diehards don't always win, despite a detailed study of the *Racing Post* to check past form, present rating and preference for soft or good ground. Perhaps some of these seasoned spectators are being blinded by their own bravado.

By all means go to the paddock and see what you are investing your money in, but there are plenty of ways to choose a likely winner without knowing much about horses. Some punters forget about the horse and concentrate on the jockey, but even A.P. McCoy couldn't win if he was riding a dobbin. Others go for the colour of the horse (Alex always backed greys) or the colour of the racing silks, although there is no evidence to suggest that when the jockey is wearing a green top and a red hat the horse will run faster than those wearing blue.

One of my friends backed a horse because he believed it winked at him while walking round the paddock; others have found success simply by selecting a horse with a nice name. If one of the runners is Victoria's Secret and your daughter is called Victoria you'd be a fool not to have a couple of pounds each way even if the *Racing Post* says it hasn't got a chance of getting in the first four.

The safest way to pick a winner isn't to look at the horse but to look at the odds. At a general election the most reliable way to forecast the result isn't to study the candidates or the opinion polls – the best information comes from the bookies. The same is true of racing, the horse with the shortest odds is the one most likely to win. You won't make a fortune from an even money bet but at least you have a better chance of enjoying the smug satisfaction of going back to the bookie to pick up some winnings.

If you pick the wrong horse in the 2.45 at Folkestone the feeling of disappointment is soon forgotten, but your decision is far more serious when buying a racehorse at the Doncaster Sales. Instead of placing £10 each way you could be spending at least £20,000 with a lot more to follow when the bills start coming from your trainer and the vet.

This is a decision even the most experienced owner should never take on their own. I've always relied heavily on our trainer, who should know a lot more about horses and has a big interest in getting successful horses into the yard. If future events prove you have backed the wrong horse at least you've someone else to blame.

At the races, viewing horses in the parade ring is optional. You don't have to look before you bet, but at bloodstock sales you are expected to look at the horse before bidding. Stable lads are only too willing to put their horse through its paces before the lot comes up for auction. While your trainer tries to come to an expert opinion your job is to watch the horse walk up and down while giving the occasional nod, smile or scowl to suggest that you know what you are looking for. Your trainer will be looking for a fluent and measured stride, a healthy coat, broad buttocks and a confident demeanour. After seeing six or seven horses, without analysing the size of their ears, the length of stride or gleam in their eye, I started to get a feel for which ones I fancied, then found I couldn't afford them. The really good looking racehorses stand out from the crowd, that's why the multi-millionaire owners push the prices over £100,000.

Most of the horses on offer have never seen a racecourse or even a saddle. There is nothing in the form book, all you have to go on is their appearance and the pedigree. The auction brochure lists past performances of the mare, and of the stallion, along with the good horses he has already produced. Beyond that you are bidding for an unknown quantity. The parentage should show whether you are buying a chaser or a hurdler, but until the horse starts running there is nothing to tell you whether it prefers left- or right-handed courses, heavy or good ground or would find it difficult to run more than 2 miles. All horses in the catalogue come with a clean bill of health from the vet so apart from noticing that every horse has long and worryingly fragile looking legs there is no indication of the extensive list of injuries that are likely to interrupt the horse's racing career.

When the bidding starts I recommend delegating the job to your trainer, who should know when to enter the bidding and you will have told him when to stop. Don't bid against yourself by catching the auctioneer's eye or waving to a friend and if you have two trainers try to ensure they don't bid against each other.

It's quite exciting, being involved in the auction. It's as tense as watching the horse run a race and unless you have the highest bid it doesn't cost any money. Although many of the lots you fancy will go way beyond your price bracket, don't worry about leaving empty-handed. Your trainer will make sure you will find something with potential to put in a horse box.

Don't be fooled by the price, you are paying guineas (£1.05p each) not pounds. In addition, expect a 6 per cent commission, VAT, transport to your trainer's yard and some vets' fees. Once your horse has been delivered to its new home the clock starts ticking on the training fees at about £35 a day.

Don't lie to your friends about the price, it is public knowledge; the details will be listed in the racing press the day after the auction and probably mentioned in the race card 'Slippery Shoeman who cost 35,000 guineas as a three-year-old has his debut today'. After a disappointing run even if you don't hear any comments from the crowd you know they will be thinking 'who in their right mind has paid so much for a horse like that!'

You could keep the price a secret by dealing directly with a trainer, breeder or another owner but, like second-hand cars, you'll never know whether you could have paid a lower price.

Whatever price you pay, my advice is to forget the figure as soon as possible, and hope you have a horse that is worth the daily training fees that you are now committed to pay.

PICKING YOUR COLOURS
AND CHOOSING NAMES

It might be very difficult to find a future champion chaser but it's easy to pick the racing colours that jockeys will wear whenever they ride your horses. There are eighteen different shades available which can be combined in thousands of ways to produce your personal, unique design. It can all be done on the internet, using a website so simple even I can work it. Play around with your favourite colours on different patterns for tunic, sleeves and hat until you find a combination that the computer says isn't already being used by another owner.

Inevitably you will have to pay a modest registration fee. Your trainer will be happy to arrange for the silks to be made ('worth getting three done, just in case') and add the cost to your next monthly bill. That's it, you now have the colours that will appear on the race card and in the *Racing Post* but no picture in the paper will look as good as seeing the silks worn for the first time when your jockey tries to find you in the parade ring.

Picking the name of your horse should be even more fun. You can give your imagination a real treat by listing a load of likely names before deciding on your favourite, but be prepared for possible disappointment. There are a number of rules which mean that some names can't be chosen.

Obviously you can't pick a name that is already being used or has been in use during the last twenty years, a rule that extends for ever to famous names like Red Rum and Shergar. You have eighteen characters to play with, which means that the total of all the letters and spaces can't add up to more than eighteen. To get a long name, some owners don't bother with any spaces and end up with names like 'Shutthedoorquietly', 'Whataloadofrubbish' or 'Shesinthekitchen', which I think are silly.

Again there is a neat website that lets you check whether your favourite name is available. Don't assume that the obvious names have already been taken. A quick recent check revealed that the following can still be used: 'Racing Certainty', 'Easy Peasy', 'Each Way Bet' and 'Don't Tell Alex' but I do wonder whether some others like 'Four Lengths Ahead' or 'Back Marker' would be ruled out for causing potential nightmares to a commentator. You certainly won't sneak through a name designed to produce an embarrassing broadcast. 'Yoovarted', 'Efinhel', 'Four Fuxake' and 'For Gas Mick' are all unlikely to get past the judge.

It is safer to stick to family names ('Ask John' and 'Popular Pete' are still available) or something connected to your pets, hobbies, house name or favourite holiday destination. Your choice of name is unlikely to make the horse jump better or run any faster and the name will be totally ignored by the stable lads who'll invent their own nickname, but every time your horse is mentioned there is the satisfaction of knowing that you dreamt up the idea.

There are other restrictions. If the horse has already been

given a name by a previous owner or breeder you can only change it with their permission (French breeders can be particularly reluctant to cooperate). If the horse has run in a race under one name you can't change it to another but at least that will spare you the £150 fee due whenever you register a new name. The £650 plus VAT you pay to set yourself up with silks and give the horse a name is small change compared with the cost of getting it fit to run in a race.

OTHER OWNERS

Owners come in all shapes and sizes, most are ordinary people, like you, who pick racing as their extravagant hobby. Your fellow owners could include Liz Hurley, Sir Alex Ferguson and Ronnie Wood, but most aren't celebrities and have never been seen in *Hello* magazine. There are some really serious owners like John P. McManus, Trevor Hemmings and Graham Wylie who have so many horses they often have several running at the same meeting and more than one in the same race (same colours, different hat). Your best-known fellow owner will be The Queen, but only a few of her horses go jumping so you are unlikely to see her at Bangor-on-Dee, Towcester or even Aintree and even if she did turn up she won't, like you, have to present her Horseracing Privilege Card after queueing at the Owners' and Trainers' entrance.

Don't be fooled, some people in the queue aren't owners or trainers. As an owner you can bring four, six or sometimes even eight guests, who may arrive on their own and pick up their badges at the gate. Others in the queue may be part of a syndicate – up to half the horses on a race card could be part owned by two friends or ten mates from a pub or golf club. If you divide the costs between ten people you all get into the parade ring but only lose one-tenth of the money.

Syndicates sound like the ideal way to get the same thrill at a fraction of the cost, but it may not work out like that. Much depends on your fellow investors, if they're a crowd of good mates your visits to a racecourse will, win or lose, provide plenty of enjoyment. You can get an extra bit of fun for your investment by dreaming up an unusual name for the partnership. Look at some of the great names in the *Racing Post* and wonder why syndicates are called The Yes No Wait Sorries, Old Boys' Network, Good Bad and Ugly and the Impulse Club.

Some syndicates don't last the test of time. Poorly per-forming horses can cause discontent among the members but disharmony is more likely to be caused by a person than a horse. Each syndicate needs a leader, someone who col-lects the money, briefs the trainer, pays the bills and very occasionally declares a dividend. The syndicate starts to crumble when some members realise that they are putting up the cash for the leader to enjoy all the best parts of being an owner. It's the person who talks to the trainer that gets the most pleasure out of planning the season's campaign and picking the right race (at an adjacent course on a con-venient date). Sure, everyone in the syndicate gets to cele-brate if the horse wins, but the organiser will expect a fair slice of the credit.

People that own a leg (25 per cent) are close to the action and the trainer probably knows their names. Members of one of the commercial racing clubs, where for about £25 a week they get a modest share in what they hope isn't a modest horse, haven't bought much more involvement than the punter who puts on £50 to win. But punters can decide on the day. If you join a syndicate you are stuck with the same horse wherever, whenever and if ever it runs.

Although the big owners' clubs claim that you are in proud possession of part of a horse, the system is close to fantasy football – you place your bet at the beginning of the season, and there is no chance of changing your bet from month to month.

But psychologically, subscribing to an owners' club is definitely one step up from being a plain punter, who imagines he owns the horse for one race only – in an owners' club a tiny little bit of the winning horse really does belong to you.

If you're lucky enough to own a horse in your own right, bank all the winnings and pay every penny of the expenses, it won't be long before you find you are not alone. It is reassuring to know that there are plenty of other people who have been equally irresponsible. Once you have joined the ranks it is important to learn how to start and hold a conversation with the people you meet in the Owners' and Trainers' bar.

At most racecourses the bar is packed but don't assume that everyone is an owner or trainer. At some courses like Carlisle and Towcester posh local people seem to have a badge that entitles them to park near the entrance and push into every exclusive nook and cranny.

You are most likely to strike up a conversation with another owner over lunch at Newbury, Cheltenham,

Bangor or Haydock where the Owners' and Trainers' badge commands more respect.

Everyone else appears to be a conversational challenge, but it only takes one question to start talking. Try 'Have you got a runner today?' 'Have you got any other horses in training?', 'Who's your trainer?', 'How's your season going?' and 'Which is your favourite course?'

There are a few tricky characters who know every-thing – every course, every trainer, every jockey – and who appear to be on first name terms with Paul, Philip, Willie and all the other top trainers. They are also friends with the stewards, and their family have been involved in racing for five generations (who all probably wore the same irritating style of tweed jacket handed down from father to son). If they have a runner you will desperately want it to lose by an embarrassing distance.

You will meet lots of owners at your trainer's Open Day. You may already know quite a bit about them; it is natural for an owner to follow the fortunes of every entry from the same stable. There may be an arrogant owner who is keen to brag about having the most successful horse in the yard but usually there is a feeling of camaraderie. By the time you have patiently watched the parade of horses, accepted a couple of glasses of champagne and settled down to the buffet lunch, your fellow owners become really friendly and genuinely wish you good luck for the new season. 'Good luck to you too,' is the reply. 'I look forward to seeing you at a racecourse somewhere during the season'.

You almost certainly will meet them again but even if you remember their face you will probably have forgot-ten their name. Don't worry, just go back to the basic question 'Have you got a runner today?' followed up with 'Which race?'

A quick look at the race card will tell you all you need to know.

TRAINERS

Every owner needs a trainer. It is quite possible to keep your future Gold Cup winner in the field at the back of your house for a few months over the summer but, in the winter, a homespun set-up suited to hacking, hunting and ponies would struggle to train and turn out a horse that could even tackle 2 miles 4 furlongs round Fontwell or Fakenham.

Be warned, trainers don't come cheap but at least they charge a little bit less than the full fees at Eton, Harrow or even Uppingham. For about £250 a week your trainer will look after just about everything to do with getting your horse to the starting line; all you have to do is turn up at the races and pay the bills.

For the fee, your horse will be mollycoddled in five star accommodation and put through a carefully crafted training schedule designed to produce a peak performance on race day. However, you won't be surprised to hear that a few extras will appear on your monthly statement – including transport (if you go to Kelso make sure your horse shares the ride with a couple more from the same stable).

Your fee doesn't usually include the cost of a farrier, or the vet, whose charges can transform your monthly account especially when it is deemed necessary to perform a major scan to monitor a minor injury.

When you go to any trainer's yard, which you must before making a decision, you'll think trainers have one of the best jobs in the world. Few managers go to work in the middle of rolling countryside, with stunning views for miles in every direction. Most yards are blessed with a dedicated team of stable lads and a powerful woman who runs the office and politely puts even the most arrogant owner back in his box. But there is a very tricky side to the trainer's job. Headteachers have a few staff problems and some of their students can cause trouble but the people who make the Head's job so difficult are the parents. Racehorse trainers are in a similar situation – they inevitably have a few staff problems and some tricky horses, but the people who fill life full of stress are some of the owners.

As an owner you can always put the next horse you buy with another yard, or move a horse from one yard to another, so it's little wonder that almost every trainer spends a fair proportion of every week exchanging pleasantries with all the owners they can find at the end of a phone. Trainers need to know a lot about racing but they must also become an expert at charming their owners.

So what are the key factors that should determine your choice of trainer?

You are going to meet your trainer at their yard and at lots of racecourses. You will meet for a drink in the Owners' and Trainers' bar, will be offered breakfast if you visit the yard and it isn't unusual to discuss tactics over dinner. With all this socialising you must find a trainer who you like. Some recruitment consultants talk about the lunch test (if you can't face the thought of lasting through lunch with the candidate don't make him or her a permanent part of your life). The lunch test is also useful when picking a trainer, but it's easier to like a trainer who produces lots of winners.

Look at the record, a crafty search on the internet will reveal the relative success of one yard compared with all the others. Don't just look at the total prize money, one good horse can cover up a poor showing by the rest of the stables. Study the ratio between the number of runners and how many win or are placed. You want a trainer who will provide you with the pleasure of watching your horse go first past the post.

But past success shouldn't be the only factor; a few top trainers will only find space for horses that cost big money at auction, and some trainers pay scant regard to their owners' opinion. To buy success you may have to pay £100,000 for a horse that has yet to be broken and then leave all the decisions to your trainer, who will be the one interviewed on television taking all the credit for your investment.

Some of the yards down the league table might record less success, but their horses usually have a more modest pedigree and the owner is allowed to voice an opinion on where and when the horse runs and who is in the saddle. Even if your advice is largely ignored, being brought into the race planning is part of the pleasure of owning a horse. Most owners prefer to be asked what they think than to be told what is happening.

Don't just look at last year. Trainers can produce dramatically different results from season to season. One year could be blighted by a virus, the next boosted by lots of rain that helps a high proportion of chasers that like heavy going. Trainers are seldom short of a reason for failure but the same excuse won't work for three consecutive seasons.

You are more likely to enjoy your racing if you pick a trainer who is based within easy reach of your home. If your trainer is in Sussex and you live in Cheshire you will seldom visit the yard and will be entered for races at Plumpton and Lingfield Park when you would prefer to go to Uttoxeter, Bangor and Haydock.

Don't decide anything until you've been to the stables. It is similar to picking a boarding school or trailing round universities with your eldest child – you will know the right answer when you get there.

There is a danger that you will be blown away by the idyllic rolling countryside or the attractive head lad. It is possible to be seduced by an array of expensive training toys – indoor water walkers, eco-friendly synthetic rubber on all four miles of the gallops to avoid knee and ligament strain, an all-weather indoor/outdoor facility to keep the exercises going when it snows and a computer that is used by the stable's dedicated horse dietician, physiotherapist and psychologist to produce an hourly analysis of every horse. Some stables are so scientifically on the ball you are left wondering why they ever lose a race.

Despite all the technology and technical support, you are more likely to be persuaded by the softer skills shown during your visit. A warm welcome, happy looking stable staff, together with fit and content horses will give all the assurance you need. Assuming it hasn't taken hours to drive there, all you need is a hearty breakfast with the prospective trainer's family and you will be hooked.

You are about to find out whether your trainer has the two vital ingredients. Are they good at finding you the right horse and do they have more than their fair share of luck?

JOCKEYS

The National Careers Service gives some helpful hints to anyone thinking of training to be a jockey. They advise that you must be fit, strong and have stamina. You will also need good eyesight and like working with horses. Your work will involve early starts and late finishes and there is a high risk of injury from falls and kicks. They should have added the need to be fearless, disciplined and underweight.

Few jobs are so dangerous that you are constantly followed by an ambulance, but the precaution is justified. Jump jockeys regularly visit the Accident and Emergency Department.

I was amazed to discover that every jockey in a race is paid the same fee. You don't have to pay extra when your horse is ridden by the champion jockey. Jump jockeys get about 40 per cent more than those on the Flat but at around £170 a race it is hardly a fortune to justify the risk of breaking your neck.

The most successful jockeys earn a fair bit more from their percentage of any prize money and some benefit from sponsorship deals, but if they only have one ride at a meeting there is little income left after paying travelling expenses and, in many cases, a fee to the agent who booked the ride.

The Careers Service should also have made it clear that jockeys need self-discipline, particularly with their diet. Some National Hunt jockeys are quite tall but they're all very thin, keeping their weight at little more than 10 stone. They must also be careful to stick to the rules of racing. Put a foot wrong and the stewards will be dishing out penalties for not trying, for trying too hard, or for overuse of the whip. These misdemeanours can lead to a several-day ban, with no income, but at least the break gives them the chance of getting a couple of square meals.

Your trainer will usually pick the jockey. Some yards keep their preferred rider on a retainer so you would often see Richard Johnson riding for Philip Hobbs and Aidan Coleman on horses trained by Venetia Williams. But even if your trainer always seems to use the same jockey there will be times when someone else will ride your horse, and if they win you'll be tempted to ask them to do it again. Occasionally your horse might be ridden by a conditional jockey, that's one still doing their apprenticeship, who is under 26 and has ridden fewer than 75 winners. Some races are exclusively for conditional jockeys; in other races they are given a few pounds advantage on the handicap. Gradually you will get to know a number of riders and will find you have favourites.

To get in your bad books a jockey only needs to a) fail to follow the trainer's race plan, b) finish down the field and c) be terse and grumpy when you meet in the unsaddling enclosure. To find favour all a jockey needs to do is win (with or without following instructions) and it is always a pleasure to talk to a winning jockey.

THE HANDICAP SYSTEM

When I was at Wadham House, a prep school in Hale just South of Manchester that closed down only three years after I left, the big event on Sports Day was the Half Mile. Every boy over the age of eight was encouraged to compete and in theory all had an equal chance of winning because the race was run off handicap. The first year I took part I started 150 yards in front of the school champion who overtook me with two laps still remaining (it was a very small track).

Most horse races are run on similar lines but instead of the poorer horses getting a head start the better runners are made to carry more weight. Experience has shown that the heavier the load the more slowly the horse will run. I guess the same principle would have worked at Wadham House but, even in the days before Safeguarding, prep school masters would have been ill advised to force little boys to be burdened with a lead-filled bag strapped to their back.

Unlike the handicap systems used for golf and real tennis, where good players get lower handicaps, in racing the best horse has the highest handicap.

Golfers are required to put three cards in before they are given a handicap. Horses follow the same routine. There are plenty of Novice Hurdle races for young horses to enter and run against other beginners on level terms, but even before the handicapper has shown his hand you will have a pretty good idea whether your horse is heading for a high or low mark.

Setting the handicaps is an art not a science. The art is practised by a panel of around eleven experts at The British Horseracing Authority who each study a particular part of the racing scene. They examine the relative performance of every horse in every race. If a horse wins or comes within the first four in both of its first two races a handicap may be awarded immediately. But some horses fare so badly during the first three races they fail to produce enough evidence to get a handicap. These poor performers were perhaps poorly ridden, fell at the first fence on each occasion, failed to finish or in some cases failed to start. If you own a horse that finds it so difficult to get an official handicap then I urge you to stop harbouring any further ideas of a racing career and help your horse to find its happiness elsewhere as a show jumper, team chaser or doing dressage at someone else's expense. Remember the training fees are exactly the same for the worst horse in the yard.

Once you have a handicap you can enter many more races and theoretically have as good a chance as every other owner in the race of finishing in the Winners' enclosure. But, if your horse keeps winning, the handicap will go up and each new race will be tougher to win.

The handicap equates to pounds of weight. Arkle, a horse that rose to the record handicap of 212, would in theory be carrying 80lbs more than Alex's best horse, Sixty Something, which has hovered around 132. But even if they were from the same era the horses would never have run against each other. Handicap races have a maximum difference of less than two stone from top weight to bottom. So better horses will go in one race and less good in another. Horses can only be entered in races with their appropriate handicap rating.

Once your horse has a handicap it will be reviewed after every race. A big win against good horses will bring a substantial increase in handicap but it won't take effect for a week. Some smart trainers run a winner again within days to beat the handicapper; they suffer a 7lb penalty due to the win, but could put up a conditional jockey, entitled to a 7lb allowance.

Perhaps I'm going too quickly, but don't worry, few people fully understand the system and although it is designed to get all the horses to the finishing post at the same time this very rarely happens. Despite the experience of the British Horseracing Authority's dedicated gurus your well handicapped horse can still finish well down the field.

Handicaps may seem to make little difference to the result of a race (although some trainers give a high mark as the main reason for a poor finish) but the handicap makes a big difference to where you go racing.

Horses rated below 85 can expect to run at Leicester on a Monday or at a wet Wednesday meeting at Towcester. To qualify for Saturdays at Newbury or Sandown it helps to be above 120 and to be certain of a run at the Cheltenham Festival try to find a horse rated in the 140s.

Although a low handicap should give you a better chance of winning it will only set you up to win a first prize of £3,000 (to make money you need to win an average of £4,000 every time your horse runs). If you want to enjoy being mentioned by Channel 4's *Morning Line* before a big Saturday meeting, read about your chances of success in the *Racing Post* and be the envy of other owners, the aim is to have a horse rated over 155. Horses that good qualify for Open races where, if there is a handicap, it is based on age – like mine was at Wadham House.

HOW RACES DIFFER

I've already explained the difference between Flat racing and National Hunt, but am now going to discuss in more detail the races that go over jumps.

Unless you buy a horse that has already raced, you may

discover that your first race is a National Hunt Flat Race – this strange contradiction in terms is designed to introduce young unraced horses to the unfamiliar routine of a racecourse and the new sensation of performing in a real competition in front of a proper crowd. These races over 2 miles, with no jumps to bother about, are often called 'Bumpers' (after the bumping action of inexperienced amateur jockeys who often used to ride in these events).

Don't be fooled by the matter-of-fact remarks from your trainer before the race – 'We're just here for the experience', 'Let's hope he enjoys the run' and 'Anything in the first six will be a bonus'. When it comes to the stable statistics, a bumper winner is as useful as finishing 1st in a serious race at Sandown on a Saturday. If bumpers are of such little competitive consequence, why do some horses run in four of them, finishing with the Weatherbys Champion Bumper at Cheltenham?

Horses usually start jumping over hurdles which are meant to measure 3½ft, exactly the same height men negotiate in the 110m hurdles at the Olympics. Hurdles are much flimsier than the 4½ft fences used for steeplechases.

Hurdle races usually cover at least 2 miles with a minimum of eight jumps. Initially your horse will run in a Novice Hurdle but hopefully, after three outings, will be awarded a handicap and the rating will indicate your place in the pecking order.

Some horses stick with hurdles throughout their career, especially those that are successful enough to attract the handicapper's eye and rise through the ranks. Most start by running in Class 4 or 5 races. The dobbins sink down to Class 7 (racing's equivalent of the Isthmian Football League

Division One North). The superstars, as their handicap shoots up towards 160, will run in upper class races. Beyond Class 1 they will qualify for Grades 3, 2 and 1 with the ultimate aim being the Champion Hurdle at Cheltenham. Another big objective, especially for the owners of mares, is to win one of the top notch 'Listed' races which entitle the winner's name to be written in 'black type', which makes it stand out when future offspring are advertised in a sale catalogue.

A lot of the hurdle races are run over 2 miles but some stayers have to go as far as 3½. After a disappointing run your trainer may suggest that the length of the race was the problem. 'We could have done with another 4 furlongs' or 'I think a drop down in distance will suit him better'. After a while you will hear another idea: 'He's built for big fences, let's send him chasing next season'.

Steeplechasers, a name said to derive from old races that were run from one church steeple to another, are normally expected to run longer races than the hurdlers. Chases can be anything from 2 to 4½ miles. The bigger obstacles include plain fences, open ditches (a ditch on the taking-off side of the fence) and sometimes a water jump (a small pond on the landing side). Some courses like Haydock have fixed brush fences which are halfway between hurdles and a proper fence and, of course, Aintree has the puissance of racing, the Grand National, with Becher's Brook, The Chair and Valentine's.

Chases have the same classifications as hurdles, from Class 7 up to Grade 1 with the top prize being the Cheltenham Gold Cup.

Entry qualifications can vary. Novice races are open only to horses that haven't won a race before the season started and most other races have a handicap limit which is usually set by the Class. If a race is oversubscribed, it is normally the lowest handicapped horses that are balloted out.

There are plenty more variations. Juvenile races for three-year-olds and races limited to mares-only, conditional jockeys or amateur jockeys. Some races are special qualifying heats for a big race later in the season and there is even a big prize bumper for horses bought at the latest Doncaster Sales (a special perk devised to encourage the reluctant bidder). If you are desperate to get rid of your horse you could enter it for a Seller where it will run against other fairly useless horses and the winner has to be offered for auction after the race.

With so many options to choose from it is surprising that your trainer finds it so difficult to find the right race for your horse. But despite an enormous fixture list, after races have been ruled out because the going is too soft, the meeting comes too soon after the last outing or a problem with right-handed courses, your horse, even if it stays injury free, will probably only run six times a year.

INCOME AND EXPENDITURE

You will face two big bills: the cost of buying your horse and the weekly training fees. But the price of ownership doesn't stop there.

As an owner you don't have to pay to enter the racecourse but a day's racing never comes for nothing. There is the cost of travel and the tip you give the stable lad. Few courses give you a free lunch and if you take some friends you will probably be picking up their tab as well. However, all this is small change compared with some of the extras that can creep onto your trainer's monthly bill.

On top of the basic training fee you will be charged for the transport to each race (and sometimes to an equine hospital). If you are paying for a horse ambulance be prepared for some significant vets' fees, but even while staying at home your horse will occasionally have a little niggle, a slight limp, a cough or show a loss of form which all require a visit from the vet. And of course the farrier keeps calling in times of both sickness and health.

Don't worry about sorting out the silks, or registering the details of a new horse with the authorities. Your trainer's office will deal with everything and add the cost to your bill. But trainers have a generous side and you will be given free tea, coffee and breakfast whenever you visit the yard, but you, too, are expected to show a bit of generosity. It is normal for something to be added to the December bill as your contribution to the lads' Christmas bonus.

Every owner has to bank with Weatherbys who make the administration easy. They debit your account with every entry fee (if you are balloted out or the meeting is cancelled you get your money back) and they pay the jockey on your behalf. Inevitably it is necessary to send large and regular sums to Weatherbys to keep your account in credit but the Weatherbys statement has a bright side, not seen in a trainer's bill: it shows some income among the expenditure.

Weatherbys can sort out your VAT, so follow their advice. Knowing the fickle state of racing finance and the dismal deal that owners get, many years ago, following a well-organised racing lobby, the government took pity and, in a bid to keep British racing competitive with that of Ireland and France, found a way for owners to claim back the VAT they pay on their racing bills. But to qualify, your horse must be sponsored and you must be prepared for it to parade round the ring displaying a commercial message. By playing to the VAT rules you can create a useful income from your sponsor.

There will be times when a modest amount of appearance money is shown on your Weatherbys account. Some race meetings on the calendar, particularly those held on a Sunday or Monday, offer a fee of around £100 to every owner who gets a horse to the starting line.

It is much more fun opening the Weatherbys statement than checking through your trainer's bill: Weatherbys show your winnings – a reminder of finishing in the Winners' enclosure and proof that racing can create a bit of income. But the statement also makes clear that you only get 80 per cent of the winnings; about 5 per cent goes to the stable lads, 6 per cent to the jockey and 8 per cent to the trainer. Despite this share in success Alex insists that following a win we must send a case of wine or a luxury hamper to our trainer to say 'Thank You and Well Done!'

In most sports like tennis, golf and football the performers are well rewarded for the part they play in providing both the bookies with something for punters to bet on and the venues with an event to attract paying spectators and significant sponsorship. In football a good slice of the money is paid out to the players but horseracing doesn't provide the same sort of incentive.

The Racehorse Owners Association (ROA) Annual Report puts prize money at the top of its agenda. They point out that 27 per cent of the horses that ran during 2014 didn't ever win any money (over 10 per cent of horses in training never even got to a racecourse but at least their owners were saved the cost of the entry fee, transport and the stable lad's tip). Only 7 per cent of horses won more than £30,000 in the year, and fewer than 20 per cent won more than £7,500. With the annual cost of keeping a horse being somewhere between £20,000 and £25,000 (much more if I follow my accountant's advice and add depreciation) I reckon your chances of showing a profit are about 10/1 against.

If you are lucky and win the Grand National your Weatherbys account will be boosted by £561,000 and even 3rd in the Cheltenham Gold Cup will bring nearly £60,000. But it is better to be realistic and see what you would get for finishing in the frame following a Class 6 race at Chepstow on a Monday where the first prize is £2,588 and for fourth you get 192 quid.

You need a very good horse that wins some high class races for income to exceed expenditure.

RACECOURSES

In many ways racecourses are very much like each other but it won't be long before even the most blinkered owner spots some significant points of difference.

All courses have bookies, badges and bars, customers can pay a modest entry fee and stand on the rail while, at some of the posher places, other racegoers pay much more to watch from a box (but not at Bangor-on-Dee which doesn't even have a grandstand). At every meeting vets and doctors are in attendance as are kiosks selling burgers, espresso and the *Racing Post*. Every course has a weighing room, a paddock, a starter, a finishing line and stewards perfectly poised to hold an enquiry. The facilities, whether recently built or desperately needing a coat of paint, seem to attract the same crowd of young men in suits ignored by girls wearing high heels and party dresses, while the long-serving male members favour tweed jackets with highly polished brown brogues.

Most spectators visit only their local course plus an annual trip to Cheltenham, Ascot, The Derby or the Grand National. Owners, however, visit lots of courses (I've been to over 30). As you go from track to track you will detect a difference in local accent (although the tweed wearers in the Members' bar will try to sound the same wherever you are).

It is important to train the trainer to enter your horses into meetings as near as possible to home. That makes it easy for you to be there to watch the race (which is one of the few real pleasures you get for your money) and, assuming the trainer is fairly close, it keeps down the transport cost.

We are lucky, our three most accessible courses are all within an hour's drive and give spectators a decent day out. Uttoxeter gets about 7/10 for the Owners' and Trainers' facilities, but their marketing department always seems to attract a good crowd by giving nearly every meeting a special theme (you are surrounded by spectators enjoying a day out without being too bothered about the racing).

Bangor-on-Dee is where Point-to-Point ends and National Hunt starts. With a perfect view from the bank that overlooks the course there is no need for a grandstand. Being less than 45 minutes from home, we are bound to bump into plenty of familiar faces, which was always a worry when they put a few pounds on Alex's horse.

Haydock and Aintree are the most grown up of our local tracks, where we have been involved in some serious Saturday racing, but so far have avoided winning a big race or being interviewed by Clare Balding. Haydock clearly wants to look after us with a free three-course lunch which I give 7/10.

When you first become an owner you will cancel everything in your diary and travel to wherever your horse is running, however long the journey takes. After a time you are tempted to stay at home and watch the race on television but there is no point in being an owner if you always miss out on the excitement of saddling up, discussing the race plan with your jockey in the parade ring and listening, tight lipped, after the race to the jockey's reason why you were pulled up three from home.

Even now, after over twelve years and 10,000 miles of travelling, often to watch our horse finish well down a mediocre field, I feel slightly guilty if I don't turn up to watch any race which is within two-and-a-half hours of home.

As a result we got to know, but not always love, a number of courses within reasonable driving range. Ludlow, Stratford and Warwick are not too far from our Cheshire home. Ludlow is where our first horse had his first run, at Warwick we had our first winner and after our first run at Stratford, jockey Richard Johnson advised me that our first horse, Transatlantic, should abandon racing and find his happiness elsewhere.

All of these courses give an acceptable welcome to

the owners and trainers, but a bit further down the road at Hereford owners were met by a bad-tempered car park attendant and then we were stuffed into an Owners' and Trainers' bar that was slightly smaller than a modest village cricket pavilion. Few owners would have been sorry when the Hereford closure was announced in 2012, an event that then made Leicester my least favourite racecourse – for me Leicester lacks any charisma.

Alex wasn't very keen on Huntingdon when, after a four-hour drive, she arrived in time for Henry Daly to tell her that he'd decided to withdraw her horse. Huntingdon returned to favour two years later when, for the first and only time, Alex had 1st and 2nd in the same race.

Towcester is one of the courses where you feel the members are much more important than the owners (there is no Owners' or Trainers' car park) so if I've got to drive nearly three hours to get to a course I would rather go to Chepstow where, on our first visit, we got a warm welcome on a very cold day, and won the big race. You tend to like a venue if your horse wins. It was a long journey home from watching mediocre performances at Taunton and Exeter.

Our horses have run at some courses that I've never seen – we have always missed our performances at Folkestone, Lingfield Park, Ffos Las, Musselburgh and Market Rasen.

Nor have we ever seen any of our runs at Southwell, but we have been there. About twenty years ago, long before Alex persuaded me to buy that first racehorse, we were staying nearby in Uppingham and decided Southwell sounded an attractive place to have a day out. My only previous visit was in 1962, during my time as a Nottingham University student, when I was part of a party that got thrown out of

The Saracens Head for stealing their 'Charles II slept here' blue plaque.

Southwell Racecourse has even less charm than Leicester, mainly Flat and all weather, it seems to have meetings every week, including the occasional National Hunt card. We went on a cold and windy day when nearly all the 500 or so racegoers were stuck in the bar, betting and watching the races on television.

Apart from Southwell we've been to several other Flat-only courses including Chester, only ten miles from home – the oldest course in the country – and Windsor, where we went to one of their regular Monday evening meetings. We went to Ascot, in 1983, long before we even thought of ownership, though it wasn't the big Royal Ascot week, which I now regard as a nuisance because the crowds keep regular customers away from our shoe repair shop down the road. Ascot has jump meetings and we have had a runner, but due to a diary clash we had to watch on television at home. We have also been entertained at York, Newmarket and the very attractive Goodwood.

Perhaps the best day out is Ladies' Day at Aintree, but an ordinary Aintree meeting has hardly any atmosphere. It is the same at Doncaster. These are courses designed for big crowds, so an ordinary race day has no buzz.

Cheltenham always has atmosphere, not just during The Festival, but at every other meeting and much the same can be said of Newbury and Sandown.

Every course can produce happy memories, especially if you get good weather – it is a pity our only visit to Kelso was in driving rain – and if you get a winner. We were never lucky at Worcester.

Part of the enjoyment of being an owner is the opportunity to visit lots of courses. Without the racetracks we wouldn't be able to run our horses, but they need to remember that without our horses they wouldn't have a business.

RACEGOING

Before Alex ever owned any racehorses we went racing about twice a year. If we were invited to enjoy the hospitality of banks, accountants or lawyers we felt obliged to spend time in the corporate tent, but I preferred just paying at the gate, free to roam round and take in the scene.

You don't just go to the races to watch horses, you are there to watch the other people. A sizeable proportion of the spectators seem to stay in the bar or hang around in a restaurant; I like to wander and take in the sights as I go. I see the important people in the paddock while I weigh up form alongside more professional punters who lean on the rails beside me.

When I place my bet with a bookie or on the Tote, I find it impossible to guess whether the person ahead of me in the queue is going to put on a bet of £200 or £2 – serious gamblers aren't easy to spot.

By the time I reach a vantage point to watch the race a healthy proportion of the drinkers and diners will have left the sweaty atmosphere of the bar to reveal clear evidence that for most race meetings you can make up your own dress code. There are women dressed for a wedding and men in shiny suits. Girls in very high heels and some scruffy guys in trainers who will probably have been banned from smarter bars.

After, hopefully, a return trip to collect my winnings, it's back to the paddock to pick the next winner. Following the same sequence for the six or seven races on the card was a great way to spend the afternoon. I always found it fun watching others having fun.

Once I found I was married to an owner, race days followed an entirely different routine.

Nowadays I never have to pay to go in. The car park ticket will have arrived by post from Weatherbys with a charming letter from the racecourse thanking you for entering the horse and saying how pleased they will be to see you on the day. They also tell you about the fabulous food and dress code in the Owners' and Trainers' bar.

You don't need to be there until an hour before your horse is due to run, but if you arrive after the meeting has started the Owners' car park will probably be full. This is normal; patrons, stewards and members seem to be more important.

With an air of calm superiority you take your privilege card to the Owners' and Trainers' entrance where you might be cross-examined by a gate keeper before claiming your badge and a free copy of the race card.

If you have time to spare, take advantage of the free cup of tea in the Owners' and Trainers' bar and watch the next race, but make sure you are ready for the appearance of your horse, being led by a stable lad to the saddling enclosure. You may be treated to a few leisurely circuits of this private parade ring before your horse is taken to one of the stalls to be saddled up. This is the time to be brave: as the owner, you are expected to join your horse in the stall, where you will shortly be joined by your trainer carrying a saddle that has just been collected from the weighing room. It is normal, but not essential, to give the horse a good luck pat, and this is the time to press £30 into the stable lad's (or girl's) hand. Your main job is now done and you can leave the team to tighten the tack and stick a sponge in the horse's mouth (which I presume provides the same sort of boost a swig of lemon barley water gives to Andy Murray before he walks on court).

You are free to walk nonchalantly into the centre of the paddock without looking at the spectators leaning on the rails who you hope are jealously looking at *you*.

It will be about seven minutes before the jockeys arrive, and during that time you should closely examine the horses, as they go round you, while appearing to talk earnestly to your trainer. A tip here: if Clare Balding or anyone else approaches with a microphone they almost certainly don't want to talk to you. Leave them to your trainer.

When the little pack of colourful jockeys appears there is usually a worrying moment when you think your guy can't work out who or where you are, but soon you are united and listening to the last-minute instructions. It usually goes like this. Trainer: 'Are there any wanting to make the running?' Jockey: 'Two or three will go at a good gallop.' Trainer: 'Keep him handy for the first mile then take it from there.' I suspect that most groups have come up with exactly the same plan.

Almost as soon as the jockey has arrived, smiled, shaken your hand and talked through the tactics he, or she, has gone to join your horse and disappeared onto the track. It is time for you, too, to leave the paddock and pick your place to watch the race. Alex always liked to watch alone, I go with the trainer.

We seldom say a word. If things look to be going well I don't want to break the spell, if we are struggling at the back of the field there is very little that needs to be said. As soon as the race is over we break our silence – instant joy and even a hug if we have won, calm, 'Not bad!' for a place and a lot more silence if we didn't even finish.

We head off to meet horse and jockey in the Winners' enclosure, or, if we failed to finish in the first four, at another area where other owners are waiting for an explanation from their losing jockey.

Although you try to be cool and calm as you pick up the prize after a win you should be feeling a real buzz because that is as good as racing ever gets.

Once your race is over it is time go home, you have seen what you came for and there doesn't seem much point in staying any longer. But after a win, there's one more duty to perform. You are normally invited into the office for a glass of champagne, while watching a replay of the race. Then, clutching your modest trophy you can proudly push through the crowd and find your car at the far end of the Owners' and Trainers' car park.

Being there is so much better than watching a winner on television.

PLACING A BET

It doesn't make much sense to back your own horse, when, as an owner, you've already invested so much money and past experience has proved that you seldom win. Forget the idea that owners benefit from inside tips. Their trainers are prone to encourage false hopes with tips that tend towards the bullish side of optimistic.

I just feel that if I don't place a bet I'm being disloyal to the horse. My mother and father would never have approved, which is probably why I felt guilty when I furtively queued to place a bet on the 1979 Grand National at the seedy little John Peel shop in Alderley Edge – no television screens, lavatories, seats, or free little biros in those days.

Today I'm a frequent visitor to Betfred, Ladbrokes, Coral or William Hill; not that I have an addiction to gambling but they are the only places where I can watch our horses race when I am touring round our shops. I place my £10 each way to support the horse and so, with a clear conscience, I can fill my pocket with their little biros.

I don't bet on our runners when we watch at home on Channel 4, At the Races or Racing UK. I have always thought that opening an online betting account is the start of a slippery slope that could lead to compulsive gambling.

I only place simple bets, never more than £20 and usually a lot less. I don't make fancy forecasts; my bets are placed for either a win or a place. In the days when I went to Belle Vue dog track I confidently went up to the bookies and asked for 'traps 2 and 5 reversed', indicating two bets on dogs 2 and 5 to finish 1st and 2nd or vice versa. That is as complicated as my betting ever got. Although I was a mathematician at school I've never mastered spread betting or bothered to understand the workings of the Exacta, Quadpot or Trifecta that are offered on the Tote. I've visited Vegas several times but never had the courage to sit down to play pontoon or poker. On my last visit I found the fruit machines were so complicated I gave up after the first $10 and spent my money on watching David Copperfield and Bette Midler.

BEGINNER'S GUIDE TO BETTING

As this part of the book is meant to enlighten the infrequent racegoer I will stop talking about complications and give you a beginner's guide to betting.

If we entertain a racing virgin they are often bemused before reaching the racecourse, because I buy them a copy of the *Racing Post*, which tells you everything and a lot more on top. The list of runners, riders, owners and trainers in each race includes a picture of the racing colours, age, rating, past form and whether the horse is wearing a tongue strap or blinkers. At the bottom of the list will be the forecast betting odds and an expert opinion on how things will work out. Move to another page (if you know where to look) and you can find full details of the last five races and the tips from every national newspaper. If you have the time you can check which horses have travelled furthest to the course (it is for you to decide whether you believe the trainer thinks it well worth the trip or that the horse will be too tired after the journey). In addition there is the recent record of every trainer and jockey in the race. Having baffled our guest with all the facts they sensibly decide to back the horses with pretty names.

Before I move on from the *Racing Post* I should explain that the paper isn't just a catalogue of racing statistics; the front few pages give a detailed report on yesterday's racing followed by an analysis of who will win today. I like the back pages, which, starting with football, analyse the likely odds on snooker, rugby league, rugby union, cricket, boxing, golf and tennis. If there is a world tiddlywinks championship it probably would appear in the *Racing Post*.

Holding a *Racing Post* as you walk round Newbury or Cheltenham is almost as important as wearing tweed and a tie. Even better if your horse gets a mention in the editorial and better still if you appear on the list of important birthdays.

Back to betting and the beginner's guide. The first-time spectator has nothing to worry about – however hard you try there is little chance of losing as much as the racehorse owners. There are three places to bet. On the Tote, at the on-course betting shop or with the bookies.

The Tote tries to make life complicated as soon as you arrive by promoting their Placepot and Jackpot bets that require a forecast of six races during the day. I think these bets are best ignored. It takes a lot of time and trouble to fill in their lottery-type betting slip; you will have to stay all day to find out if you are a winner and when I did win the Placepot on a big day at Aintree I was one of over 1,000 winners and received a dividend of £4.85. As a beginner it is better to bet for your horse to either win or be placed (that usually means in the first three but can differ depending on the number of runners). 'Each way' means a bet for a win and a place so it is two bets and £5 each way will cost you £10. You have no idea what odds are being offered by the Tote until the race is over. It all depends how much is staked on each horse. The Tote takes a meaningful percentage as profit and the balance is handed out to the winning punters.

At the on-course betting shop you have the choice between

the odds quoted when you place your bet and the starting price. If you don't win it doesn't matter which one you pick.

The Betfred shop to be found at the races is little different from the one on your local high street but you won't be able to bet with Honest Joe the bookie in the middle of Bolton or Basingstoke. Bookies add to the fun of a day at the races. Don't just pick the most honest looking one with an attractive girl typing the bets into a laptop that has sadly replaced the big ledger. Simply search for the best odds and when you think you have found them, pounce – pass over a tenner and declare '£10 win Archer's Hideaway' or '£5 each way Bobby Dazzler', put the ticket in your pocket and make a note where you need to return to collect your winnings.

Once the bet has been placed, move away. If you are tempted to look at any more bookies I'll guarantee you will spot some more favourable odds and feel like a bit of a loser before the race has even started.

Don't be surprised if you win – first-time gamblers often get lucky but I can guarantee that your luck won't last. At the races, owners and punters lose money but the bookies make a profit.

THE SUPPORTING CAST

Although I can be quite critical of the way owners get such a poor deal with pathetic prize money and some second rate facilities, I would never want to manage a racecourse. Many of our major National Hunt venues have racing on fewer than twenty days a year – Aintree only has eight and three of those make up the Grand National meeting. For the rest of the time they have to seek hospitality income from weddings, corporate dinners and conferences. Course directors are to be congratulated on being so commercial, with a special award to Chester which has a thriving pub in the middle of the course.

It must be a nightmare putting the team together for the few days when racing takes place. All of a sudden you need a small army of gate keepers, car park attendants and caterers, who will be joined by bookies, burger bars and the security guards from G4S.

The real stars are the stable handlers, the starter and the stewards who make sure the racing runs smoothly. Then we have those who are there to help when things go wrong – the vet, the doctor and the ambulance that follows every race (having viewed one race from a vet's car that circled the track, I got a proper idea of the speed horses go. I'm not surprised there are so many injuries).

While all these other people are working behind the scenes you will regularly see the same trainers, jockeys and other owners. However, among these familiar faces are a few characters who seem to turn up everywhere but you can't work out why they are there. They seem to know everyone, often appear in the paddock, but never finish in the Winners' enclosure.

They are the Breeders and Bloodstock Agents here to study form and oil their lines of communication. They are the property dealers and merchant bankers of racing, keeping below the radar like a footballer's agent but making a percentage out of many of the deals that are done. I suspect they make a healthy profit helping owners to buy the horses that will almost certainly lose them money.

RACING DICTIONARY

Each hobby and profession has its own language and racing is no exception. I've therefore compiled a selection of racing jargon and terminology to give the novice owner a head start before meeting their peers in the Owners' and Trainers' bar. Newcomers to the game may find it fairly easy to look the part, but can fall down on the buzzwords. This list may help.

Ante post A betting term that refers to sentiment in the run up to a race. The ante post favourite three days before the 2015 general election was Ed Miliband.

At the post Nothing to do with Royal Mail – this is another way of saying 'at the start'.

Backward Generally used by trainers in the phrase 'a bit backward' to explain why your horse needs many more months of training fees before being ready to race, and to prepare you for a disappointing first appearance.

Ballotted out Provisional race listings often list far more entrants than the race can safely accommodate (there is usually a limit of between eighteen and 24). Many will withdraw to race elsewhere but if there are not enough withdrawals, the horses with the lowest ratings will be balloted out. If this happens to you, any promises made to you by the racecourse – e.g. warm welcome, free carvery – are likely to become worthless.

Bleeder A bleeder is a horse that has burst a blood vessel – the blood usually appears through the nose. This could be a sinister sign of a serious health problem so if it happens before a race the vet will step in and your horse will be withdrawn.

Blow out A short training run of about a mile, a day or so before running a race.

Blow up Quite the reverse – when a horse blows up it runs out of puff and is left way behind the rest of the field.

Bolted up This phrase can be used to describe a horse that shoots ahead of the other runners and wins easily.

Bottle Can be applied to horses or jockeys – having the courage to be competitive. Bottle is also a term used by bookmakers – it's betting slang for odds of 2/1.

Boxed in Hampered by other horses, so unable to run freely. Don't be hard on the horse, blame the jockey – as in 'he allowed himself to get boxed in'.

Break in Training a young horse to wear a saddle and get used to being ridden is called 'breaking in'. Some trainers send young horses away to a specialist who will break in your horse (for a fee!).

Broken down If the commentator says your horse has broken down, fear the worst. It may not have fallen at a fence but injuries can happen between fences. It happened to one of Alex's horses, 300 yards into its first race – it not only broke down, it broke a leg and had to be put down.

Brought down The sort of bad luck that you have to take in your stride. Just on the day when your horse has never looked better and is jumping out of its skin a clumsy jockey jumps across you and brings you to the floor. The *Racing Post* will simply report that you fell at the fourth but you know that you would have won if your horse hadn't been brought down.

Bumper   Using this term demonstrates that you know a fair bit about the sport. Bumper is an alternative term for the National Hunt Flat races, designed to give inexperienced horses their first sight of a racecourse. Trainers often claim bumpers aren't about winning, but although they say, 'I just hope he/she enjoys it', they're desperately keen to finish in front. Bumpers are nearly always the last race on the card, so, even if you saddle the winner, most spectators will have left for home before you step up to receive your bottle of champagne.

Cheek pieces   Quite attractive bits of sheepskin attached to the bridle. They are not there to make the horse look prettier; the object is to aid concentration by making it difficult for the horse to look backwards.

Connections   A word to cover anyone who is involved with the horse, particularly the owner and trainer, but could extend to the stable lads, the guy who drove the horse box and perhaps the dog next door. It is a particularly useful word for commentators who can't remember the owner or trainer's name as in 'I'm sure the connections will be more than pleased with this performance'.

Cover or covering   Words used to describe mating, an expensive game if you own the mare but a money spinner for the stallion's owner and the guy who runs the stud farm.

Covered up   Nothing to do with mating, it's when a

jockey tries to keep the horse among a group of other runners to stop it running too freely.

Cut   If your trainer talks of 'a bit of cut in the ground', he is describing a course that is getting a bit soft so you can expect galloping horses to leave a trail of mud. If on the other hand the trainer talks about your horse having 'the cut' then you will be getting a bill from the vet – it's another term for gelding.

Dark horse   Nothing to do with its colour, this refers to a horse with hidden potential. The talent may have been deliberately concealed by the trainer carefully picking races that don't reveal the real horse until springing a surprise off a generous handicap.

Drifter   This does not refer to a wayward horse that fails to concentrate but is applied to those that fail to impress the punters so that the odds go up (drift) in the betting.

Drop in class   Having failed to do well, pick a race against inferior horses. If the handicapper has done a good job you still won't win.

Drop in trip   Enter for a shorter race, usually after failing to feature in a previous race.

Dwell at the start   Setting off after the rest of the field has already gone due to a reluctant horse or lack of concentration on the part of the horse or jockey.

Entire horse   A horse that has not been gelded, perhaps in the hope that it will earn a future fortune as a busy stallion.

Front runner   Some horses like to be in the front of the field. It is rare to lead from start to finish but it has happened a few times for Arctic Ben, the only Timpson winning horse ridden by A.P. McCoy.

A front runner usually gets overtaken well before the finish but while in the lead no one can bring you down, you are well seen on television and get plenty of mentions on the commentary.

Gelding   A horse that has been castrated. The operation is thought to give an advantage over jumps but will seriously hamper the chance of earning any stud fees.

Get a leg   Basically this is bad news. Obviously a horse has four legs but if your trainer says your potential champion has got a leg then one of the four has a problem. Every injury from tendon trouble to 'a little niggle' will lead to some substantial vets' fees and many months before your horse will be fit enough to race again.

Get handy   An expression generally used in conversation between jockeys and trainers in the paddock before the race. 'Get handy and see where we are with half a mile to go' is a phrase designed to build the owner's confidence but can be loosely translated as 'I don't think we have much of a chance but try and keep up with the others and pray for a miracle'.

Get the trip   A term used when a horse is still running well at the end of a race, while others have started to struggle far from home (see 'off the bridle').

Go through the card   This generally means much more than simply casting your eye over the race card. This describes the ultimate success of winning every race at a meeting. It is normally punters or tipsters who go through the card; it is a very rare feat for a jockey, and even the wealthiest owner is unlikely to have enough horses in training to make it a possibility.

Going   The going, or the state of the ground whether firm, good, soft or heavy, is often quoted by trainers as the reason why a horse has been withdrawn, or has performed below expectations. Some trainers spend most of the season looking for the right ground only to find the going was far too soft.

Going down   Even if they have to run uphill horses are always said to go down to the start.

Green   For the first few races expect your trainer to blame any lack of success on the horse being 'a bit green'. It means that your horse still has a lot to learn, which is presumably what we pay the trainers for!

Hacked up   In general use the phrase means something pretty nasty like maimed, mutilated or mangled but in racing it takes on an entirely different meaning. A horse has hacked up when it wins easily – so easy it might as well have been out on a hack.

Jocked off   Not as rude as it sounds. The term is used when a jockey, who has already been booked to ride in a race, is replaced by another rider. As well as being jocked off, the original jockey will be pretty hacked off especially if the horse then hacks up.

Keen   As soon as your trainer uses the phrase 'a bit keen' before a race you can probably forget any thoughts of winning.

   Keen is a kind way of saying the horse is so overwrought, nervous and excited it uses up lots of energy before the start and has nothing left to give if it manages to reach the finish.

Long shot   A horse with little chance of winning, as indicated by the big odds offered by the bookies. The owner of a long shot still has high hopes, but the reason for the low rating is usually very clear well before the end of the race.

Non-runner This is a horse that the trainer has declared as a runner at the last entry stage (usually by 10.00am on the day before the race) but, despite having committed the owner to pay an entry fee, withdraws the horse from the race.

The trainer will have several good reasons – also entered for another race that seemed a better place to go, change in the ground, injured on the journey or decided the competition was too hot. All this isn't so bad if your horse is withdrawn before you set off from home, but it isn't much fun doing a 250-mile round trip to watch a non-runner.

Non-trier When a jockey fails to get the horse to perform at its full ability it is deemed to be a non-trier. The implication is that the horse is being held back for a good (or in reality bad) reason. The plot could be to protect a high handicap and surprise the bookies on a future outing, but the motive may be even more sinister. This is so serious that all concerned, jockey, trainer and owner, could be banned from future racing.

Off the bridle If the commentator says that your horse is already off the bridle with more than a mile to go you can probably forget any ideas of the Winners' enclosure. Jockeys don't just sit on your horse and hope they are in control. Think of the bridle as a touch on the brake, the way your jockey keeps at a steady pace – once your horse is 'off the bridle' the horse is running out of get up and go and instead of holding back the jockey starts making eccentric moves to make it go faster.

Usually 'off the bridle' means you've lost.

Off the pace   Used to refer to a horse that is well behind the rest of the field. This may not be a problem if your horse is in the first few furlongs of a 3-mile race, but it is not good news to be off the pace with half a mile to go.

One paced   Some horses have an irritating habit of raising your hopes by leading the field for five-sixths of the race only to be overtaken in the home straight and finish out of the first four. These horses are one-paced – when the jockey puts a foot on the accelerator by coming off the bridle nothing happens. One-paced horses seldom win unless all the rest of the field falls down.

Out of the handicap   The highest-handicapped horse in a race will normally carry the maximum weight of 11st 12lbs; the other horses carry a pound for every point difference in handicap. But there is usually a minimum weight of 10 stone so any horse that has a handicap more than 28 lower than the top weight has to still carry 10 stone and is said to be out of the handicap. But as my father said whenever I played against much better golfers, 'You might not win but it is good experience'.

Overweight   You will be pleased to hear this is a term which applies to jockeys not owners. It always seems unfair on people who eat only lettuce leaves to publicly point out that they have put on a couple of pounds, but jockeys who ride the lowest-handicapped horses may have to weigh in at 10 stone, if not they are overweight and the horse has to carry the extra pounds.

Pulled up   A horse is pulled up by a jockey who decides it is in no one's interest to finish the race. Don't be alarmed – the horse probably isn't lame, but once the jockey sees no chance of any prize money it makes sense to stop and save the horse for what will hopefully be a better performance next time.

Rule 4 Although this is purely to do with betting, the simple mention of Rule 4 shows you know your stuff. Rule 4 states what happens to a bet placed before a horse withdraws and becomes a non-runner. It means the odds are adjusted and any winning punter will get less than they hoped – if they ask why, just say 'Rule 4 applies'.

Scope Tricky word because racing folk use it in two ways. A horse is said to have scope if it matures with age – a useful concept for trainers who want their owners to keep paying training fees for poor performers.

Scope is also a medical term to describe an inspection of the respiratory system. After a surprisingly poor performance your trainer may suggest having a scope. If it comes back as a bad scope your vets' fee will get much bigger.

Second string If an owner has two horses in a race the one less likely to win is called the second string. It is also normally ridden by a jockey wearing a different hat from the owner's usual colours. If a trainer is running two horses in the same race the less experienced jockey will be riding the second string.

S.P. Simple betting abbreviation for starting price.

Springer Another betting term, this describes a horse whose price reduces dramatically.

Stewards Usually picked, by the British Horseracing Authority, from the local worthy great and good gentlefolk who were riding ponies before they could walk, stewards (three at each meeting), are in charge of the racing and sit in judgement if there is any dispute.

Stewards' enquiry   If a horse or jockey is thought to be guilty of infringing the rules during a race the three stewards review a replay and decide whether to change the finishing order or punish the jockey (the horse gets away with it).

Stipendiary steward   An extra steward sent from head office to advise the local stewards (although I expect they think they know it all already).

Tongue strap   This is literally a strip of material that ties the horse's tongue to the lower jaw to stop the horse swallowing its tongue during a race. It is a rather unpleasant procedure to watch when your horse is being saddled up.

Turned out   A phrase that can be used in two ways. At the end of the season the horse will be turned out into the fields – good news for the owner because the training fees are replaced by much lower keep fees.

Before many races an award is made, usually by the sponsor's wife or girlfriend, to the best turned out horse. Good news for the stable lad or lass who has prepared the pretty horse but an omen for the owner – the best turned out runner seldom wins the race.

Under orders   When the horses are all lined up ready to go and the starter lifts his flag they are 'under starter's orders' and no more bets can be placed. (It is for a somewhat different reason that it is also the title of this book.)

Weighed in   The jockey, holding the saddle, sits on the scales in the weighing room before the race to make sure he is complying with the handicap. After the race those jockeys who are placed repeat the procedure. If all is correct the announcer declares they are 'weighed in', the finishing order is confirmed and winning bets are paid out.

Winners' enclosure   A good place to finish this list. It is difficult to hide the smug expression on your face if, after a race, you can stride towards the Winners' enclosure to receive an upbeat briefing from the jockey. It is not a bad feeling if you are placed 2nd, 3rd or 4th but being a winner is to be cherished – it doesn't happen very often. A few spectators will watch your horse return for the moment of triumph but only a few will stay long enough to see you pick up the trophy.

I have now given even the greenest racegoer enough information to understand what follows, as I take you through some of the trials, tribulations and occasional triumphs of the last few years.

Before I weakened and bought Transatlantic, Alex's first horse, a friend of ours told me to expect a few disappointments but added that they are more than compensated for by the thrill of watching a winner go past the post. He didn't mention much about the cost, but simply added that owning a racehorse is a marvellous way to lose money.

2008–2009

THE HORSES

When I look back at Alex's first four years as an owner it is hardly surprising she came to the conclusion that she needed to own several horses to get an active season. When we only had Transatlantic it was a long wait between races and there was always the danger that one injury would wipe out an entire season. It was five years before Alex got her first win. By 2007/08 she had six horses and was getting used to regular visits to the Winners' enclosure. This proved Alex was right to point out that with more horses you are likely to have more winners, but I also noticed that you will lose more money. Even in a successful season each horse will cost an average of £10,000 assuming a little bit of prize money and only a modest bill from the vet.

Before the start of 2008/09 Arctic Ben was purchased to replace Transatlantic so we kept the number of horses up to six, which I hoped would provide plenty of excitement for Alex and put a decent amount of prize money into the Weatherbys account.

The line-up at the start of the season was:

TRAINED BY HENRY DALY:

Thievery age 7 grey gelding (rating 79)

Last season Thievery recorded his first win and was never out of the first four in five starts. Alex has always been particularly fond of Thievery who has shown how much pleasure you can get from a horse rated in the 70s.

Ordre de Bataille age 6 grey gelding (rating 115)

Due to a succession of persistent niggles Batty hasn't run since December. With a rating of 115 we are expecting to travel further than Bangor-on-Dee to see him race in competitive company.

Timpo age 5 chestnut gelding (rating 112)

Won two of his only three outings last season and has already attracted the handicapper's interest with a mark of 112. With plenty of promise we are hoping for a good season.

Arctic Ben age 4 grey gelding (novice)

Our biggest ever purchase at nearly £100,000 comes on the back of a bumper win and with plenty of promise. Shouldn't be long before we see him performing in his first Novice Hurdle.

Cobbler's Queen age 4 brown mare (novice)

Has run only two races – both in hot company, both decent prize money, mares-only bumpers at Sandown and Aintree – which, despite being well down the field on each occasion, brought warm words from jockeys Richard Johnson and

Mark Bradburne. We are looking for some good results in novice hurdles leading to a competitive handicap.

🐎 TRAINED BY PAUL WEBBER:

Key Cutter age 4 bay gelding (novice)
A new boy who is highly regarded by the yard, but you don't win any prize money on the gallops at home. We hope to see him in a bumper well before Christmas.

OTHER DISTRACTIONS

My life changed during the summer of 2008. Our son Edward surprised the rest of the family when he decided to enter the world of politics early in 2007 and was adopted as the prospective Conservative parliamentary candidate for Crewe and Nantwich. With the seat held by the experienced and popular Labour MP Gwyneth Dunwoody, Edward's chances of success at the next general election were pretty slim. But in April 2008 Gwyneth suddenly died and after a high profile by-election Edward won the seat with a majority of nearly 7,000. Twenty-four hours later, at Uppingham Speech Day, I introduced myself to a stranger, 'I'm John Timpson.' She replied, 'Are you any relation to the man who has just been elected to Parliament?' Since then people refer to me as Edward's father.

Edward's victory was helped by the unpopularity of Gordon Brown, who was heading towards an economic crisis. Fortunately, the subsequent bank collapse and slowdown in retail sales had little impact on the Timpson business. While other retailers struggled, we had a big stroke of luck that helped increase the number of our shops from 600 to 830 and grow profits by 40 per cent.

While Edward was canvassing in Crewe, his elder brother James, our CEO, was negotiating to buy a chain of about 50 photo and dry cleaning concessions in Sainsbury's. They both achieved success on the same day.

In December 2008, we got a bigger, and totally unexpected, opportunity when Bowie Castlebank, owner of the Max Spielmann and Klick photo processing shops, went into administration. The switch from analogue spools of film to digital cameras had completely changed the photo world. Sales fell dramatically and the shops were making a loss. But, when a business goes into administration, its property leases come to an end. In a very weak property market we were able to negotiate better terms including, in most cases, at least six months rent free. In our first year, this previously loss-making business turned in a £3 million profit.

We also sowed the seeds for future expansion when we opened a ten-shop trial of Timpson concessions within Tesco. They were tiny units inside modest parts of the Tesco portfolio, but we did well enough to be given the chance to open many more a few years later.

In December 2008 the Countess of Wessex officially opened our refurbished offices in Wythenshawe, a revolutionary open plan design that incorporated two traditional phone boxes and a fireman's (or, to be politically correct, 'firefighter's') pole. The Countess took it all in her stride until she revealed that her shoes needed heeling. Our while-you-wait job provided the perfect photo opportunity.

Top of our discussion with the Countess was the way we had started to actively employ ex-offenders, and our first, recently opened prison workshop in Liverpool.

Despite our increasing commitment to racing we had four holidays in France. Twice to meet up with friends, once to join son James and his family, and a two-night trip to Paris so we could see Celine Dion in concert. We also had our usual fortnight on Mustique and four short spells at our holiday home on Anglesey.

Visits to Wits End, our Anglesey cottage, have taken on a business dimension since Alex took on the challenge of buying the local pub. She was so successful with The White Eagle that we undertook an even bigger task down the road by buying The Maelog Lake Hotel near Rhosneigr. Visits to Anglesey have become a mixture of business and pleasure.

We enjoyed one other short break abroad, to Vegas where we went to watch Bette Midler. It was a record year for concert going. You can get a flavour of our taste in music when you see some of the names we saw live in concert – Bruce Springsteen, Liza Minnelli, Michael Bublé, Elton John, Tina Turner and Lionel Richie.

It was probably the first year that I realised that, with no executive responsibilities, I was now approaching retirement. As a result, Alex and I threw ourselves into a quest to pack in lots of the pleasures that had been missing from our past. We welcomed horseracing as a significant part of our new life, but saw no reason to give up the rest of our interests. So Alex spent most of her time helping past and present foster children. I became a Vice Chairman of Trustees at Uppingham School while playing plenty of snooker, tennis, real tennis and golf, but still found time to visit over 600 shops a year.

Racing was the new hobby that we fitted happily into the rest of our schedules. None of our passions and pastimes make a profit so it was easy to accept that horseracing would lose us money.

We started the new season with high hopes.

THE RACING SEASON

Friends, trying to show an interest in our hobby, ask 'How are the horses doing?' If the question is posed between May and October there is seldom anything to report.

The National Hunt season ends with a big meeting at Sandown on the third Saturday in April. Although the next season starts on the following day we are unlikely to have another runner until the end of October. Alex isn't keen on summer racing – she thinks firm ground and warm sunshine are designed for the high heels and floral dresses worn at Ascot and Epsom. Jump racing suits softer ground, Hunter wellies and the tweed jackets seen at Cheltenham.

We usually enjoy a break from full training fees and race meetings. It's the perfect time to reassess our performance and plan ahead, but for most of our summer is forgotten.

Racing stables operate every day of the year. Any parent whose child has a pony quickly discovers that horses require constant attention. However, on most summer days our trainers probably don't need to do much more than count the number of horses in their fields to make sure none have run away.

It's a good time for trainers to take a holiday but they may have a few horses racing in the summer and must keep up the public relations through regular contact with their owners. Their phone calls and emails can be a cause for concern. Our first reaction is 'what has gone wrong now?' Usually there is no need to worry – we get emailed pictures to prove that the horses are all fit and coming on nicely with a plan to appear sometime in October. Occasionally we are told about a new niggle and the need to check with the vet. This kind of call is nowhere near as expensive as the one when the trainer starts: 'I've just found a fantastic looking grey with incredible credentials who will be ready for hurdle races after Christmas'. I'm a soft touch, usually agreeing to buy a new horse with a fraction of the research we carry out on a new shoe repair shop, which is certain to be much, much more profitable.

Although we take a break, jump jockeys continue to look for as many rides as possible. Summer success scores just as many points towards the jockeys' championship as a win in the winter. Coming first at Uttoxeter in June or Worcester in August adds the same points to their tally as winning the Cheltenham Gold Cup. There are a few big jump meetings in the summer, but even with a first prize of £20,000, a National Hunt meeting on a hot summer day doesn't feel like the real thing.

Alex was adamant – we don't go racing in the summer. It is the time to take stock, talk about past successes, try to forget the failures, and dream of next season. Without any runners there is no chance of success or excitement but we don't have to face up to failure or disappointment. We try to visit our horses at their stables, with either breakfast at the yard or lunch at the local pub and after plenty of warm words from the trainer leave full of confidence that the horses will be in perfect condition for the start of our new season. By the end of the summer all of our past pessimism has been replaced by blind optimism that looks forward to a new season with loads of winners leading to ultimate success at the Cheltenham Festival.

The *Racing Post* in June and July is of little interest. The headlines are about Flat racing – National Hunt meetings are few and far between.

All Alex's horses are put out to grass, unlikely to be seen on a racecourse until October and Presence of Mind, in which she had a quarter share, will never be seen on a racecourse again. His four-year career showed promise that was never fulfilled. Presence of Mind taught us a lesson – use a trainer close to home. He was with Emma Lavelle near Andover, convenient for the rest of the syndicate, but a long way from Cheshire. Turning up to see his attempts to tackle fences at Fontwell Park and Folkestone meant an overnight stay. Consequently, apart from one trip to Exeter, we watched Presence of Mind at the bookies or on satellite TV. We followed his final appearance at Lingfield Park at the end of April on a website in Mustique. He was pulled up 2 miles into a 3-mile race and, three weeks later, was sold for a modest price which was given to charity.

On our return from the Caribbean we entered the world of politics. Our son Edward was the Conservative candidate at a by-election at Crewe and Nantwich, a high profile affair, well covered by the national press, which repeatedly reported Labour claims that Edward was nothing but a 'Tory Toff from Tarporley', living in a big house with a collection of llamas in his garden. Although Edward doesn't own a top hat and the llamas belong to a neighbouring farmer, it was probably fortunate that we weren't seen posing in a paddock during the by-election.

Shortly after buying our first horse, Alex was told you need to own at least five and probably ten to guarantee an annual appearance in the Winners' enclosure. The disappointment of Presence of Mind emphasised the point – only a small percentage of racehorses go to Cheltenham.

Six years ago Alex discovered the Doncaster Sales. She was looking for greys, limiting our choice and increasing the price I have to pay. On that first visit we picked three possible prospects and left Henry Daly to do the bidding. When the first came into the ring Henry never even raised his arm. Two of the big bidders, perhaps a McManus or Hemmings, were interested and quickly took the horse out of my price range. But Henry bought our second choice, a grey called Thievery (stable name, George) who has turned into an honest runner and a winner (once Henry found the right race for horses rated 0–90). George hasn't produced a profit, but he's certainly given Alex a good run for my money.

Last year at Doncaster we decided to go for it. Keen to find a Cheltenham contender I was prepared to substantially increase my budget. The best horses look so good, even I could recognise class, and we picked three for Henry to purchase. My irresponsibly high guide price proved paltry in the face of bids from one of the big hitters. Henry returned from Doncaster empty handed.

This year the Doncaster Sales coincided with Edward's by-election and instead of joining in the bidding, Alex was driving the Conservative Campaign Minibus round Crewe and Nantwich. But this didn't deter our trainers, Henry Daly and Paul Webber:

'There's your sort of horse coming up tomorrow,' said Henry.

'But I can't come to Doncaster,' I replied, 'I'm in Crewe.' 'Seriously,' said Henry repeating himself, 'it's worth a good look, just won a good class bumper and will come on even more next season.' The foolhardy figure I gave him to work on was good enough to buy another addition to Alex's stable – Arctic Ben.

Paul Webber waited until after Doncaster. 'I bought a three-year-old,' he said. 'It's big and it's grey.' Alex called at Cropredy, Paul's yard, and reported back. 'It's only just a little bit grey, but I like it.' And to seal the deal she said, 'That's it! Seven horses will be enough, I won't want us to buy another for some time.'

I rang Paul and accused him of painting the horse grey to secure Alex's approval, but still agreed to buy the horse. It needed a name. In the past we have used names connected with our business – Cobbler's Queen and Key Cutter. This time I suggested While-U-Wait, but Alex wanted something associated with the by-election. I suggested Floating Voter, Edward rejected Tarporley Toff and Alex, who had the casting vote, chose Llama Farmer. He should have his first race in 2009.

Goodbye July, another month that has gone by without any of Alex's horses seeing a racecourse. The only reminder about racing was the training bills – with all horses out to grass they were a fraction of the normal amount and were almost a pleasure to pay.

I first started thinking about the forthcoming season while I compiled my diary for the rest of the year. Alex says that by planning so far ahead I'm wishing my life away, but I need to work out how to fit everything in. First the priorities: holidays, days out with Alex, board meetings, family birthdays, school trustee dates, golfing holidays, snooker nights and real tennis. Then I pencil in my business travel – I aim to visit each of our 640 shops every eighteen months. But I have to be flexible: weddings, parties, and other invitations I can't refuse invade my carefully prepared programme, but the main disruption is caused by football and racing.

I blame Sky for fiddling with the football fixture list. During June I got advance warning of every Manchester City match. Most games were due to kick off at 3 o'clock on Saturday afternoons, but by mid-July it had all changed, a quarter of the fixtures had been moved to Sunday afternoon or Monday night. Our racing calendar is even more uncertain. When it comes to horses there is no such thing as a racing certainty.

Henry Daly thought our first race could be in October and Paul Webber even mentioned September, but I didn't take much notice. Last year we had no runner until November. We can't forecast when the action will start and certainly don't know where it will take place. I could fill my diary with all the possible meetings: Stratford, Uttoxeter, Ludlow, Hereford, Worcester, Haydock, Newbury … but there isn't much point, we could be running anywhere, at any time. The only way I'm going to see one of Alex's horses run is to cancel some shop visits, break an engagement or change the date of a board meeting. Otherwise I will have to watch all the races in Ladbrokes, William Hill or Betfred. I have, however, put one meeting in my diary – on Wednesday 3 November I hope to be at Warwick, where in 2006 and 2007 Mrs A. Timpson won the Novice Hurdle (two of the three races ever won in her colours). We are keen to make it a hat-trick, but nothing is certain. Our entry at Warwick depends on the trainer. Does he think it is a good idea, have we got the right horse for the race and will the going be too soft or too firm? So Warwick is only written in very light pencil, but at least it's in my diary – the only firm racing day in my calendar between now and Christmas. But I intend to go to lots more. Anyone with an arrangement to meet me from November onwards, for business, pleasure, golf or tennis, should be warned – I'm totally unreliable and may cancel at short notice. I don't want to miss Alex's next appearance in the Winners' enclosure.

I was right about Warwick – the going was too soft and with the race being a bit hot none of our horses made the trip – I used the gap in my diary to good use and took Alex out for lunch.

With none of Alex's horses competing during the summer I had almost forgotten about horseracing, when I opened a letter from Henry Daly advising Alex of a small increase in his training fee:

'I hope you will understand this is unavoidable,' he wrote. 'I know Gordon Brown tells us that inflation has changed very little in the last two years, but that is simply not true of us. The cost of a bag of racehorse nuts alone has gone up by 20 per cent in the last twelve months.' Humour, tact and diplomacy all in a short note, a prime example of the essential asset needed by any trainer – customer care.

The thought struck me, is there a manual to help trainers to keep even the most critical owners happy? If not, here are a few thoughts that could appear in a Trainers' Phrasebook:

HOW TO HANDLE AN OWNER

The week before a race – The object is to convince your owner that you have done everything possible to bring their horse to peak fitness without raising hopes of a certain appearance in the Winners' enclosure. Reassure your owner with:

'He's looking good.'
'Richard/Mark took him out this morning and was
   very pleased.'
'He's certainly ready for it.'
'He's come on a lot since I last spoke to you.'

But manage expectations by adding some measured words of caution:

'Let's hope he travels well to the racecourse.'
'It's a strong field.'

'The ground isn't ideal but he needs the run.'
'It will be a very good test.'

These phrases show the trainer has done a good job, without raising hopes that the horse will win. Hopefully the conversation will end with:

'I'll see you in the Owners' and Trainers' at 1.30.'

Owners believe their trainer has nothing more important to do than watch their horse every time it runs. They expect him/her to saddle it up, talk to the jockey and be there in the Winners' enclosure. Any trainer that can't be there needs a good excuse:

'We've got three horses running at Cheltenham.'
'I've a meeting in London.'
Or 'I'm taking the kids skiing.'

These are all acceptable, but don't try them more than once a season.

On the day:

In the Owners' and Trainers' bar – Give more measured assurance:

'He was jumping well yesterday.'
'As far as I can see he had a good journey.'
'It's all a bit new, he's never been to Warwick before.'
'We could have done with some rain.'

Saddling up – It's time to press the pessimistic button a little bit harder:

> 'He looks a bit keen.'
> 'The experience will do him nothing but good.'
> 'I hope 2½ miles isn't asking too much.'

The Parade Ring – Even the owner of a rank outsider becomes optimistic when they enter the Parade Ring. To dampen false hopes point out the quality of the opposition:

> 'Look at No.3, a horse built for big fences.'
> 'That yard's horses always do well here.'
> 'You can see why he's favourite.'
> 'That grey is much more mature.'
> 'We've still got a bit of growing to do.'

Greeting the jockey – Show you have a race plan but don't let your owner know too much about it:

> 'As we discussed, Richard, give him a good ride and
>   enjoy the race.'

Then leave your jockey to do his own bit of customer service.

During the race – Simple tip here: keep quiet. Communicate only by nodding or shaking your head. Towards the finish you need to pick the best phrase to explain your defeat.

After most races – Only one horse can win each race. All the others lose. Although the jockey will have already put the right spin on the horse's performance you will still need the following phrases:

> 'Not bad considering the going.'
> 'That was very good experience.'
> 'Considering he lost 10 lengths at the start, it was a good run.'
> 'Eighth in a strong field is real progress.'
> 'It's certainly been a very good test.'
> 'I was pleased with that.'
> 'He needed another half mile.'
> 'Taking into account the heavy ground it was really quite promising.'
> 'Encouraging signs for when he goes chasing next season.'

Or, for the horse that pulls up three from home:

> 'We will see what the vet says on Monday morning.'

After a win – Stay calm but look pleased. Give credit to the horse in a way that shows that your yard has done an excellent job:

> 'I knew he had it in him.'
> 'That shows how much he has improved.'
> 'I couldn't have expected it to go better.'
> 'Just as we'd hoped.'

The owner will be keen to fix the next race but never reveal future plans:

> 'We've got a lot of options.'
> 'Let's see how he is when he gets back to the yard and take it from there.'
> 'We'll give him a break and look for the right race in three or four weeks' time.'

So much for my fantasy phrase book, summer is now over, Alex's horses are back in the yard, I am paying the full training fee once again and we are looking forward to the first race sometime in October, when I expect to add a few more phrases to the manual.

I was travelling back to the office having played real tennis on Monday 1 September when I heard about Sheikh Mansour's takeover of Manchester City. I took a detour to Ladbrokes in Wythenshawe, where fortunately the odds hadn't kept up with the news, and I put what for me was a substantial amount of money on City to win the Premiership at 200/1. 'Where have you been all summer?' said the lady behind the counter. In the winter I'm a regular customer. I go there whenever one of Alex's horses is running and I'm tied to the office. My last visit was in March, when she had a horse running at Huntingdon on the same day as our board meeting.

Being married to a racehorse owner has its drawbacks – the training fees, vets' bills, the amazing price some people pay for an unbroken horse that 'should have a chance of getting to Cheltenham' and the way that racing can ruin my diary. Lunch with long-lost business friends and games of golf are unravelled in an instant when our horse is declared at a meeting where we might just possibly appear in the Winners' enclosure. I have yet to reschedule a board meeting but I have given 'backword' to golf, tennis, business meetings and even Manchester City.

A bit more notice would help. Top owners can map out a winter schedule with their horses following a defined route to Cheltenham via Warwick, Haydock, Newbury and Sandown. Most owners with horses rated between 85 and 110 have no plans. We don't even know when or where we will make our first appearance of the season, but judging by the increased size of the recent invoices I know all our horses are in full training and should be fully fit.

I was planning my autumn diary when I realised Alex was looking over my shoulder. 'Lots of golf and tennis I suppose,' she said. 'You should be visiting more shops. As the father figure of our business you should talk to branch staff, not play games or sit in silly meetings.' 'But,' I protested, 'in eighteen months I've visited every branch.' 'In that case,' said Alex, 'start all over again.'

Last year I spent over 100 days on the road. My father taught me to visit every outlet, and now my son James does the same. I've been touring the high street for over 45 years.

A month ago I played golf with a guy who talked about his visit to our Bournemouth branch. He was amazed our manager not only knew me, but had met me several times. 'Do they know you are coming?' he asked. 'If I go with an area manager, everyone is prepared,' I replied, 'but on my own I get one surprise visit before telephones are buzzing.'

One day after calling at Huddersfield I arrived at a busy Bradford branch as the phone rang. I answered it. 'Just so you know,' said the caller, 'John Timpson is on his way.'

My golf pal had another question, 'What's your agenda, is there a checklist?' 'I don't look for trouble,' I replied, 'I'm not an inspector, I go for a chat. But as a result I know every shop from the front door to the lavatory, my mind keeps an up to date picture of the high street in general and our competitors in particular, but more important I know something about our colleagues' holidays, hobbies, football teams and children.'

Occasionally I stumble on a big idea. Kelvin, in Newport, showed me how to add memorial plaques to our house sign business. In 1996, Glenn, in West Bromwich, preached the potential of watch repairs and persuaded me to give the new service a big push. It is now a £12 million business growing at 15 per cent a year. My shop visits remind me that managers know much more about their business than head office, that's why we let John design his own refit at Hammersmith and probably why he has put turnover up by 20 per cent.

Recently at a business dinner, I met a man who uses our branch in Cirencester. He was amazed I knew the name of the manager, Bill O'Dell. 'You must take ages visiting your shops to know them so well,' he said. 'Doesn't your wife complain?' 'No,' I replied, 'it is Alex who pushes me out. She says it's the best way to run the business.'

As usual, Alex is absolutely right, but as a result, while Alex is enjoying a day out at Hereford or Stratford, I will be watching the race in Ladbrokes.

The long summer lay-off is over and it's all starting to happen with two horses on the same card at Cheltenham (sounds good doesn't it?). Not The Festival of course, but Cheltenham on a Saturday was good enough for both trainers to claim that we were in hot races and warn us not to raise our hopes too high. They were right to manage expectations. In the first race Key Cutter came in 11th and we had to wait until the last race of the day to see Timpo finish in exactly the same position.

We are back in the routine and the first week of November was typical. On Tuesday we were told that Arctic Ben needed a run, but Henry Daly wasn't sure whether it would be on Thursday at Stratford, Friday at Uttoxeter or Sunday at Huntingdon. 'I can't do Thursday,' said Alex, as if it was my fault. 'That's no problem,' I said, making matters worse. 'I can change my programme and visit some nearby shops so I can see the race.' 'All right for some,' said Alex. 'If it turns out to be Sunday,' she continued, 'and we have to go to Huntingdon, I have no intention of going there and back in a day to such a dreary course. Let's stay at Uppingham on Sunday night and have a decent pub meal.'

I was really looking forward to a night out in Rutland when Alex rang on Thursday morning. 'Arctic Ben's in the 12.50 at Uttoxeter tomorrow.' I cancelled golf and a haircut, but with Uttoxeter only an hour away there was no need to set off until 11.00am. We drove there with considerable misgivings – we had been to Uttoxeter seven times and never seen any of our horses finish in the first three.

I looked at the odds the night before, expecting to see Arctic Ben installed as favourite. He wasn't, but at 9/2 must have a chance. The *Racing Post* the following morning had marked him down to 8/1 with the comment – 'Arctic Ben won a modest bumper at Ludlow in May and given his dam comes from a good jumping family looks a fair prospect.' So we were full of hope when we got to Uttoxeter in good time for the race. Although not the best on the circuit, Uttoxeter looks after owners and trainers quite well and we treated ourselves to a £3 roast beef bap, I gave £20 to our stable girl and put £20 each way on Arctic Ben. (I never quite understand why I have a much bigger than normal bet on our own horse, when I've already invested so much money to get the animal to the racecourse, in the hope I might win some prize money.)

In the paddock Henry Daly looked at the opposition. 'Pretty experienced lot this,' he said. 'Our horse has a lot to learn; most of these have been running on the Flat.' 'Why,' asked Alex intelligently, 'have you entered him for this race and the next one is a National Hunt Novice in which none of these Flat horses are allowed to appear?' 'Well,' said Henry, 'it's the trip, I only wanted him to go 2 miles. The National Hunt Novice is 2½.'

We were invited, with the other owners, to watch the race from Lady Clarke's box (her late husband transformed Uttoxeter). There was no big screen that day at Uttoxeter so I watched the race on the monitor inside the box. The picture was almost as good as the one we get on our television at home.

Apart from the rare occasion when your horse is in contention at the finish, you will, at some time during every race, realise that your jockey is not going to win. With Arctic Ben this sinking feeling came between the last two fences – he finished 5th. Not bad, in line with the forecast made in the *Racing Post*. 'And,' said Alex, with some glee, 'the favourite nearly came last. It is some consolation to know that most of the owners are as disappointed as you are.'

'A bit green,' said Mark Bradburne, as he jumped off Arctic Ben, 'but a nice ride. He was running on well over the last two fences.' 'Yes,' said Henry smiling, 'I think we need 2½ miles next time out.'

Monday isn't a great day to go racing. As I understand it, many of the racecourses get extra money to open on Mondays and when Thievery was entered at Warwick in a Monday meeting it certainly wasn't convenient for me. Travelling round some of our shops in the West Country I needed to find somewhere to see the race. I managed to spot a bookmaker in Ilminster. I was his only punter, he didn't have Racing UK so I never saw the race, all I got was the commentary. Still, the commentary couldn't have been better, my £10 each way bet was enough to encourage Thievery to jump the last fence in 1st place and run on to win by 2½ lengths. I smiled and the man behind the grille looked glum. His only transaction of the afternoon, my £10 bet had cost him £54.

Later that week, Alex had an unexpected phone call from Henry Daly. 'I want to run Thievery again,' he said. 'He's only got a 7lb penalty. If I wait for the handicapper he would go up 9lbs which might be too much – it's Hereford on Sunday.'

The weather was appalling, and we expected the

meeting to be cancelled and even if it went ahead felt Henry was sure to withdraw Thievery – two runs in a week on soft going was probably asking too much. The rain persisted and so did Henry – Thievery (better known by the stable as George) went to the start in storm conditions with the bookies offering no better than 11/10 on.

Henry was right. A handicap of 7lb wasn't enough to stop him winning and 9lbs would have been too much – he won by half a length, just edging ahead in the last 50 yards. Alex stepped up to receive the prize before we were invited into the racecourse office for a victorious glass of champagne. Everything suddenly seemed easy – two runs, two wins, with almost enough prize money to pay for a month's training fees. We were looking forward to racing the following weekend, with Key Cutter at Uttoxeter on the Saturday, a birthday party in London on Saturday night, followed by Timpo at Cheltenham on Sunday afternoon.

I'm beginning to understand why people say that being an owner is character building. Key Cutter wasn't expected to do well, but after starting at 20/1 finished with some bookies at 8/1 – they clearly saw something that I didn't. My instinct was correct, Key Cutter was well down the field. 'He was hanging right all the way round,' said jockey Will Kennedy. 'Don't know what happened – ring you tomorrow morning,' said Paul Webber. Paul was on the phone within an hour. 'Lost a shoe,' he said, 'that's the reason. Can't believe it!'

Neither could I. 'Lost a shoe' has been added to my list of reasons for a disappointing run.

Cheltenham wasn't a lot better. Timpo did okay at the start, was exactly where Henry wanted, but made no headway until the last 500 yards, when suddenly he started running faster than any other horse in the field. He finished 11th. 'Disappointing,' said Henry, 'expected better than that. He's a bit green, spent half the race looking round wondering what was going on, but in the last few yards he showed plenty of ability.' I started to wonder whether Mark Bradburne was carrying his mobile phone to compare notes with Henry before he jumped off Timpo for the inquest. Mark came towards us. 'Bit green,' he said. 'Spent half the race looking round, but the way he came on at the end shows he's got plenty of ability.'

'Still, I suppose,' I said to Alex, 'we've had a nice day out.' Cheltenham's not a bad place for an owner. I'd sent an email ahead and booked a table in the Owners' and Trainers' restaurant – a decent free lunch only matched on my travels by the hospitality at Haydock and certainly miles better than the Owners' and Trainers' shed at Hereford, where you are crammed together on a wet day like battery hens. Still, despite the lack of facilities, Hereford has happy memories – never mind the lunch, we finished in the Winners' enclosure.

Despite my career in the retail trade I'm a reluctant shopper – but I always try to come up trumps when buying Christmas presents for Alex.

Since Alex became a racehorse owner the on-course photographers have provided another type of present. When Thievery had his two wins at the beginning of November I received photographs of Alex's favourite horse from every angle – jumping the last three fences, passing the winning post and receiving the applause as he arrived in the Winners' enclosure. But you don't have to win to attract the attention of the course photographer, almost any excuse will do. Ordre de Bataille's third at Ludlow brought another package of pictures and the photographers were not deterred by Arctic Ben finishing 5th at Uttoxeter and Timpo 11th for the second consecutive time at Cheltenham, they simply snapped away and sent the pictures in the post, confident that I'd be tempted.

What a perfect Christmas present. I resisted the temptation to ask our IT Department to digitally airbrush the words 'Proof Only' and provided the course photographers with the orders they were expecting and probably deserved. I had put pictures of all Alex's horses in silver frames and wrapped them up well before Christmas Day.

With Alex out Christmas shopping and me busy in the business we failed to get to a racecourse during the second half of November. We watched the progress of Alex's horses in the bookies and on Racing UK, but we had a racing date in the diary for December. We were invited by friends to Haydock the day of the Tommy Whittle Chase. We mentioned Haydock to both Paul Webber and Henry Daly. 'If there's a suitable race it would be nice to see one of our horses run,' said Alex. Paul and Henry both obliged, a little reluctantly.

'Key Cutter might get balloted out,' said Paul.

'I've entered Timpo, but it's a bit of a hot race,' said Henry.

Key Cutter wasn't balloted out, but when Mark Bradburne brought him back a poor 12th, we wished he had been. Timpo's race was very hot, but at least two finished behind him. 'Not bad,' said Simon, who was looking after Timpo in Henry Daly's absence. 'Oh, by the way, I've got something Thievery won at Warwick a few weeks ago.' The prize was a picture of Thievery in a silver frame – although Alex's Christmas presents were already wrapped, labelled and tied up with ribbon in her Manchester City racing colours, I added this new one to the pile.

'Guess what?' said Alex three days before Christmas. 'I've got three runners on Boxing Day.' Pressgang (Alex has a quarter share) was running at Kempton while Thievery and Ordre de Bataille went to Huntingdon. 'I'm not going to travel that far on Boxing Day,' said Alex. 'I'm watching them on television so you can go to the football on your own.'

Our son Edward was born on 26 December and his birthday treat is nearly always a trip to watch Manchester City. On Boxing Day morning Alex made her selections from four meetings and I visited Coral, in Tarporley, to place her bets. It took longer than expected, not just because she had selected twenty horses in eighteen races (a total bet of £160), but I'd forgotten that The Tarporley Hunt starts its Boxing Day meet at the Swan Hotel in the middle of the main street.

I was glad I went to the football, City beat Hull 5–1. On my return I watched recordings of Huntingdon and Kempton. Ordre de Bataille won, Thievery came a creditable 4th and at Kempton, in the race immediately after Kauto Star's success in the Stan James King George VI Chase, Pressgang was heading for an easy win when he jumped almost sideways at the third from last, was not much straighter at the next, but squeezed home for Alex's second win of the day. Coral paid out a total of £163.30 on the twenty bets – the profit of £3.30 paid for the petrol I used to pick up the winnings with a few pence to spare.

With two winners in one day I am now waiting for more photos to arrive in the post, which I will frame for Alex's birthday in April.

'It will be fun,' we were told by horseracing friends when we talked about buying our first racehorse. They pointed out the positive bits, watching your horse over the gallops for the first time, waiting for him to enter the Winners' enclosure and reading speculation in the *Racing Post* with your name appearing as a new and up-and-coming owner.

But they never talked about the tricky times.

We were never warned about travelling through driving rain to watch a horse race at Huntingdon only to find it's been withdrawn two hours before the start. We weren't prepared for four weeks of snow with no racing while the bills still appear with a full training fee. Nor were we alerted about holidays. As a National Hunt owner January and February can be pretty important, but that's when we always go away – two weeks in Mustique to celebrate our wedding anniversary. 'But,' said a permanently optimistic member of our party, 'you can always watch them run on satellite.'

As it turned out, with so many meetings cancelled due to bad weather, this was a good year to be away. But, halfway through our holiday Pressgang was due to run at Sandown. I tried hard to find out how I could watch the race online. Roger Pritchard, managing director of Mustique and racing enthusiast, nearly had the answer. A punt with Betfair usually gets access to their pictures over the net. But, unfortunately, that day they could only offer Wetherby, no pictures being beamed from Sandown. The best we could do was live commentary broadcast on the Sporting Life website. We had just watched Manchester City on Fox Sports (with Spanish commentary) losing 1–0 to ten-men Stoke City when the commentary commenced from Sandown.

This was easily the best race any of Alex's horses had entered – five fancied horses fighting for prize money of £55,000. Any sort of decent performance would ensure Pressgang was on the way to the Cheltenham Festival.

From the start Pressgang was tucked in just behind the leaders, the commentary was encouraging, I imagined the sight of Pressgang (a big horse) starting to dominate the field. As far as we could hear everything looked good until Pressgang fell at the seventh. We listened to the commentary until after the photo finish hoping to hear news of the fallen horse, but there was nothing.

We were on Macaroni Beach when Paul Webber rang with the bad news.

'It's been a disastrous day,' said Paul. 'Dominic Elsworth, our jockey, heard a crack as they approached the seventh fence.' 'We were committed to jump,' said Dominic. 'There was nothing I could do.'

And that was it – Pressgang had to be put down.

Paul Webber, who was clearly very distressed during our telephone call, said it all in a subsequent email:

Dear John and Alex

What a desperate day, for all your patience and trust to be rewarded like this is very cruel. Everybody has put so much into the preparation of this talented, but testing horse, just as he was showing how good he was this instance strikes from nowhere.

I replied:

Thank you for your email. We are so sorry that all your diligence has ended in such tragedy. Alex is fine, I think she was always aware that an owner may face some dark days, she is relieved to find that Dominic suffered no serious injury. Our concern now is for yourself and your team, particularly those who have been with Pressgang every day. We know he was much loved and recognise how much he will be missed.

Racing isn't always as much fun as we were led to believe.

Every time we've acquired a new horse we think we've bought a future superstar. But our hopes have often been dashed within the first three races, despite the encouraging remarks of jockey and trainer: 'Plenty of ability there', 'Could be a good chaser', 'You'll have some fun with this one'. You know the fun is more likely to be at Hereford or Market Rasen rather than Newbury and Cheltenham.

But Pressgang was different. He went to The Festival in

2006 and came 2nd in the bumper. He was going to bring us our free owners' ticket to Cheltenham this year, until he broke his leg at Sandown and was destroyed. But, we had a lifeline: Ordre de Bataille was entered for the Thursday of The Festival.

Batty had won on Boxing Day and was clearly good enough to be considered, but all depended on his big race at Newbury, the Arkell's Brewery Novices' Handicap Chase. 'It's simple,' said Henry. 'We just need a win.'

That morning the headline on the racing page of *The Sun* said: 'ORDRE OF THE DAY' and the article, next to a picture of Henry Daly, announced that Batty was their nap selection – a really good chance of winning.

Newbury values its owners and trainers, recognising that without us they couldn't run a horse race. There were some seats outside the Owners' and Trainers' bar, well placed for the roast beef barm cake kiosk and the parade ring. My selection in the first three races all came 4th. A good run for my money but I got nothing back from the Tote. I'd already placed my bet on Batty when we saw Henry Daly striding across the paddock with the saddle. Alex nervously walked round Batty to slip £20 into the lad's hand (although of course, she wasn't a lad). And as we went to the paddock I looked up at the odds – the punters didn't agree with *The Sun*, Batty was 7/1.

Jockey Christian Williams appeared in our light blue and white Manchester City colours. It was his first ride for Alex, and I could see she approved. The twinkle in his eye was enough to get her on his side. We went with Henry to the stand taking everything in our stride, but eventually every owner gets a little nervous. My nerves kicked in after a mile. Batty was well placed, but it is the last four fences that matter most. Just before the third from home Batty took the lead, which is where he stayed until the second last. 'I thought I was going to win,' said Christian as he returned to the unsaddling enclosure, 'but the weight was too much, I was giving the best part of a stone to the three that finished in front of me.'

For the fourth time that day I had put money on the horse that came 4th. Batty wasn't going to Cheltenham, nor were we.

Having whinged all season about the inconvenience of getting short notice about horses that ran miles away from our home on dates that don't fit our diary, we had a purple patch. It started at Uttoxeter, a course where in thirteen visits we had never got into the first three. That day's runner, Arctic Ben, had disappointed on every appearance – his only win was for his previous owner who sold me the horse at a handsome price on the back of that success.

Uttoxeter could not have been in a better place that Saturday. In the morning I was at Uppingham School for a trustee meeting. Uttoxeter is almost exactly halfway home and the race at 3.45pm gave me ample time to meet up with Alex before Arctic Ben appeared in the parade ring. Everything went according to plan. I was on time and Alex was there to greet me, but Arctic Ben had not read the script – he came 2nd, given another furlong it could have been 1st – a very happy start to the weekend.

Seven days later Ordre de Bataille was at Bangor, the

closest course to our house. It was perfect timing. With his race at 3.30pm I had plenty of time for 18 holes of golf in the morning. We were there early. 'Batty', our name for Ordre de Bataille, had been balloted out of the Cheltenham Festival, so this was his next best thing. And he certainly took advantage, winning easily. Alex beamed as she accepted the bottle of champagne, which, incidentally, was handed back so it could be given to the winner of each successive race.

The following day we disappeared for a few days in Las Vegas. We aren't gamblers, it's just the buzz that gets to us and, on this occasion, the chance to see Bette Midler in concert. While away we had two runners at Towcester. Every casino has a big area given over to sports betting, showing horse races from across the States, alongside baseball, golf, tennis and American football. I hoped to see Cobbler's Queen and Timpo on a big screen in Vegas, but the bloke behind the information desk looked bemused when I asked him about racing from the UK – he hadn't even heard of Towcester. So I relied on my BlackBerry. Neither horse was mentioned, although we discovered back home that Timpo had been placed 3rd – if there are only seven runners my BlackBerry just reports 1st and 2nd.

Still suffering from jetlag, we went back to Uttoxeter the following Saturday to see the first race (again I had time to play my 18 holes of golf). We had seen Key Cutter at Paul Webber's yard two days before disappearing to Vegas. Frankly, although I'm not an expert on these things, he didn't look like a winner and certainly hadn't impressed in his previous three outings. But today was going to be different. Alex, being superstitious, didn't want to go into the stand so I was just with Paul when Key Cutter shot past the odds-on favourite to win by 3 lengths. We both hope no one took a picture as we hugged each other in excitement. The odds of 14/1 fully reflected everyone's expectation including ours, but I still had the courage to put £20 each way on the Tote and having drunk the free celebration glass of champagne and watched the DVD of Key Cutter's performance I returned to the Tote window to collect the largest amount of money I've ever won on a bet.

I knew our luck would run out – Key Cutter's next appearance at Ludlow was desperately inconvenient for both of us. Alex was in London visiting our daughter and grandchild, I was calling on shoe repair shops near Reading. The race was at 5.00pm – I'd earmarked Ladbrokes in Kidlington as the place where I was going to watch, but hadn't taken account of Bank Holiday traffic on the A34. I didn't make it, which turned out to be good, Paul Webber withdrew Key Cutter after the meeting started (the course had been watered and then it rained). Another lucky escape.

It was a good month for owner Alex Timpson and her husband – we only lost a little bit of money.

There was a lot at stake when Cobbler's Queen went out for our last run of the season at Huntingdon. She is our only mare and the only horse, apart from bumper runner Llama Farmer, who had not been placed this season.

I was starting to put her disappointing performance down to the name. Alex is the owner but because I pay the bills she gives me naming rights. The name 'Cobbler's Queen' was selected for obvious reasons. Thankfully that evening at Huntingdon proved I had not put a jinx on her performance – I thoroughly enjoyed listening to the commentator shouting out the name I had chosen as she went first past the post.

With that race over all our horses were put out to grass and we were ready for a summer break from racing. No *Racing Post*, no diary changes to get to a meeting at short notice and, the best part, much lower training bills. We did go to Goodwood and enjoyed the spectacle but Flat racing just doesn't seem the same. There are no jumps and each race is over in no time at all.

Just when the racing scene had gone out of my mind, Paul Webber rang. 'I'm going to Doncaster next week, for the sales,' he said. 'With the recession, prices are bound to be well down this year, I reckon there's a few bargains. I've picked out a few prospects – all greys. I'm sure Alex would be interested.'

Alex was interested and on the second day of the sales I was at the other end of Paul's phone listening to him bidding successfully for our next horse.

By the time we went to Paul's yard to view our latest acquisition and eat an excellent breakfast (full English with sensational sizzling sausages) I had a list of new names, which we fed into Paul's computer to see if any were available. My favourite, 'Photo Finish' (in recognition of the Max Spielmann photo shops we'd just purchased), was already taken. I was particularly disappointed to find that someone had already got there first and used the name 'Sole Trader' so our new horse will be called 'The Crafty Cobbler'. After all, the name hasn't done Cobbler's Queen much harm and perhaps we can create a winning line of horses known throughout the racing world as 'The Cobblers Collection'.

SEASON 2008–2009

2008–2009

HORSE	DATE	COURSE	RACE	DISTANCE	PRIZE MONEY	JOCKEY	RATING	POSITION	RUNNERS
Thievery	3-Nov-08	Warwick	Hand. Chase	2m	3K	Andrew Tinkler	79	1	11
	9-Nov-08	Hereford	Hand. Chase	2m	6K	Richard Johnson	85	1	8
	26-Dec-08	Huntingdon	Hand. Chase	2m ½f	3K	Mark Bradburne	91	4	12
	18-Jan-09	Towcester	Hand. Chase	2m ½f	3K	Richard Johnson	91	2	11
	5-Mar-09	Carlisle	Hand. Chase	2m	3K	Andrew Tinkler	94	8	12
	21-Apr-09	Towcester	Hand. Chase	2m ½f	5K	Richard Johnson	94	6	9
	24-Nov-08	Ludlow	Chase	2m 4f	5K	Richard Johnson	115	3	8
	26-Dec-08	Huntingdon	Nov. Chase	2m 4f	3K	Mark Bradburne	115	1	10
Ordre de Bataille	27-Feb-09	Newbury	Nov. Hand. Chase	2m 6½f	6K	Christian Williams	121	4	9
	21-Mar-09	Bangor-on-Dee	Hand. Chase	2m 4½f	9K	Andrew Tinkler	121	1	9
	16-Apr-09	Cheltenham	Nov. Hand. Chase	2m 5f	6K	Andrew Tinkler	126	4	9

(continued)

103

HORSE	DATE	COURSE	RACE	DISTANCE	PRIZE MONEY	JOCKEY	RATING	POSITION	RUNNERS
Timpo	18-Oct-08	Cheltenham	Hand. Hurdle	2m 5f	12K	Richard Johnson	114	11	16
	16-Nov-08	Cheltenham	Hand. Hurdle	2m 5f	15K	Mark Bradburne	113	11	19
	20-Dec-08	Haydock	Hand. Hurdle	2m 4½f	16K	Michael McAvoy	128	9	12
	26-Feb-09	Ludlow	Hand. Hurdle	3m	4K	Michael McAvoy	110	6	9
	25-Mar-09	Towcester	Nov. Chase	2m 4f	5K	Andrew Tinkler	105	3	7
	5-May-09	Exeter	Hand. Chase	2m 1½f	3K	Richard Johnson	105	9	11
Cobbler's Queen	26-Oct-08	Towcester	Nov. Hurdle	2m	3K	Andrew Tinkler	–	8	15
	23-Nov-08	Towcester	Nov. Hurdle	2m 5f	3K	Andrew Tinkler	–	5	13
	11-Dec-08	Huntingdon	Nov. Hurdle	2m 3½f	5K	Dominic Elsworth	–	13	14
	28-Feb-09	Doncaster	Nov. Hand. Hurdle	2m ½f	3K	Andrew Tinkler	83	2	16
	25-Mar-09	Towcester	Hand. Hurdle	2m 3f	3K	Jack Doyle	85	9	17
	6-May-09	Huntingdon	Hand. Hurdle	2m 4½f	3K	Richard Johnson	84	1	10

(continued)

HORSE	DATE	COURSE	RACE	DISTANCE	PRIZE MONEY	JOCKEY	RATING	POSITION	RUNNERS
Key Cutter	18-Oct-08	Cheltenham	Nat. Hunt Flat	2m ½f	3K	Dominic Elsworth	–	11	17
	15-Nov-08	Uttoxeter	Hurdle	2m	6K	Will Kennedy	–	6	8
	20-Dec-08	Haydock	Nov. Hurdle	2m 4f	4K	Mark Bradburne	–	12	14
	28-Mar-09	Uttoxeter	Maiden Hurdle	2m 4f	2K	Mark Bradburne	–	1	12
	20-Apr-09	Kempton	Nov. Hand. Hurdle	2m 5f	4K	Mark Bradburne	108	8	18
	31-Oct-08	Uttoxeter	Maiden Hurdle	2m	2K	Mark Bradburne	–	5	16
	24-Nov-08	Ludlow	Nov. Hurdle	2m 5½f	5K	Mark Bradburne	–	8	9
Arctic Ben	12-Jan-09	Fakenham	Maiden Hurdle	2m 4f	2K	Richard Johnson	–	5	13
	14-Mar-09	Uttoxeter	Nov. Hand. Hurdle	2m	6K	Richard Johnson	107	2	10
	11-Apr-09	Haydock	Hand. Hurdle	2m ½f	8K	Andrew Tinkler	112	7	10
Llama Farmer	26-Apr-09	Ludlow	Nat. Hunt Flat	2m	2K	Will Kennedy	–	7	13

	RUNS	1ST	2ND	3RD	4TH
Thievery	6	2	1	0	1
Ordre de Bataille	5	2	0	1	2
Timpo	6	0	0	1	0
Cobbler's Queen	6	1	1	0	0
Key Cutter	5	1	0	0	0
Arctic Ben	5	0	1	0	0
Llama Farmer	1	0	0	0	0
Total	34	6	3	2	3

	TRAINING FEES	ENTRY FEE/ JOCKEY	TOTAL COST	WINNINGS + SPONSORSHIP	NET COST
2008–2009					
Key Cutter	17,186	525	17,711	1,600	16,111
Timpo	17,136	2,185	19,321	3,819	15,502
Cobbler's Queen	17,365	1,364	18,729	6,510	12,219
Arctic Ben	16,435	1,575	18,010	4,650	13,360
Ordre de Bataille	16,309	1,710	18,019	14,550	3,469
Thievery	17,156	1,200	18,356	12,065	6,291
Llama Farmer	16,215	335	16,550	3,120	13,430
					£80,382

2009–2010

THE HORSES

With the addition of The Crafty Cobbler we now have seven horses in training so this is the line-up for the new season:

 TRAINED BY HENRY DALY:

Thievery age 8 grey gelding (rating 92)

Although Thievery will never be good enough for Cheltenham, as long as his handicap stays around 90 (he starts the season on 92) we always reckon he has a chance of winning a Handicap Chase. The prize money is never going to be big but we hope he will give us the chance to pose in the Winners' enclosure.

Ordre de Bataille age 7 grey gelding (rating 126)

This is our big chance for a Cheltenham Festival appearance, but he will have to do well in Handicap Chases early in the season to get his rating up from 126 towards 140.

Timpo age 6 chestnut gelding (rating 105)

Despite our high hopes last season was a disappointment. He just didn't have the speed to feature over hurdles in spite of tackling races up to 3 miles. Showed more promise in his two races over fences, although this was admittedly against very moderate opposition, but we will have to be patient. A little niggle that appeared after his disappointing run in May has led to a long period of recovery that could mean that he won't be able to run before Christmas.

Arctic Ben age 5 grey gelding (rating 111)

We remain hopeful that his high purchase price will be justified by future performances. So far we have hardly seen any return on our investment, but he looks good back at Downton Stables and we are hopeful that he will improve during the season.

Cobbler's Queen age 5 brown mare (rating 92)

With last season ending with a win we are hopeful that this horse, which seemed full of promise when purchased at the Doncaster Sales, will start to come up to expectations. The plan is to stick to hurdle races of about 2½ miles.

HORSES WITH PAUL WEBBER:

Key Cutter age 5 bay gelding (rating 108)

We are quietly confident that Key Cutter will turn into a superstar, especially when he starts going over fences. Everyone says he is a natural chaser who can only come on with the experience of another season under his belt.

Llama Farmer age 4 brown gelding (novice)

It is too early to say what we can expect from this horse after a mediocre performance in his bumper at the end of last season. We wait with interest to see how he will perform over hurdles.

The Crafty Cobbler age 3 grey gelding

The yard are quietly confident that this horse really has the potential to become a classic chaser, but we will have to wait until after Christmas before he gets a chance to show what he can do in a couple of bumpers followed by a possible hurdle race before the end of the season.

MUSTIQUE

For the first time in over 25 years we took a four-week holiday, a chance to relax in the Caribbean sunshine on Mustique, where we have been regular visitors since 1994.

We discovered the island by chance. In 1993, to celebrate our silver wedding, we took fifteen friends to Richard Branson's Necker Island; it was a great success and considerably less expensive than it is today. We had the island to ourselves for ten days with everything included from boat trips to bottles of champagne on the beach, all for about £65,000. None of us had ever experienced luxury like it before and, a year later, our friends asked us to find a similar set-up at a price we could all afford. I found Mustique in a travel agent in the middle of Prestbury, Cheshire. Without even consulting Alex, I booked a house called Plantations at the north end of the island. When we arrived, we discovered our next door neighbours were Princess Margaret and Patrick Lichfield.

It adds a bit of buzz to be alongside celebrities (Mick Jagger and Steven Spielberg were also there), but, for us, the main appeal of Mustique is its peace and privacy. I guess that is why so many famous names go there to escape prying eyes and the paparazzi.

Alex and I have been back almost every year since that first visit, renting different houses with a resident team. For the first ten years we seldom joined the social side apart from my regular tennis coaching from pro Richard Schaffer, the weekly cocktail party at the Cotton House and daily visits to Basil's Bar.

I now have a number of Mustique friends and enjoy their company but can still find plenty of time to read books, drive round the island in a Kawasaki Mule or sit on Pasture Bay watching the big waves. I never leave Mustique without booking a return visit – the focus of thinking during dark winters and wet summers back home.

But this four-week holiday was bound to be less relaxing than our usual fortnight in January when we timed our holiday to include our wedding anniversary and the Mustique Blues Festival.

We booked a big family house called Yemanje perched on the top of a hill with an amazing 360 degree panorama and a bird's eye view of Macaroni, Mustique's most popular beach. We had the big house to ourselves for a week, a chance to relax before our grandchildren started to arrive – eight of them plus their parents.

For months I was looking forward to the warm Caribbean sunshine but as soon as the children started to arrive the weather changed and they spent several wet days watching films on the television and driving round the island looking for tortoises (there are always lots around after a shower of rain). Our three-year-old granddaughter Tilly was transfixed by a DVD of *The Wizard of Oz* which she watched seven times. I had to take my turn to see snatches of the Open Championship from Turnberry and Tom Watson just failing to win and become the oldest Open Champion.

I had expected a totally horse-free month but had forgotten about the Mustique Equestrian Centre where I had to settle a sizeable bill for a number of trails and pony rides. The amount looked substantial in East Caribbean dollars but once translated into sterling was only a fraction of my monthly training bill.

Mustique inevitably brought back memories of last season's low point when Pressgang had to be put down at Sandown while we were on the island at the end of January. With our best horse now never able to fulfil his promise we will have to look elsewhere to find one that can give Alex a winner at the Cheltenham Festival.

In the brief interludes when we were excused from our grandparent duties we escaped on our own to Basil's Bar for a bit of people watching and a rum punch. Inevitably our conversation got round to horses but we didn't spend long lingering on our memories of a mixed but, on the whole, successful season. Our thoughts were already focussed on our future hopes when, as Manchester City supporters and season ticket holders, we are bound to face some difficult decisions.

A combination of hot sun and strong rum filled us full of fantasy as we wondered whether our first runner in the autumn would clash with City beating Manchester United 4–1 as we climb to 2nd in the Premiership. A little light headed, we also began to worry whether watching City take a 6-point lead at the top of the table by beating Stoke at The Etihad on Boxing Day would make us miss Ordre de Bataille's easy win at Kempton, that should make him a short odds favourite to win at Cheltenham.

As I ordered a second drink, the heat was clearly causing Alex to allow her ambitions to get out of hand. 'We still need to strengthen the squad,' she said and I agreed. 'A couple more quality players in defence will make all the difference.' 'I'm not talking about football,' Alex continued looking slightly irritated, 'I'm talking horses.'

THE RACING SEASON

It was time to return to reality – despite Alex's dream of buying more horses our line-up for next season will remain:

Thievery
Ordre de Bataille
Timpo
Key Cutter
Cobbler's Queen
Arctic Ben
Llama Farma
The Crafty Cobbler

Despite the strong rum in my Mustique Whammy I stood my ground – I have no plans to strengthen our squad before the start of the season.

We are getting withdrawal symptoms, it seems a long time since Llama Farmer came home in the middle of the field in a bumper at Ludlow in May and since then it's been an uneventful summer. There were no big vets' fees, or panic phone calls from Henry Daly or Paul Webber but Henry did ring to tell me about a really good horse he thought would be a great addition to our string. I'm a bit of a soft touch and forgot about the firm stance I took in Basil's Bar when I flatly refused to consider buying another horse. I don't know why I changed my mind but with one telephone conversation Alex now has horse number nine and I've decided to call it Cobbled Together.

On the first Saturday in September, we were reduced to watching Flat racing on Channel 4. I chose to be the bookmaker and Alex was my only punter. Alex backed all the greys and I lost. During September there are very few jump meetings on the calendar, so even if Alex's horses had been fit and ready to go there was nowhere to go to.

It's been a very wet September, so wet that everyone seems to be grumbling. But the rain suits me just fine – it is certain to stimulate the demand for shoe repairs. Wet pavements and a few puddles soon find the holes in the soles of your shoes. A wet week can increase a cobbler's sales by over 30 per cent. The rain is also good news for our horses: it should mean that we don't get the usual early excuse of – 'It's too dry, we need softer ground, we'll have to wait for four weeks.' But I suppose this year the reason for not running will be 'Too wet, and too heavy'.

The summer was so wet that racing at Cartmel was nearly cancelled when the going was quoted as 'heavy to soft' or perhaps it was 'soft to heavy'. Cartmel looks a great place to go horseracing – a small course with an intimate holiday atmosphere, I've seen Cartmel a couple of times but never been there on the day of a meeting and probably never will because although they stage National Hunt fixtures it's only open for business in the summer.

I probably got a flavour of the Cartmel experience when we were taken for a day's racing at Killarney during their August Festival. We were staying with our son James's in-laws Frank and Geraldine and their Irish son-in-law Jeremiah who seemed to know everyone in town. He smoothly talked us in through the turnstiles, got us all a member's badge and posh seats in the Owners' and Trainers' area. Everyone seemed to know nearly everyone else, the course was full of fun and laughter, a great day out for everyone apart from the five horses that fell badly and had to be put down. The big fields running that day made it a dangerous sport, but these deaths didn't dampen any enthusiasm of the grinning Guinness-filled crowd. Irish racing is more informal but in some ways more serious than racing in the UK.

We would love to run a horse at Killarney but our instructions to Henry and Paul state that unless it's a big race at Kempton, Sandown, Newbury or even Cheltenham our horses run close to home. We don't want more than a two hours' drive. So you can usually expect to see us at Bangor, Haydock, Aintree, Uttoxeter, Warwick, Stratford, Ludlow and just about as far as Hereford or Worcester.

'I reckon Thievery will be the first one to appear on a racecourse this season,' I said to Henry Daly when he rang to tell Alex that there were no problems. 'How did you know that?' he asked. 'Simple,' I replied, 'that was the first horse you started charging full training fees for.' A sure sign that we'll soon, yet again, be legitimately sitting in an Owners' and Trainers' bar.

Suddenly the call came – Henry Daly rang with a long list of dates – Stratford, Uttoxeter, Haydock, Ludlow – providing possible races for Thievery, Arctic Ben, Ordre de Bataille and Cobbler's Queen all within the next fortnight. 'But,' advised Henry, 'if we don't get rain I doubt whether any of them will run. I'm not starting the season on the wrong ground.'

The rain started almost as soon as Alex put down the phone – our season was about to begin.

I was committed to a tour of some of our shops in East Anglia when Alex went to Ludlow. We have the luxury of a company plane which makes it possible to cover the country without spending too many nights away from home. The plane operates from Hawarden near Chester and gets us to most parts of the UK within an hour – with Martin our driver waiting to meet me I can get to almost any shop before 9.00am having left home at 7.00am. That day I was back in the Chester branch of Ladbrokes in time to see Arctic Ben in the 3.55. As soon as I placed my £10 each way bet the odds shortened and Arctic Ben started as 9/2 joint favourite. I now know enough to recognise some signs of potential success or failure – the first half mile did not look good: Arctic Ben was 'too keen', his head fighting in all directions in an effort to go faster than Richard Johnson wished – using up energy that would be needed nearer the finish – predictably we finished well back in 3rd and I collected £19 for my £20 bet.

Thievery was in the 5 o'clock by which time I was in Coral, Tarporley, where I placed another £10 e/w bet. While I was waiting for the race, our odds drifted from 9/2 to 13/2. Fair price I thought for a horse probably handicapped too highly. But Thievery, who always tried hard, came steadily through the field to come 2nd. I collected £23 – £2 up on the afternoon.

Alex rang as she left Ludlow. 'Good news,' she said. 'Henry was really pleased with Thievery and although Arctic Ben was short of pace he thought the trip will have done him good.'

On Saturday we went to Stratford, not a great viewing course – it is much better to watch the race on the screen than try to pick them out on the racetrack – so I saw the picture I would have seen in Coral or Ladbrokes. I had unsuccessful memories of Stratford – on my only previous visit I watched our very first horse, Transatlantic, run his last race finishing well down the field in a mediocre Class 5 hurdle race.

Ordre de Bataille has much more ability – twice a winner last season he was one of six runners in the feature race of the day, a Class 3, 2½-mile chase.

He was looking relaxed until complacently jumping straight through the fifth fence – but still looked well placed coming to the last, alongside three other horses – one fell, the other two sprinted to the line leaving our Batty in 3rd place – with only six running the Tote kept all of my £15 e/w bet.

'That was OK,' said Henry, seeing my slight disappointment,

'the run will have done him good. See you on Friday at Uttoxeter,' he said as Alex and I headed for the car park. 'Cobbler's Queen in the 3.30, the going won't be quite to her liking – but she needs the run.'

Cobbler's Queen did better than we expected on the good ground at Uttoxeter and finished 4th in a field of fifteen. She was still running on good ground nineteen days later at Leicester when she won a mediocre race off a handicap of 92. Still a win is a win.

Not a bad start – so far every one of our runners has picked up some prize money and we still have to see Key Cutter and Llama Farmer who are ready to run in November.

After such a good start to the season (a winner, a 2nd, two 3rds and a 4th) things were bound to go wrong and they did. The last few weeks have been full of bad news.

We had only just registered the name of one of our two new horses, 'The Crafty Cobbler', when Paul Webber rang to tell us that the three-year-old was out on the gallop when he had a heart attack, collapsed and died. Alex said my suggestion that this would save on our training fees was heartless and in bad taste.

A few days later we hit a problem with the other three-year-old. He was destined to be called 'Cobbled Together' but the stubborn French breeder refused permission for a name change, so my plans to create a stable of cobblers had two severe setbacks within a week. Our latest horse has to be called Safran de Cotte.

Timpo continues to be confined to quarters on extended convalescence and Thievery has been out of sorts for the last three weeks (I wonder if horses can get the swine flu that is currently headline news).

Arctic Ben was 'coming on well' until he slipped and fell while training and was thought to have bruised some muscles.

Towards the end of November we only had four horses available for racing. When we went to Ludlow on a Monday we still had two runners – Llama Farmer, in what Paul described as a 'hot' Novice Hurdle, and Ordre de Bataille, who was favourite for the big chase of the afternoon ('we will have to see if he likes the heavy going,' said Henry Daly).

The meeting started with some good news. We met Arctic Ben's vet who declared he was 'all but sound but he should rest a bit longer'. I suppose 'all but sound' means we can expect a few more vets' fees. The bookies were quoting Llama Farmer at as much as 200–1, and the one I picked had a broad grin when he pocketed my £20 – they thought he would dislike the heavy going and gale force wind. They were correct: he was pulled up with half a mile to go. But, I was told by Andrew Tinkler: 'It was good experience, he is still a big baby and needed the run. He has the looks of becoming a good chaser one day' (always give the owner a glimmer of hope).

Ordre de Bataille, despite being thought worthy of a decent sized headline in the *Racing Post*, struggled to complete the course and finished 4th. He clearly didn't like the going. Disappointing!

The heavy rain stopped all of our horses for a fortnight, but two were entered on the same Thursday that we were returning from a three-day break in Austria. This was one in a series of city breaks that we planned as part of our geriatric gap year. Although for most of our travels we booked first class flights and five star accommodation, we had a more economic approach to the city breaks – preferring to rent an apartment found on the internet at a modest price. This tactic worked quite well in Venice, Tuscany and Paris so we tried the same technique in Vienna. At the airport our taxi driver showed some surprise when I gave him a slip of paper with the address. Reluctantly he took us to a soulless street and stopped outside a grey apartment with a black front door – we collected a set of keys from the housekeeper who showed us to our flat on the top floor. The welcome pack was a litre of milk, a loaf of bread and four small bottles of beer – the beds were hard, the television didn't work and the flat smelt damp. We looked at each other with the same thought. I was pleased I'd asked the taxi driver to wait but pretty irritated that I had carried our suitcases up four flights of stairs. Our deal demanded payment on arrival – I was happy to hand over the modest amount to the caretaker as we went back to the taxi asking the driver to 'Please take us to the best hotel in town.'

We had two very happy days in the Hotel Sacher, which was only ten times the cost of our apartment.

Paul Webber rang while I was on the streets of Vienna: 'It is a competitive handicap and Key Cutter is 25/1 in the morning papers (i.e. don't expect to win) but he should go well. I am hoping for the first four. Oh and by the way, Llama Farmer had a little nick while out training yesterday. We need to watch him carefully – he won't be running at the weekend.'

While Key Cutter was at Huntingdon, Cobbler's Queen was being withdrawn due to heavy going at Ludlow and we were in the air on the way back from Vienna, looking forward to watching the races on Sky Plus. We had to stop off at Maastricht to refuel and there was a message on my BlackBerry from my PA Christine titled 'Key Cutter'. Should I open it up or wait to watch the recording at home? We couldn't wait, the message read 'Key Cutter came in 2nd at 33/1'.

Perhaps we are in for a better month.

The Christmas freeze went on so long we wondered whether we would see any of Alex's horses run before our holiday at the end of January. There were a few false hopes – Alex received a welcome letter and car park sticker for meetings at Warwick and Ffos Las but one meeting was cancelled and at the other the going was far too heavy.

When we finally found ourselves with a declared entry the prospect was hardly exciting – Llama Farmer was running at Haydock, thankfully the nearest jump racecourse to our home, in a Novice Hurdle. Indeed two of the builders currently working on our house were planning a day at the races. 'See you in the Winners' enclosure,' said Alex, jokingly. Llama Farmer was unplaced at 100/1 in his last outing at Ludlow – his first attempt over hurdles. Overnight he was being quoted at 66/1, long odds for a seven-horse race.

Our race was the last on the card so there was plenty of time to play golf, have lunch and get to Haydock in time to place a modest bet on the winner of the third race. Against my better judgement I used the winnings to put £10 each way on Llama Farmer.

I must say he looked good in the paddock, bigger than all the other horses. The field was down to six and our odds were now 33/1; I was not confident.

I was interrupted as I made my way to the stand to see the race: 'Hi John' – it was Nigel, the manager of our shoe repair shop in Rochdale. 'What's it like?' he asked. 'Up to you, he clearly isn't the favourite,' I replied before moving on quickly to watch the race.

Llama Farmer kept in touch with the field until the last fence where he outjumped the favourite and went on to win comfortably by 3 lengths. Alex proudly picked up her trophy in the Winners' enclosure, while I went back to the Tote which was paying nearly 40/1 on the winner.

On Monday the builders were more than happy, they thought Alex's comment about the Winners' enclosure had been a serious hint so they piled in at the bookies at Saturday morning odds of 66/1. Nigel, our manager in Rochdale, had taken my tip and never placed a bet – I rang him to apologise.

We had three more runners the following Wednesday at Huntingdon. The conditions were not ideal, all three horses would have preferred much firmer ground but both Paul Webber and Henry Daly said we can't be picky, they need a run.

We had a problem. For the first time ever Alex had two horses in the same race. Paul had entered Key Cutter in a Novice Hurdle and Henry had put Cobbler's Queen in opposition. We needed to choose a different cap to establish our 'second colours'. We wouldn't have red (Man United) and we couldn't have white or blue (our existing colours) so Alex chose pink which she thought would look good with her sky blue and white Manchester City colours.

The meeting at Huntingdon was perfectly placed for our travel plans. We were in London for a dinner the night before and Huntingdon was only a modest detour on our way back home to Cheshire.

After a welcome bar lunch in the town centre we arrived in driving rain as the jockeys were returning to the paddock after the first race.

It was a day for huddling in the Owners' and Trainers' bar while we worried about how to cope with two horses at one time. I came with enough cash to tip three stable lads and Alex had a plan to be polite to two trainers at the same time.

We took a trainer each while the horses were saddled up but formed a friendly group in the middle of the paddock waiting for jockeys Will Kennedy (Key Cutter) and Richard Johnson, who were briefed at a discreet distance, where I asked an indiscreet question. Two days later we were leaving for another holiday in Mustique – knowing that Richard Johnson had been there during his relationship with Zara Phillips, I asked what he thought of the island – he discreetly said nothing.

I watched the race with Henry Daly. He was quiet as we saw Will Kennedy, according to plan, take Key Cutter straight into the lead. As the field passed the grandstand Henry shook his head, 'She doesn't like this ground,' he said, 'doesn't like it at all.'

Key Cutter continued to lead round the second circuit and with no big video screen it was difficult to spot Cobbler's

Queen until the commentator pointed out, 'Mrs Timpson has got 1st and 3rd with three fences to go.'

Henry was still shaking his head when Cobbler's Queen jumped the last fence just ahead of Key Cutter and went on to win by nearly 4 lengths while Key Cutter ran on to secure 2nd place. A one-two for Mrs Timpson and this was the first time she had two horses in the same race.

It was all smiles in the Winners' enclosure where Alex was pictured with both horses and jockeys. It doesn't get much better than that.

We were well set up for our holiday but there was still another race, Ordre de Bataille was running in the 3.40. What a contrast! Batty started at the back, jumped badly and never made any progress. Richard Johnson decided a mile and a bit was enough, pulled Batty up and gave us his view in the unsaddling enclosure, 'Got a niggle somewhere that is putting him off jumping – need to check him out.'

A disappointing end to a great week which gave us some very happy memories to take over to Mustique.

Alex certainly had a purple patch at the end of January, which continued while we were away on Mustique. Safran de Cotte, the horse that should have been called Cobbled Together, was running in his first bumper at Market Rasen. By the swimming pool I was checking my BlackBerry for the result when I received an email from Mustique's managing director, Roger Pritchard, 'Congratulations, an emphatic win.' Our winning streak had followed us to the Caribbean – that afternoon I even won my game of tennis. Safran de Cotte's first time out bumper win gave Alex three wins and a 2nd in five outings. On our return we went straight from Gatwick to Hereford to watch Cobbler's Queen run in a qualifier for the Mares' Final at Newbury on 27 March. Despite being top weight by over a stone we finished a comfortable 3rd and the Newbury meeting is firmly in our diary – racing was beginning to be an easy game.

Two races further down the Hereford card saw the return of Thievery (a plodder that operates well off a handicap in the low 90s). Thievery – stable nickname 'George' – is Alex's favourite but has spent most of the winter at home with a nasty virus.

Thievery started as favourite but the front runners went off too fast and for the last half mile Richard Johnson brought him home at a gentle pace. 'Too quick,' said Richard when he returned to the paddock, 'but he will be better for the outing. With that run under his belt and perhaps a couple of pounds from the handicapper he could enjoy more success on a similar trip in three weeks' time.'

While we were in Mustique I received several enthusiastic emails from Paul Webber – attached to one was a picture of 'Cheval en France'. The emails confirmed that the animal was Alex's preferred colour (grey) and he went on to use the phrases 'something out of the ordinary', 'very special indeed' and 'over budget'. We arranged to go to France the week we returned from the Caribbean.

We flew in a small plane from Chester and picked up Paul and bloodstock agent Claude at Oxford en route to Rennes. Jacques, a trainer and the owner of 'Cheval en France', drove us at speed to an amazing facility (gallops galore) provided by the local authority and used by all the local trainers.

We watched Cheval take a few jumps, run on the Flat and parade before us in the yard. We pretended to know what to look for until Paul and Claude produced a few tips. Claude clearly knows his stuff:

'He looks relaxed.'
'Big behind and big ears ... Both are good.'
'When he walks watch the feet, the back foot should
    go down beyond the point where the front leg
    has been.'
'Head slightly down when racing ... Good sign.'
'After exercise went straight to the manger.'
'He's big for a horse born less than three years ago.'

The list went on, there were no negatives. These were all reasons why Cheval was over budget, but price was not mentioned. We headed for lunch.

Jacques took us to a local small town but drove past several attractive restaurants and parked outside a grey hotel with little character. We went inside and he received a warm welcome.

I don't know why we bothered to look at the menu. Jacques spoke to the proprietress and we all had scallops followed by sole (sharing an enormous fish that was proudly presented and to which Jacques gave his final approval).

Lunch was superb – I hadn't noticed the Michelin star. Over champagne, wine, cheese, a dessert plate, pudding wine and more champagne, Claude confirmed that 'Le Cheval' ticks all the boxes. Price was still never mentioned.

'Le Cheval' arrived at Cropredy (Paul's yard) six days later. We are calling him 'Sole Survivor'.

I suppose it is my fault for not giving up the day job (having just had my 65th birthday in March 2008 I am certainly old enough to retire). I'm still conscientious enough to turn down a day at the races in favour of a prior commitment at the office. On the day Alex watched Key Cutter run at Ludlow I was presenting a Leadership programme in Wythenshawe. Even worse, the training course was running at exactly the same time as Key Cutter so I couldn't even watch the race in our local Ladbrokes. I had however used Sky Plus to record the race on Racing UK.

When I got home I walked straight past Alex. 'Don't tell me,' I said anxiously, 'let me watch the race for myself.' I wanted to see whether we had recovered from the previous poor performance at Bangor where the left-handed track was blamed for a disappointing run. Ludlow is clockwise.

I found the programme and pressed fast forward only to find the recording ended at 2.30 – the race was at 3.00pm. I had only recorded the Racing UK Freeview. So I had to ask Alex, to discover that Key Cutter liked the change in direction and came a very good 2nd.

At least I was able to go to Newbury – twice. If I were to draw up my personal league table for racecourse hospitality, Newbury would be in the top three. Free lunch in a pleasant room with a great view of the course, streets ahead of the stingy welcome we receive at some courses where we are huddled into a hut.

The first visit to Newbury was to see Arctic Ben come 3rd, winning more than enough prize money to pay for the horse box and part of our travelling expenses.

Our second Newbury trip promised a bigger payout – over £22,000 to the winner of the Mares' Hurdle Final. In qualifying, Cobbler's Queen's rating had shot up from 90 to 120, enough to push her well up the weights and this had sent the starting price up to 33/1.

Due to the odds we were pretty pessimistic. Cobbler's Queen travelled well for 2 miles staying within the first four until fading with 3 furlongs to go. We were keen to know what happened at the end of the race. We met Richard Johnson back in the paddock, while owners of the first four smugly sauntered to the Winners' enclosure. 'Could have been better,' said Richard. 'But I got jostled two from home and lost my stick. Might have been 4th or 5th. Perhaps give her a 3-mile outing before the end of the season. Should do well over fences next season.'

March wasn't great for the Alex Timpson stable. Ordre de Bataille, who was clearly unhappy over fences, was entered in a hurdle race to build up confidence – it didn't do the trick. I suspect we are facing a few more vets' fees with no more racing for Batty until the autumn.

Thievery came 5th in a moderate race at Wincanton (a long way for the horse box to travel and nothing to pay for it!). But the lack of success brought some good news: Thievery's handicap is now down to 89, he is back in with a chance.

Irritatingly I could not go to Haydock where we had entered both Llama Farmer and Safran de Cotte. Alex went to the races and I headed for Burnley to watch Manchester

City. On the outskirts of Burnley I found a branch of William Hill in time to watch Llama's race, the 4.35.

With his odds coming down from 20/1 to 9/1 in ten minutes before the race my hopes were raised. My view of the race was obscured by the 4.30 from Carlisle which set off late and dominated a split screen showing both races. By the time I got a proper view of our race Llama had lost contact with the leaders.

My disappointment was short lived. Within seven minutes of the kick-off, as the leaking roof in Burnley's visitors' stand dripped directly onto my head, Manchester City were leading 3–0, going on to win 6–1. The European Champions League now seemed much more possible.

Safran de Cotte was in the bumper at 5.45 (just when City went in at half time 5–0 up) but I had taken care to record the proper programme on Racing UK.

Alex had gone upstairs by the time I arrived home so I went quietly into the drawing room to watch the race. Our Sky wasn't working. I tried the only trick I knew and switched the Sky box off at the mains. It didn't make a difference, I had to ask Alex to tell me the result. 'Look at the DVD,' she said, a remark that told me all I needed to know. You are only given a DVD if you win. And what an emphatic win it was: 12 lengths with no hint of a reminder from jockey William Biddick.

Alex says that even Henry Daly was excited. We are now dreaming of what Safran de Cotte will do over hurdles next autumn. I am hopeful that at the very least he will win enough money to pay for the horse box.

Every year we enjoy a stress-free race day – Ladies' Day at Aintree, on the day before the Grand National. You don't need a runner to enjoy the buzz, excitement and most of all the Liverpudlian fashion flair. 'That should be the end of the season,' said Alex who can't see the point of jump racing in the summer. But it was only early April and Alex still had several horses in training.

Arctic Ben taught us a lesson. We have only bought two horses with previous racing experience. Transatlantic had been successful on the Flat and Arctic Ben had won his only race, a bumper, by a distance. With the price reflecting his one success Arctic Ben was, still is, and hopefully will always be our most expensive horse. Transatlantic cost considerably less – but after winning £22,981 in Flat races he only won £864 in attempts over the sticks.

Arctic Ben is still looking for his first win in the Alex Timpson colours – indeed, after two years, he has seldom been in the first three, living proof that when it comes to horses you seldom get what you pay for.

Arctic Ben tried again at Uttoxeter starting as favourite but it was another bitter disappointment. Already well beaten into 2nd place at the last fence, he was overtaken by two more horses approaching the post and yet again failed to finish in the frame.

With April dominated by the general election Alex and I spent quite a lot of time in Crewe and Nantwich supporting our son Edward in his successful battle for re-election as their Member of Parliament. As a consequence we didn't see much racing, but our trainers kept us up to date on the telephone. For some reason Sunday morning is the preferred time to ring with a weekly progress report giving us a list of possible entries and a horse-by-horse report. Most of the good news is given at the start of the call:

> 'He has recovered well from his excellent run at
>   Bangor.'
> 'Richard rode her on the gallop last Thursday and was
>   delighted, he thinks she should be in with a shout
>   next Friday.'

Other horses don't command the same enthusiasm:

> 'Working well but is still four weeks away.'
> And, 'I still haven't found the right race for him.'

Bad news usually comes at the end of the call:

> 'He had a bit of a knock while in the stable, so we will
>   now have to wait until next season.'
> Or even worse, 'I'm still waiting for a final verdict
>   from the vet but injuries like this can take a
>   long time.'

Early in the month I had a surprise call from Paul Webber. A half-brother to our successful new horse Safran de Cotte was listed in a sale at Cheltenham. I made a snap decision and bought the horse for Alex's birthday.

Alex's birthday started badly when I filled my diesel-driven car with petrol. I managed to remain cheerful when Alex drove us in her car to Ludlow where she celebrated her birthday with lunch at The Winning Post before going to watch Key Cutter in the 3.05. Paul Webber, who joined us for lunch, persuaded Alex to visit the stables as soon as we got to the racecourse to give Key Cutter a lucky pat on the back. But Alex was greeted by a different horse adorned with sky blue and white ribbon – it was her surprise present. It was a French horse that I was allowed to rename as long as I picked something that began with the letter S. I decided to call Alex's birthday present Sixty Something.

At 3.05 we discovered that Key Cutter had needed a much bigger pat on the back. After leading for well over a mile he quickly lost ground and finished 7th.

My two visits to our local Ladbrokes the following week were even more disappointing. On Wednesday in the 2.30 at Southwell, Thievery (normally a very solid jumper) was very awkward at the first fence and three from home Richard Johnson was catapulted into the air as if he was on a flying trapeze. 'A race too far' was Henry Daly's verdict. Thievery won't appear again until October by which time I have no doubt Henry will tell us, 'He needs the run'.

Luckily, on Thursday I was too late to place a bet. By the time I got to Ladbrokes the race had started. Timpo, running his first race after being injured all season, started at the back of the field, which is where he stayed.

'That's it,' said Alex when I got home and described Timpo's run as 'pretty poor'. 'I don't like summer racing,' she continued, 'it is time for a break.'

Henry telephoned the following morning. 'I was happy with Timpo. A good effort considering his long lay-off. Should run again in three weeks!'

SEASON 2009–2010

HORSE	DATE	COURSE	RACE	DISTANCE	PRIZE MONEY	JOCKEY	RATING	POSITION	RUNNERS
Thievery	22-Oct-09	Ludlow	Hand. Chase	2m	5K	Richard Johnson	92	2	9
	14-Feb-10	Hereford	Hand. Chase	2m	1K	Richard Johnson	92	8	14
	12-Mar-10	Wincanton	Hand. Chase	1m 7½f	3K	Richard Johnson	92	5	6
	28-Apr-10	Southwell	Hand. Chase	1m 7½f	2K	Richard Johnson	89	UR	7
Ordre de Bataille	24-Oct-09	Stratford	Hand. Chase	2m 5f	11K	Andrew Tinkler	126	3	6
	23-Nov-09	Ludlow	Hand. Chase	2m 4f	7K	Andrew Tinkler	125	3	7
	12-Dec-09	Doncaster	Hand. Chase	2m 3f	13K	Mark Bradburne	123	5	15
	27-Jan-10	Huntingdon	Hand. Chase	2m 7½f	5K	Richard Johnson	122	PU	10
	14-Mar-10	Towcester	Hand. Hurdle	2m	6K	Mr W. Biddick	117	13	15
Timpo	29-Apr-10	Hereford	Hand. Hurdle	2m 4f	2K	Richard Johnson	105	7	8
	30-Oct-09	Uttoxeter	Hand. Hurdle	2m 5½f	4K	Andrew Tinkler	92	4	15
Cobbler's Queen	16-Nov-09	Leicester	Nov. Hand. Hurdle	2m 4½f	4K	Richard Johnson	92	1	12
	27-Jan-10	Huntingdon	Hand. Hurdle	2m 4½f	2K	Richard Johnson	99	1	13
	14-Feb-10	Hereford	Nov. Hurdle	2m 4f	3K	Mr W. Biddick	110	3	13
	27-Mar-10	Newbury	Nov. Hand. Hurdle	2m 4½f	22K	Richard Johnson	120	10	18

(continued)

HORSE	DATE	COURSE	RACE	DISTANCE	PRIZE MONEY	JOCKEY	RATING	POSITION	RUNNERS
Key Cutter	14-Nov-09	Uttoxeter	Hand. Hurdle	2m 4f	5K	Will Kennedy	108	6	9
	10-Dec-09	Huntingdon	Hand. Chase	2m 4½f	3K	Will Kennedy	105	2	16
	27-Jan-10	Huntingdon	Hand. Chase	2m 4½f	2K	Will Kennedy	110	2	13
	3-Mar-10	Bangor-on-Dee	Hand. Chase	2m 7f	6K	Will Kennedy	113	6	7
	25-Mar-10	Ludlow	Hand. Chase	2m 5½f	5K	Will Kennedy	113	2	13
	25-Apr-10	Ludlow	Hand. Chase	2m 5½f	6K	Will Kennedy	118	7	13
Arctic Ben	22-Oct-09	Ludlow	Hand. Hurdle	2m	4K	Richard Johnson	111	3	9
	12-Feb-10	Kempton	Hand. Hurdle	2m	2K	Mr W. Biddick	112	4	16
	6-Mar-10	Newbury	Nov. Hand. Hurdle	2m ½f	6K	Mark Bradburne	112	3	11
	21-Apr-10	Southwell	Nov. Hurdle	1m 7½f	3K	Mr W. Biddick	115	4	8
Llama Farmer	23-Nov-09	Ludlow	Nov. Hurdle	2m 5½f	4K	Andrew Tinkler	–	PU	9
	23-Jan-10	Haydock	Nov. Hurdle	2m 1f	3K	Andrew Tinkler	–	1	6
	20-Feb-10	Haydock	Nov. Hurdle Grade 2	3m 1f	17K	Andrew Tinkler	–	5	7
	3-Apr-10	Haydock	Nov. Hand. Hurdle	2m 4½f	11K	Andrew Tinkler	125	PU	13
Safran de Cotte	9-Feb-10	Market Rasen	Nat. Hunt Flat	2m ½f	1K	Jake Greenall	–	1	11
	3-Apr-10	Haydock	Nat. Hunt Flat	2m ½f	1K	Mr W. Biddick	–	1	5

	RUNS	1ST	2ND	3RD	4TH
Thievery	4	0	1	0	0
Ordre de Bataille	5	0	0	2	0
Timpo	1	0	0	0	0
Cobbler's Queen	5	2	0	1	1
Key Cutter	6	0	3	0	0
Arctic Ben	4	0	0	2	2
Llama Farmer	4	1	0	0	0
Safran de Cotte	2	2	0	0	0
Total	31	5	4	5	3

	TRAINING FEES	ENTRY FEE/ JOCKEY	TOTAL COST	WINNINGS + SPONSORSHIP	NET COST
2009–2010					
Llama Farmer	14,957	1,872	16,829	5,645	11,184
Crafty Cobbler	5,223	320	5,543	1,000	4,543
Arctic Ben	18,301	1,070	19,371	2,780	16,591
Thievery	18,230	785	19,015	3,555	15,460
Ordre de Bataille	16,421	1,275	17,696	4,505	13,191
Cobbler's Queen	16,881	1,060	17,941	8,565	9,376
Key Cutter	16,694	1,325	18,019	5,140	12,879
Safran de Cotte	12,765	260	13,025	3,950	9,075
Timpo	14,540	290	14,830	1,750	13,080
Sole Survivor	3,814	–	3,814	750	3,064
Sixty Something	2,053	–	2,053	500	1,553
					£109,996

2010–2011

THE HORSES

With both trainers making encouraging remarks about our horses we should be in for a good season, although it is difficult to see an entry for the Cheltenham Festival this year. However with our two new additions both getting rave reviews from their yards a Festival runner can't be far away.

We start the season with the following team:

WITH HENRY DALY:

Thievery age 9 grey gelding (rating 85)
Affectionately known as 'George' by the stable lads Thievery has been an honest and consistent performer in modest company, competing for mediocre prize money. It was a surprise, towards the end of last season, when Thievery parted company with Richard Johnson at Southwell, but that was probably no more than a blip and we look forward to another assured season in Class 4 and 5 company.

Ordre de Bataille age 8 grey gelding (rating 122)
'Batty's' confidence took a severe knock at Huntingdon in January when Richard Johnson pulled him up suspecting some sort of pain at every fence. A step back to hurdles at

the end of the season should have helped, despite finishing well down the field. It would be great to see 'Batty' back to winning form.

Timpo age 7 chestnut gelding (rating 100)
After only one race last season we reckon Timpo is fully restored to rude health and will get the chance, at last, to show his true potential. His first outing could come right at the beginning of the new season, but after almost twelve months without a run I hope to see plenty of appearances and a significant improvement in his rating.

Cobbler's Queen age 6 brown mare (rating 118)
It is time to go chasing with this mare. Two wins over hurdles have shown that she has ability and the experts tell us that she is built for fences. For the first time we will be entering mares-only chases and will get a handicap advantage in mixed company. The longer we have this mare the better she seems to perform.

Arctic Ben age 6 grey gelding (rating 113)
Although Arctic Ben was in the first four in all four races last season he was still falling short of our expectations. This time we are switching him to chases, every jockey says that he will be better over fences. We will soon see if they are right.

Safran de Cotte age 4 grey gelding (novice)
An attractive horse that the stable lads say has loads of character. Bought during last season, he quickly established his credentials by winning two bumpers in impressive style. Fingers crossed, we might have found a superstar.

HORSES WITH PAUL WEBBER:

Key Cutter age 6 bay gelding (rating 118)
With three second places last season it can't be long before Key Cutter is a winner having steadily moved up the handicap rating and competed with better company. We secretly think that Key Cutter could be the one to take us to The Festival.

Llama Farmer age 5 brown gelding (rating 123)
Some say that last season's win over hurdles at Haydock was a total flash in the pan, but Llama was always expected to make his mark over fences. Our plan is to go chasing and look forward to seeing another win before long.

Sole Survivor age 3 grey gelding (novice)
This fairly expensive result of a day trip to France is a big horse, bigger than any other being stabled by Paul at Cropredy – so big many are in awe of his potential. We feel we have a very special horse in Sole Survivor and can't wait to reveal his latent ability at a racecourse.

Sixty Something age 4 grey gelding
This birthday present to Alex has the same sire as Safran de Cotte; let's hope he has the same ability. We look forward to seeing him run his first race.

THE RACING SEASON

By the beginning of May most of our horses were out in the fields enjoying a break. Our trainers, Paul and Henry, no longer needed to telephone to tell us why a horse would not run for at least a month ('going too soft', 'needs to come on a bit', 'can't find the right race'). Nor do they need to manage our expectations before a race ('it's a hot race, anywhere in the first six would be a good result', 'not the ideal distance but he needs the run').

We will also have a break from the optimistic inquest that jockeys manage to produce after a devastating defeat ('he will have gained a lot from the experience', 'should do well over fences next season').

We, too, can spin a good story when asked 'How have you done this season?' … 'Pretty well,' I reply. 'Five winners including our one-two at Huntingdon, and Safran de Cotte a double bumper winner is a great prospect for next year.' My enthusiasm ignores the truth that our expenditure was much greater than the prize money. 'But,' Alex said, 'what did you expect? At least we enjoyed ourselves.'

At the end of May Timpo was still in training and had been entered for a Sunday meeting at Worcester. It was our first visit to a course that concentrates on summer racing, a policy that appears to pay off. The compact racecourse was crowded with casual racegoers ignoring the heavy rain and enjoying a funfair in the centre of the track.

The Owners' and Trainers' bar was far too busy to bother with, especially as Alex was struggling with an arthritic hip, so she found a seat near the parade ring while I was sent to press pound notes into the hand of the stable lad who saddled up Timpo.

Early in his career Timpo filled us full of hope – he came 6th in a classy bumper at Newbury and won his first race over fences. Since then things have not gone too well. Today, on the advice of Richard Johnson, he was stepping up to 3 miles. 'Not so sure,' said Henry Daly. 'We shall have to see.'

The bookies put Timpo at 20/1 – bottom of the field – but both Henry and the punters should have had more faith. Richard was wearing a broad grin as he led Timpo back to the unsaddling enclosure in 3rd place. 'After a short break he should do well in a Novice Chase.'

On 17 June Alex had an operation to replace a painful hip and with all ten horses plus their owner expected to be fully fit by September we are looking forward to another successful season.

Even if her horses had been running over the last eight weeks you would not have seen Alex at a racecourse. On 17 June she had a hip replaced and, since then, hasn't travelled far.

During June and July we seldom heard from our trainers Paul and Henry but at this time of year no news is good news.

All Alex's horses should be out in a field having fun. The only reason for Henry or Paul to telephone is to report a health problem. Apart from 'a tiny wind operation' to Llama Farmer the news has been vet-free, so we are looking forward to an active season. 'They will all be in by next week, ready to start doing some serious work,' reported Henry the other day. 'Key Cutter should be the first to go,' said Paul. 'We are aiming for early October – not many meetings until then.'

The phone calls signalled a significant increase in the weekly training fees – next month I could anticipate much bigger bills. Alex, however, with the new hip already promising much more mobility, was anticipating an exciting season. But she has a big worry:

'What happens if we have a winner and I get caught by Clare Balding?' she asked me. 'I wouldn't have a clue what to say – all the other winning owners seem to know everything about racing in general and their horses in particular.'

'There is nothing to worry about,' I said, hopefully with confidence. 'Just say nice things about the horse, its trainer and the jockey, using some familiar phrases that are bound to get Clare nodding in agreement. Sprinkle the interview with words like: He has come on really well during the last month … Henry (or Paul) and his team back at home have done a cracking job … There is no doubt we liked the better ground … The extra 2 furlongs made all the difference …'

Alex wasn't convinced. 'If I see Clare heading towards me with a microphone I'll leave her to you.'

To build Alex's confidence I proposed a bit of role play – 'I will be Clare interviewing you after Thievery has won the Cheltenham Gold Cup – see how you get on.'

'But Thievery will never even get an entry to any meeting at Cheltenham,' said Alex being awkward. 'I know that,' I sighed. 'Can we just give it a go?'

Our cat looked bewildered as I used the television remote as a pretend microphone and asked my first question:

'This is Alex Timpson the proud owner of Thievery, winner of The Gold Cup. Alex, explain how you feel.'

'Obviously this is a dream come true,' said Alex talking into the remote control. 'I am just so delighted for everyone back at Ludlow. Henry and his team have done a fantastic job.'

'Talk us through the race Alex,' I continued. 'Did it go according to plan?'

'Richard gave him a fantastic ride and Thievery showed great character,' said Alex warming to her role. 'Before the race we were worried about the step up in distance but we needn't have bothered, he's come along a lot in the last month and the firmer ground helped but he really showed the determination to dig deep when it mattered.'

I moved the remote towards my mouth.

'Where next?' I asked. 'What are your plans for next season?'

'First things first,' replied Alex, 'I will speak to Henry tomorrow morning to check how he is and we will take it from there.'

I put down the remote, the interview was over. 'Well done!' I said in genuine admiration. 'But I didn't really say anything and I made most of it up,' said Alex. 'Doesn't matter,' I replied, 'you sounded just like a winning owner. That's what most of them say.'

One of the dubious duties of being the owner (or in my case the owner's husband) is the constant need to respond to friends wanting inside information. Before every race Colin, the builder who is working at our house, and Paresh, our Finance Director, need to know, 'What are the chances?'

The briefings from trainers Paul and Henry don't tell us enough to answer the question. 'Needs the run', 'It's a competitive race' and 'We may need softer ground' are remarks designed to manage our expectations; we seldom have a clue whether we are onto a winner.

Last season we had a great start – five out of our first six

entries finished in the first three. This year has been different. Key Cutter, Cobbler's Queen and Timpo have all come
2nd (all Novice Chases) but Thievery, starting his first race
of the season as favourite, finished well down the field.

Alex and I went to Stratford on a Saturday, hopeful that
Ordre de Bataille would do better, but he never bothered to
race and was pulled up with half a mile to go – only three
finished and if he had taken the trouble to jump the last
three fences at least we would have picked up over £300
(Batty arrived back at the paddock full of beans!).

The following Sunday we went to Huntingdon on a
very wet day to watch Arctic Ben who started as favourite to
win a 2½-mile chase. He never entered the race, was tailed
off at the start and stayed detached from the field until
Richard Johnson pulled him up. On the long drive back
we were talking on the telephone to a lifetime National
Hunt follower. 'That's racing,' he said in sympathy – it
didn't cheer us up.

Alex takes a philosophical view to these setbacks; after
all she has a somewhat pessimistic long term plan. She has
created extra paddock space in the fields at the back of our
garden so they can all come and live with us when they
retire from racing.

Despite our disappointments we went to Bangor-on-Dee
full of hope. It was Safran de Cotte's first run over hurdles
after two winning bumpers last season.

He looked good in the paddock and was awarded 'best
turned out'. I told Henry Daly it was 'the first win we've had
this season', but I don't think he was amused.

Safran put our season back on track. He led from the
start and when challenged by J.P. McManus' 6/4 favourite,

Richard Johnson hardly had to ask for a response. We won by 1¾ lengths.

Buoyed up by the win we went to Ludlow the following day where we had two runners in the same race – Key Cutter and Batty. The only other time we have had to pick an alternative hat to distinguish our colours was at Huntingdon last season where Cobbler's Queen and Key Cutter gave us a one-two. After the first circuit with both horses handily placed in 3rd and 4th I was beginning to wonder whether we were in for a repeat performance but Batty soon faded and was pulled up with nearly a mile to go. Although Key Cutter came 2nd I still felt a twinge of disappointment.

We stayed at Ludlow for another hour so we could watch Thievery run in the 3.40 at Taunton. The race made me a bit more miserable – Thievery parted company with Andrew Tinkler four fences from home.

I wondered whether both Thievery and Batty would soon be coming to live in our back garden but the news next day was full of hope. Andrew Tinkler was convinced Thievery was running well enough to win and the scan on Batty (which will no doubt stand out on my next monthly invoice) showed an infection which should soon disappear.

A mixed start to the season but, as they say, 'That's racing.'

There is no doubt that being married to a racehorse owner is more fun when her horses are winning money. With Safran de Cotte coming 1st at Bangor (three races, three wins) I was so keen to see his next outing at Haydock I arranged to cut my Saturday morning golf from 18 holes to 9 – the race was at 12.35. I was really excited, the prize money was a bit better than we are used to and it was a Listed Race.

We never went to Haydock, Henry Daly decided the race was too hot, he was reluctant to risk our unbeaten record so I played a full 18 holes (and won £2).

Neither did we go to Towcester on the Sunday where Thievery fell in a race he could have come close to winning. But things got better on Monday. It was a board meeting day so I had to watch the races with non-exec director Patrick in Ladbrokes near our office. But Alex was at Ludlow to watch Timpo come 2nd and stayed on to watch the feed from Kempton where Key Cutter won a 3-mile chase. Not a bad day – £75 won from Ladbrokes and over £4,500 going into my Weatherbys account.

We went to Newbury on the Friday to see Llama Farmer fade in the last half mile coming 6th (in line with the odds of 12/1). Little did we realise that this would be our last race meeting for nearly a month.

We had runners entered at Exeter, Huntingdon, Leicester, Taunton, Cheltenham, Doncaster and Uttoxeter and a few more. Most of the meetings were cancelled and most of our horses were unable to train for the few that took place. We were hit by snow and ice. Instead of missing a race that was too hot we were thwarted by courses that were too cold.

It is disheartening to see the only fixtures featuring all-weather Flat racing from Southwell and Lingfield Park in the middle of the National Hunt season. I have become an avid viewer of the week's weather forecast on Sunday's *Countryfile* hoping for news of a warm front but was forced to cross out a few more fixtures from my diary.

We are still paying the training fees so hopefully when the thaw comes we will be back on the track. But with plenty of others in the same position loads of horses will need a run and instead of being ruled out by the weather we could miss out in a ballot.

To make matters worse snow and ice are killers for cobblers – our shops have had a miserable month. I can't believe the forecasters can look so cheerful when they tell me, 'With the wind moving back to the north a further bout of winter weather will hit the whole of the British Isles at the end of the week.'

What happened to global warming?

Apart from a disappointing performance by Key Cutter at Newbury a week before Christmas we went through the whole of December without a runner. The snow and ice interfered with training and whenever we did enter a horse the meeting was abandoned.

We needed a change of luck and where better than the New Year's Day meeting at Cheltenham. A big meeting with a 25,000 crowd expected – quality racing on a Saturday and we had two runners – Alex and I drove down dreaming of a great day.

The first day of January must have been the quietest day on the roads for years. With nothing on the motorway through Birmingham we arrived at Cheltenham more than two hours before the first race, but we were not alone. The car parks were already getting busy, the bookies were arriving and punters were munching their first burgers of the day.

We had Safran de Cotte in the first race and Sole Survivor in the bumper at the end of the day. I can't remember the last time we watched every race on a card.

Alex and I were the first to arrive in the Owners' and Trainers' restaurant, so early that they were still giving the staff their briefing on speedy service. We sat down and read the papers. None of the tipsters fancied either of our horses but with sixteen in each race that was hardly surprising. However with Safran having won three races out of three and Sole Survivor getting rave reviews from the jockeys who had ridden him at Paul Webber's yard we knew we had two really good chances.

Cheltenham is one of the racecourses that offers owners a proper free lunch. It is not as good as Haydock, there is usually a long queue, and the drinks are quite expensive but at least it is better than the complimentary cup of tea on offer in some Owners' and Trainers' bars. Unless you are in a big party you have to share a table; it's the luck of the draw who you get. We were lucky; the gang on our table had a horse in the 3.15 so we were on our own for most of the time – that was the only bit of luck I had all day.

I was amazed that so many people turned up on New Year's Day. Despite a late night and lots of lingering hangovers more than the expected 25,000 racegoers enjoyed a cold but sunny day. It wasn't as busy as The Festival but I had to jostle through the crowd to get to the pre-parade ring.

Having a runner at Cheltenham is a special experience for any owner. There are no races for plodders – appearing in the paddock shows that you have a proper horse with the potential to run in good class races. I could sense a touch of arrogance among my fellow owners who were mostly dressed for the occasion (tweed trousers, tweed skirts, tweed jackets, tweed waistcoats and tweed hats). We all tried to look nonchalant – totally at home because we have a runner or two at every Cheltenham meeting.

As soon as I saw Safran de Cotte slipping back down the field in the first race I knew we were in for a bad day. Sole Survivor fell away with 2 furlongs to go and every horse I backed in the races in between was a loser. Our best two horses had been well beaten – the day that promised to be an important step on the way to The Festival in March ended in bitter disappointment.

With the snow gone I was sure things would improve and they did – a bit. Thievery managed to complete a race for the first time in four outings when finishing 4th at Leicester and Safran de Cotte overcame a stumble three from home to come 3rd in a pretty hot race at Warwick.

We were due another win and had every chance when Arctic Ben and Timpo were entered in consecutive races on a Thursday meeting at Ludlow. I was visiting some of our shops in Yorkshire but Alex was ready to go to the races when the meeting was abandoned due to frost.

Two miserable months on the trot – surely February will be better.

When you become a racehorse owner your mind is full of positive thoughts – putting a plan together that finishes at the winning post before being presented with the first prize back in the paddock. It takes time for reality to kick in – only one horse can win a race and that horse is often ridden by A.P. McCoy or trained by Paul Nicholls – it is unlikely to be yours.

If you have a sequence of runners that fail to finish remind yourself that it could be worse:

- All the meetings could be cancelled
- Your horse could be severely injured
- You may have a horse that doesn't run for a whole season
- You could win a big race and then be disqualified by the judge.

All these are good reasons why nearly every owner loses money but that seldom dampens their enthusiasm.

Having spent January waiting for some good news I came to the conclusion that we were just having a decidedly difficult season.

Bad fortune followed us on holiday to Mustique. Admittedly, on the eve of our departure, Cobbler's Queen came in 2nd at Huntingdon but only four horses started the race and later in the meeting we watched Arctic Ben finish at the back of a mediocre field.

We only had one entry while we were away, Safran de Cotte in a competitive hurdle at Kempton Park. We followed the race on the radio in the Mustique Company office with managing director Roger Pritchard, who cheerfully told us our horse was tipped to win in the *Racing Post*.

We heard about Safran's smooth run down to the start, how he settled in quietly at the back of the main pack and then steadily moved up into a challenging position. Then that was it, the name Safran de Cotte never got another mention, for all we knew he had fallen at one of the last four fences. He didn't fall but by the time he reached the finish the commentator had lost interest – our horse had simply run out of puff.

We were not alone, it was somewhat reassuring to know that the other Henry Daly horses were showing a similar lack of speed over the last half mile. The one horse that bucked this trend was Timpo who came 2nd in a decent race at Huntingdon.

While we were suffering with Henry's horses most of Paul Webber's were enjoying a good run but we didn't share the same success as other Webber owners. Sole Survivor, our future superstar, came a disappointing 2nd in his second bumper at Bangor, and Llama Farmer was so badly cut in a collision with another horse at Leicester that it is unlikely he will race again until next season.

Timpo gave us some hope by coming 2nd again at Ludlow but we and Arctic Ben came back to earth after he was hampered at the third from home at Kempton when he looked certain to end Henry Daly's 66-day run without a winner. A nasty fall nearly ended Arctic Ben's career – another horse that won't see a racecourse again until next season. Two days later Andrew Tinkler was the likely winner of a moderate 2½-mile chase on Cobbler's Queen when she made a mistake two from home and he was lucky to just stay in the saddle. They finished 3rd.

Last week Alex made the seven-hour round trip to watch Thievery run at Chepstow – I had a trustee meeting at Uppingham so watched on At The Races. It didn't go well – Jake Greenall took him a bit too fast early on and he failed to have enough left for the finish. The commentator in summing up the race said, 'That must have been the poorest 0–90 handicap that has taken place for many a year.'

The following day I got my monthly bank statement from Weatherbys. I normally look straight at the income column to enjoy the positive pleasure of seeing prize money hitting the account. But this month there was next to nothing – I had to put in a bigger than normal cheque to keep the Alex Timpson racing enterprise in the black.

Yet again we watched the Cheltenham Festival at home on television. Perhaps next year you will see us in the Owners' and Trainers', but for now we can only look forward to Ladies' Day at Aintree. We won't have a runner but there will be plenty to look at and keep us entertained without bothering too much about the horses.

Alex and I visited Aintree on both Friday and Saturday – Ladies' Day and the Grand National in glorious sunshine – some of the best racing of the season. Over the two days I must have backed more than 30 runners without finding one winner.

After eight years as an owner you might expect us to pick up some inside information, but our betting system doesn't show any sign of the professional punter. Alex backs every grey. Whatever the form or tipster advice it is the colour that matters to Alex even if the *Racing Post* reports 'This horse never justified the £25,000 price paid at Doncaster three years ago. Pulled up ten times on nineteen starts its highest finish (4th) was in a five-horse race. One day it could find a race to win but not today – Avoid.' Despite such strong advice, if it is grey Alex picks it and I place the bet. At least it is easy to spot our runner – but often the grey is seen at the back of the pack.

If there is no grey horse in the race, it's a more difficult decision, but Alex still ignores the form. She faithfully backs any runner from the Henry Daly or Paul Webber stables and is certain to follow a horse with a name connected to one of our grandchildren – Pride of Patrick, Topical Tilly and Special Sam all get the nod, whatever the odds.

Some days Alex's 'system' does surprisingly well, but it let us down badly that day at Aintree. I lost so much money that on Sunday morning I made an unscheduled visit to the hole in the wall, but by then I knew our visit to Aintree had been unexpectedly expensive in another direction.

On National Day we were being entertained and sat on separate tables. 'Had an interesting lunch,' said Alex. 'I was next to trainer Venetia Williams and we had a long chat about this and that – I have asked her to look out for a horse for us. She knows it will have to be a grey.'

Within a week we were at Venetia's yard between Hereford and Ross on Wye – another day bathed in sunshine which I suspect will lead me to another grey and more negative cash flow.

'We need a new horse,' commented Alex. 'Thievery is unlikely to keep going after this season.'

Alex was right about Thievery who ran his last race at Hereford the day before the Royal wedding. He was placed 5th and not disgraced but it is clear that Thievery would struggle to add to his record of three wins and we decided to retire him with fond memories of the wonderful week when he won two races in six days.

By now we were learning to live with the lack of success during a disappointing season. The run of bad luck lowered our expectations so we were realistic about Cobbler's Queen's chances in a 3-mile chase at Uttoxeter. A competitive race, but with only five runners, top-weight Cobbler's Queen could have a chance.

Andrew Tinkler had to work hard, Cobbler's Queen found it difficult to concentrate for the full 3 miles but she paid attention when it really mattered, sweeping into the lead with 4 furlongs to go and won easily. Fantastic. Suddenly our troubled season was forgotten as Alex courageously stood close enough to Cobbler's Queen for a photograph before accepting a bronze horse's head that will be proudly displayed in our 'trophy room'.

We looked forward with confidence to what may be our last day out before the break. Sixty Something was due to appear for his first outing in a bumper at Worcester. After training all season it was certainly about time we saw him on a racecourse. But we didn't go to Worcester.

Paul Webber rang a week before the meeting. 'He's lame, I don't know why yet but he won't be racing before October.'

So, after buying the horse a year ago and months of full training fees, all I can expect is another bill from the vet.

'Still,' said Alex, 'it means we can look forward to three new horses next season.'

'Why three?' I asked.

'Well,' replied Alex, 'there is Sixty Something, the grey Venetia is looking for and of course we will have to ask Henry to find a replacement for Thievery.'

'But …' I said, starting to point out her mistake before I quickly realised that Alex was making a statement of fact.

SEASON 2010–2011

HORSE	DATE	COURSE	RACE	DISTANCE	PRIZE MONEY	JOCKEY	RATING	POSITION	RUNNERS
Thievery	21-Oct-10	Ludlow	Hand. Chase	2m	3K	Richard Johnson	85	6	8
	11-Nov-10	Taunton	Hand. Chase	2m	2K	Andrew Tinkler	78	UR	10
	21-Nov-10	Towcester	Hand. Chase	2m ½f	1K	Michael Murphy	78	F	6
	13-Jan-11	Hereford	Hand. Hurdle	2m 1f	1K	Richard Johnson	78	4	9
	12-Mar-11	Chepstow	Hand. Hurdle	2m	2K	Jake Greenall	77	5	9
	28-Apr-11	Hereford	Hand. Hurdle	2m ½f	1K	Andrew Tinkler	73	5	12
Ordre de Bataille	23-Oct-10	Stratford	Hand. Chase	2m 5f	7K	Timmy Murphy	122	PU	8
	11-Nov-10	Ludlow	Hand. Chase	3m	6K	Richard Johnson	113	PU	9
	28-Dec-10	Ffos Las	Hand. Chase	2m 5f	6K	Andrew Tinkler	107	PU	12
Timpo	6-Jun-10	Worcester	Hand. Hurdle	3m	2K	Richard Johnson	100	3	11
	6-Oct-10	Ludlow	Hand. Hurdle	2m 5½f	3K	Richard Johnson	100	6	17
	29-Oct-10	Wetherby	Hand. Chase	3m 1f	2K	Andrew Tinkler	98	2	10
	22-Nov-10	Ludlow	Nov. Hand. Chase	3m	3K	Andrew Tinkler	96	2	9
	26-Jan-11	Huntingdon	Nov. Hand. Chase	2m 7½f	2K	Richard Johnson	98	2	6
	23-Feb-11	Ludlow	Hand. Chase	3m	3K	Jake Greenall	98	2	12
	23-Mar-11	Warwick	Hand. Chase	3m 5f	3K	Jake Greenall	98	PU	6

(continued)

HORSE	DATE	COURSE	RACE	DISTANCE	PRIZE MONEY	JOCKEY	RATING	POSITION	RUNNERS
Cobbler's Queen	5-Nov-10	Fontwell	Chase	2m 3f	3K	Richard Johnson	–	2	6
	16-Dec-10	Exeter	Nov. Chase	2m 3f	4K	Richard Johnson	118	5	7
	27-Jan-11	Ffos Las	Nov. Chase	3m	3K	Richard Johnson	113	2	4
	8-Mar-11	Exeter	Nov. Chase	3m	3K	Andrew Tinkler	111	3	12
	26-Mar-11	Newbury	Nov. Hand. Chase	2m 6½f	17K	Andrew Tinkler	115	UR	9
	30-Apr-11	Uttoxeter	Nov. Hand. Chase	3m	2K	Andrew Tinkler	110	1	5
Key Cutter	6-Oct-10	Ludlow	Chase	2m 4f	3K	Will Kennedy	118	2	8
	11-Nov-10	Ludlow	Hand. Chase	3m	6K	Will Kennedy	118	2	9
	22-Nov-10	Kempton	Chase	3m	3k	Will Kennedy	119	1	5
	15-Dec-10	Newbury	Nov. Hand. Chase	2m 7½f	5K	Will Kennedy	122	12	16
	25-Apr-11	Huntingdon	Hand. Chase	2m 7½f	4K	Dominic Elsworth	119	3	6
	12-May-11	Ludlow	Hand. Chase	3m 1½f	6K	Will Kennedy	118	7	11
Arctic Ben	31-Oct-10	Huntingdon	Hand. Chase	2m ½f	6K	Richard Johnson	113	7	9
	25-Nov-10	Taunton	Nov. Chase	2m	4K	Andrew Tinkler	113	2	3
	27-Jan-11	Ffos Las	Nov. Hand. Chase	2m 5f	3K	Richard Johnson	113	4	6
	5-Mar-11	Kempton	Nov. Hand. Chase	2m	3K	Andrew Thornton	111	F	5

(continued)

HORSE	DATE	COURSE	RACE	DISTANCE	PRIZE MONEY	JOCKEY	RATING	POSITION	RUNNERS
Llama Farmer	26-Nov-10	Newbury	Nov. Hand. Chase	2m 2½f	7K	Dominic Elsworth	123	6	10
	29-Dec-10	Newbury	Nov. Hand. Chase	2m 6½f	5K	Dominic Elsworth	120	PU	15
	11-Jan-11	Leicester	Nov. Hand. Chase	2m	2K	Dominic Elsworth	115	7	9
	8-May-11	Uttoxeter	Hand. Chase	3m 2f	3K	Dominic Elsworth	110	4	6
Safran de Cotte	10-Nov-10	Bangor-on-Dee	Nov. Hurdle	2m ½f	3K	Richard Johnson	–	1	12
	1-Jan-11	Cheltenham	Nov. Hurdle	2m 4½f	6K	Richard Johnson	–	10	15
	15-Jan-11	Warwick	Nov. Hurdle Grade 2	2m 5f	14K	Leighton Aspell	–	3	8
	2-Feb-11	Leicester	Nov. Hurdle	2m 4½f	3K	Richard Johnson	120	6	12
	1-Jan-11	Cheltenham	Nat. Hunt Flat	1m 6f	8K	Dominic Elsworth	–	15	16
Sole Survivor	2-Mar-11	Bangor-on-Dee	Maiden Nat. Hunt Flat	2m ½f	1K	Jake Greenall	–	2	7
	23-Mar-11	Haydock	Nat. Hunt Flat	2m	1K	Dominic Elsworth	–	9	10

	RUNS	1ST	2ND	3RD	4TH
Thievery	6	0	0	0	1
Ordre de Bataille	3	0	0	0	0
Timpo	7	0	4	1	0
Cobbler's Queen	6	1	2	1	0
Key Cutter	6	1	2	1	0
Arctic Ben	4	0	1	0	1
Llama Farmer	4	0	0	0	1
Safran de Cotte	4	1	0	1	0
Sole Survivor	3	0	1	0	0
Total	43	3	10	4	3

	TRAINING FEES	ENTRY FEE/ JOCKEY	TOTAL COST	WINNINGS + SPONSORSHIP	NET COST
2010–2011					
Safran de Cotte	16,559	1,915	18,474	7,280	11,194
Arctic Ben	16,210	945	17,155	3,975	13,180
Cobbler's Queen	17,748	1,600	19,348	6,975	12,373
Timpo	17,249	1,670	18,919	6,230	12,689
Ordre de Bataille	16,827	1,040	17,867	2,500	15,367
Thievery	17,838	1,430	19,268	2,780	16,488
Key Cutter	18,096	1,555	19,651	8,580	11,071
Llama Farmer	18,425	1,555	19,980	2,805	17,175
Sole Survivor	15,400	840	16,240	2,890	13,350
Sixty Something	16,159	–	16,159	2,500	13,659
King of Keys	188	–	188	100	88
Upbeat Cobbler	630	–	630	200	430
					£137,064

2011–2012

THE HORSES

After eight years of ownership we now feel we are getting the hang of it. Our third trainer, Venetia Williams, brings an added dimension to the team and, although Thievery has retired, new purchases have increased the size of Alex's string to what she reckons is about the right number. We certainly should have a good chance of finding a few more winners even if we face the certainty of losing a lot more money. We start the season as follows:

WITH HENRY DALY:

Ordre de Bataille age 9 grey gelding (rating 102)

After an injury sustained at Huntingdon eighteen months ago his promising career has gone totally pear shaped. He showed considerable consistency in three chases before last Christmas, by being pulled up on every occasion. An infection revealed by a scan may have been part of the problem and meant that Batty hasn't raced since December. After such a long lay-off and with his rating right down to 102 we are hopeful that he will get back to his old winning ways.

Timpo age 8 chestnut gelding (rating 98)

With four 2nds in a row last season Timpo is certainly due for another win. He has become a useful performer in modest chases up to 3 miles and while he remains with a handicap under 100 has every chance of being in the frame, but he will never be good enough to compete for big prize money.

Cobbler's Queen age 7 brown mare (rating 110)

Although last season ended with a win, Cobbler's Queen somehow picked up a leg strain that is taking so long to get right she is likely to miss the first half of this season. As a seven-year-old there is still plenty of time to move up in class. Perhaps she will see some truly competitive racing after Christmas.

Arctic Ben age 7 grey gelding (rating 111)

We are still waiting for Arctic Ben to justify the faith we had when we paid a substantial purchase price on the back of a promising bumper win. He has a habit of being too keen in the early stages and running out of steam well before the winning post. After a useful 2nd place at Taunton we thought he was settling down when two races later a nasty fall at Kempton nearly ended his career. After an amazing recovery he is ready to race from the start of the season.

Safran de Cotte age 5 grey gelding (rating 120)

After a 100 per cent record in two bumpers Safran started last season with a win over hurdles at Bangor where Henry Daly declared him to be 'a true Saturday horse'. Although he failed to find another win in pretty respectable company we still think this is our banker-to-be at Cheltenham in

March. Don't expect him to appear until the season is well under way. He loves heavy going so we need plenty of rain.

Upbeat Cobbler age 3 grey mare
A French mare who seems to tick all the boxes, with a strong physique and composed temperament but we won't really know what she is like until she visits a racecourse. First bumper should be after Christmas.

 WITH PAUL WEBBER:

Key Cutter age 7 bay gelding (rating 115)
Showed plenty of promise when he went chasing last season although a disappointing final run at Ludlow suggests that he has found his level with a handicap at around 115. Likes firm ground so we can expect him to be racing in October but may take a break if the ground gets too sticky.

Llama Farmer age 6 brown gelding (rating 105)
Llama needs to produce another good performance to prove that his win at Haydock wasn't a flash in the pan. That sudden bit of form over hurdles caused the handicapper to rate him at 125 and despite failing to get into the frame over fences it took all season for his rating to fall to a more realistic 105. We hope that against more modest company he will find his way back to the Winners' enclosure.

Sole Survivor age 4 grey gelding (novice)
This big horse bought in France was never made for bumpers so we are not surprised that he didn't record a win last season. The switch to hurdles should bring much

anticipated success. Everyone who rides this horse gives him high marks – he has the makings of growing into a class chaser over the next couple of years.

Sixty Something age 5 grey gelding

After spending a year eating grass and being honed to perfection on full training fees this well-thought-of horse went lame so never saw a racecourse. With so much schooling he will probably skip the bumpers and go straight into hurdling.

King of Keys age 3 brown gelding

A new horse bought during the summer that has already become popular at the yard. Described as a genuine horse with a pleasing disposition, we hope that he will be a successful addition to Alex's team. It could be well into 2012 before he runs his first bumper.

WITH VENETIA WILLIAMS:

Miss Tique age 3 bay mare (novice)

This, our first horse with Venetia, comes from France having already had experience over hurdles. The French start their horses jumping as three-year-olds. We hope to find a juvenile hurdle race before Christmas as the prelude to a fairly full season for this exciting prospect.

NEW PLANS

During another family holiday on Mustique – three weeks of sun, tennis, rum punch and close encounters with our eight grandchildren – Alex and I started to think about next season with high hopes that this would be the year that we would finally find one of our horses going to Cheltenham.

The last time we were on the island in February we still hoped that following a disappointing start to last season our luck would change. It didn't. Apart from a happy visit to the Winners' enclosure with Cobbler's Queen at Uttoxeter we had little to shout about.

Despite this unsuccessful and expensive experience, Alex's string, like Manchester City's squad, is still getting bigger. Thievery has left on a free transfer – we decided the handicapper would never do enough to make up for his lack of pace but Thievery has character and under his nick name 'George' has always been a stable favourite. He is remaining at Downton Hall with Henry Daly as an inspirational stable mate for others in the yard, and there are plans for him to go hunting.

None of our horses ever need to worry about the knacker's yard. Alex's long term plan includes a retirement home, which is now being created around our house – twenty acres of land lovingly prepared to accommodate any horse that reaches the end of its racing career. So far the fields have only seen her first horse Transatlantic but, judging by the amount of tree felling, fertilising and fencing going on, Alex expects to care for a considerable collection of horses living in luxury to a ripe old age.

Since May we have bought three new horses so yet again approach a new season with blind faith and high hopes.

One of these future superstars is with a new trainer. Venetia Williams enthusiastically followed up a chance meeting with Alex at the Grand National and after a summer of searching sent us film of an 'exciting three-year-old prospect' winning a hurdle race in France with several lengths to spare. Although the horse was out of our price bracket, the name 'Miss Tique' with its close connection to our favourite holiday destination made the mare irresistible.

We have had name problems with the new horse bought by Henry Daly. We planned to call her Tradesman's Daughter but French breeders expect owners to stick to the name given at birth so commentators may have to cope with an unpronounceable French tongue twister. Bearing in mind what we paid for the horse we should at least be allowed to pick the name, just more evidence why the EEC is bound to end in tears. Fortunately we found a loophole – the French agreed to change the name as long as it begins with the letter 'U' (they change the letter each year) – I picked 'Upbeat Cobbler'.

No naming problems with the new horse bought by Paul Webber. King of Keys was approved without any problem and hopefully will at least equal the success of stable mate Key Cutter.

It may be next year before these three new horses appear on a race card but we hope to see one horse in its first bumper in October and he should do well. Sixty Something, bought in May 2010, went lame within days of his first scheduled appearance in March but he is back in training and with all that practice and maturity I am sure must be more than a match for the competition.

I look forward to October with renewed confidence – it will be great to get the regular reports from each trainer and the jockey's reasons why we didn't win this race but might win the next one and, hopefully, it will be fantastic to experience the thrill of seeing Alex's light blue and white Manchester City colours in the Winners' enclosure.

But I do have a big worry. Two weeks ago we went to Goodwood, where Alex remarked, 'You know I think I could get to like Flat racing after all.' I will try to ensure she doesn't take this new interest too seriously.

THE LONDON MARATHON

Over the last few months racing has taken a bit of a back seat, but I have a good excuse. I am currently Master of The Worshipful Company of Pattenmakers, a City Livery with shoe trade connections (pattens were a form of footwear in the Middle Ages, a bit like a health sandal on top of a big piece of metal which raised the wearer well above the filth that flooded the streets).

The Master's role includes a lot of dinners, mostly in London, supporting our charities and maintaining old traditions. I have discovered there are tons of old traditions to maintain. I was there at the Quit Rent Ceremony (it would take me too long to explain), The Silent Ceremony and The Lord Mayor's Banquet. The nearest I got to a horse was when I rode in a carriage in the Lord Mayor's Show. I also ran in the London Marathon.

My marathon entry was prompted by Simon Goodman, my successor as Master Pattenmaker. After dinner and a couple of glasses of wine we were discussing how to raise more money for our charitable fund. Every year the Pattenmakers Company has a few places in the London Marathon, so I foolishly suggested that I might run while I was Master and Simon quickly pledged £100 if I completed the course. With little thought I accepted his challenge.

Secretly I'd always wanted to have one last go at the London Marathon. I had already run five marathons but the last was in 1984. I ran the second and third London Marathons and was proud to finish – although I took over four hours I nearly beat a man wearing a hippo outfit and one person breasted the tape three hours after me.

But I underestimated the effect of a 28-year gap.

Within days of taking up the challenge I had my first trial run. It took me nearly an hour-and-a-half to complete a convenient circuit that took me near to the racing circuit at Oulton Park – I got back home in less than 90 minutes and was pretty pleased until I retraced my steps by car and discovered that I had covered just over 6 miles. It didn't take me long to work out that at that pace a marathon would take me nearly eight hours. I clearly had a lot of work to do.

Needing all the help I could get, I went to a proper running shop to buy some shoes. They put me on a treadmill to track the characteristics of my running style, which required a pair that cost well over £100.

Each time I tackled the 6-mile circuit I went a bit quicker and within six months it was taking no more than an hour – still about a five-hour marathon pace but not too embarrassing. With another five months to get into shape perhaps I would be close to my PB.

By Christmas I was already sponsored for £10,000 and with my promise to double the donations my run was already worth a lot of money. But the winter weather that brought racing to a stop also made it impossible to go out running. I tried a few half-hearted efforts on a running machine but soon got bored so I went out for a short run in the snow, slipped on some ice and twisted my knee.

I wasn't short of advice. My children bought me a bagful of energy sachets, which were guaranteed to give me a boost if taken every 40 minutes during a run. I spent several hours with Sheena the physio, who massaged my knee, and a fitness fanatic from my golf club emailed me some tips after spotting my eccentric running style as he drove past me on the road to Chester.

In February I did an 18-mile run in three hours twenty minutes and was really pleased. Perhaps that personal best was still possible.

I was spending several nights in London so started early morning running on the Embankment. It was then that I realised that everyone else was running more quickly than me. The jogging commuters sped past me and I never overtook another runner. I then noticed I have also become a slow walker – whenever I go to London by train from Crewe it takes me longer than anyone else to walk from the car park to the station.

We had a trial run – the Wilmslow Half Marathon which took me just short of three hours and didn't do my knee much good. With only three weeks to go to the big event I gave up training and hoped that the knee would gain enough strength to get me round 26 miles.

I had plenty of family support. Our daughter Victoria was running with her husband Jonnie. Our son Ollie, an extremely unfit 32-year-old, did no training and was enjoying several cigarettes at the start. I ran with Edward, a regular London Marathon competitor who was giving up all thoughts of a quick time to look after his father.

Edward told me to take it steady at the start because, he explained, it is so much better to be overtaking people in the latter stages of the race. As pacemaker Edward set off at a very modest pace and I struggled to keep up. It took over three hours to reach Tower Bridge which is not quite halfway. We seemed to give the spectators some pleasure – as I passed several shouted 'Come on Grandad' and to relieve his boredom Edward started to run backwards, kidding the crowd that he was trying to set a world backwards running record.

By the time we finished, in just under six-and-a-half hours, most of the spectators had drifted off for a cup of tea and the course was being narrowed to allow traffic to flow again.

I wasn't proud of my performance but I still studied the statistics. Victoria beat her husband, both finishing in under four-and-a-half hours. Ollie, despite minimal training and a few cigarette breaks, got round in five hours. But at least Edward's tactics paid off and during the second half of the race we overtook more than 1,000 fellow competitors.

The 2011 London Marathon will definitely be the last time John Timpson will ever go running.

It seems unlikely that I will see many racecourses this side of March 2012 when I hand over to my successor as Master Pattenmaker, so I expect to be a regular visitor to Ladbrokes for the next few months.

THE RACING SEASON

The season got off to a steady start with Arctic Ben, Key Cutter and Timpo finishing in the first three. So when I did get the chance to go to Bangor-on-Dee to watch Ordre de Bataille I was hoping to witness Alex's first winner of the season. We were in the first race – he looked fantastic in the paddock as the odds shortened to 5/1, which looked a good bet as he was towards the front of the field for the first mile, but then he quickly faded and was pulled up with 4 furlongs to go. 'It's more mental than physical,' said Andrew Tinkler. 'Goes back to when he hurt his shoulder at Huntingdon eighteen months ago – I think he simply doesn't like it any more.'

Before the start of the second race we were heading back to the car park having decided it was time for Ordre de Bataille to retire and enjoy a life of leisure in the fields at the back of our house where the training fees are much cheaper.

On 16 November we had three horses running at Warwick – a rare chance to see Llama Farmer, Sixty Something and Sole Survivor on the same day (all trained by Paul Webber so presumably we saved a bit on the cost of transport). But I was away on Pattenmaker business – a degree ceremony at the University of East London, an address by the Lord Mayor at the Mansion House and supper at the City of London Boys' School.

I caught up with the first two races on my iPad on the way to the Mansion House. Llama Farmer came a creditable 6th and Sixty Something, running his first ever race, was 9th (showing enough speed in the latter stages for the stewards to ask for more details).

Although there is a branch of Coral that is pretty handy for the Mansion House I was too late to get there for the 3 o'clock so I missed Sole Survivor winning by a short head at 12/1 – our first win of the season. I am delighted that Alex and I appeared in small print in the *Racing Post* the following day which described our trip to France to buy the horse. But they failed to mention that the name Sole Survivor, although having an obvious connection with shoe repairs, is really named after our Michelin star lunch where the deal was done – superb scallops and an enormous sole – hence Sole Survivor.

Like buses, winners often come in pairs so I was not surprised when Timpo won at Towcester the following Sunday – a race I watched courtesy of At the Races on our television at home. Alex said a trip to Towcester was a step too far after her wonderful day at Warwick.

I am missing the live racing and the coded messages from our trainers and jockeys but soon I will be a Past Master of the Pattenmakers and once more will be able to hear why our horse would have done better with an extra couple of furlongs on a more galloping track with softer ground on a right-hand course. In the meantime I will leave Alex to watch the horses while I keep eating the dinners.

Owners could be forgiven for wondering whether their contribution to racing is seriously undervalued. It is not just a question of cash, although the pathetic pickings on offer are a clear indication that we must all do it for love not money.

During the season it costs about £2,000 a month to keep a horse in training plus various vets' bills and 'miscellaneous' on top. Thankfully the bills drop dramatically when your horse is put out to grass but the total cost for a year will not be far short of £20,000. If you are lucky (and most owners are not) the horse will run six times a season so will be costing over £3,000 a go before paying the entrance fee, the transport, the jockey and handing a few quid to the lad. So if you win a race good enough to pay a £4,000 first prize you haven't won, you have just about got your money back.

Despite the financial folly we are happy to pay for horses with a rating 0–90 or even 110 which are running in races where the first prize is £1,760 and the fourth horse gets £142.50.

So if owners don't do it for the money perhaps it is the promise of a five star day out with luxury accommodation, Michelin star food and free champagne. Dream on!

My highest marks go to Haydock Park, where they certainly appear to have put the care of owners pretty high up their pecking order – compared to Hereford where we have in the past got a grumpy greeting from the guy in the car park before crowding into the cramped little Owners' and Trainers' hut to claim our complimentary cup of tea.

The facilities at Leicester are miles better than Hereford but the course has the atmosphere of a funeral in fog. We picked up our first ever prize money at Leicester when Transatlantic finished 2nd in a poor quality Novice Hurdle (it was a Monday). We should have been overjoyed but came away with memories of a small crowd mainly made up of bored-looking men with nothing better to do. Some courses have an old fashioned charm; Leicester is simply old fashioned.

We were therefore a touch disappointed when Paul Webber entered Key Cutter for a Steeplechase at Leicester. We were travelling back from London to Cheshire that day and as it wouldn't take much of a detour to take in Leicester there seemed no escape. But Alex developed a migraine so we had to drive straight home where we saw Key Cutter romp in to win easily (prize money £2,145). Perhaps if we'd been there I would have felt a little bit better about Leicester.

Timpo, who won early in December, looked set up for a good season until we had a setback. The vet had given him the wrong injection and he would fail a drug test if run during the next eight weeks. This blow was nothing compared with the bad news we got the following week. Two legs were the cause of our disappointment: one belonged to Llama Farmer who had to be fired and won't see a racecourse before December 2012. Cobbler's Queen's injury is so bad she won't race again but may not retire. Alex says she 'would quite like her to have babies'; I immediately wondered how much that would cost.

Arctic Ben has a habit of coming 4th and did it again at Bangor-on-Dee to win £152.93. Checking my bill from Henry Daly I find that the cost of transporting Arctic Ben to Bangor was £72.00 and that was on top of paying an entry fee of £41.08 and a jockey fee of £148.95. But Alex said, 'it is nice to win something'.

Our next outing was at Haydock not only as an owner but also as guests of Haydock Chairman Bill Whittle. I have already said that Haydock is the tops for entertainment – that day we were looked after very well indeed.

With heavy rain changing the going from 'soft' to 'mud' we knew we had a chance with Safran de Cotte and so it proved – he loved the ground, winning a first prize of £8,846 and at 13/2 gave a decent return on my £20 each way bet. For a fleeting moment I thought that, after all, being an owner could be a paying proposition.

Even though one of our horses with Paul Webber, Sixty Something, was well down the field in the last race of the day, Henry Daly could tell that I was in a good mood when we had a drink in the Owners' and Trainers' bar as most of the racegoers battled against the driving rain on their way home.

Henry was keen to convince me that breeding from Cobbler's Queen would not be as financially foolish as I feared. It doesn't cost as much to keep a mare as it does to train it, but the stallion certainly knows how to charge for performing his role. Then when the foal arrives you have another animal to pay for. Henry kindly showed me a copy of the bills he is paying for one of his brood mares.

I should have expected the extra bills from the vet including £125 for 'scan and manual ovaries', £72 for a clitoral swab and triumphantly £39 for a positive pregnancy examination. Adding it all together including a stud fee of £3,500, quite a lot of transport and the cost of keeping mother and baby for two-and-a-half years, I reckoned the whole exercise comes to not far short of £30,000 – about the average price we have been paying at the sales. But, I said to Alex, as Cobbler's Queen has won four times the foal might sell for a lot more and we could make a decent profit. 'I wouldn't trust anyone else to look after one of our foals,' said Alex. 'We will have to keep it.'

A year ago we lost a month of racing due to the frost and snow, so, with all our grandchildren away for Christmas, we were looking forward to plenty of good days out over the holiday. Sole Survivor ran at Leicester! It was cold and windy on the Owners' and Trainers' viewing area (the bar was so cramped you had to go outside to get elbow room). Sole Survivor looked handy until the last half mile then faded rapidly. 'Probably wind,' said Paul Webber, 'often happens – I think we will give him a small wind operation to see if that does the trick.' We left the cold winds of Leicester, jumped in the car, switched on the heated seats and drove home.

On New Year's Day we went to Uttoxeter to watch Arctic Ben come home 1st in a six-horse race and won £2,742.

'I bet you are pleased,' said Alex. 'Not only a good win to finish the year but we must be making money.' I thought it best just to smile and resist making any comment.

Alex and I were a long way away from Musselburgh when Key Cutter set off as favourite in a 3-mile chase boosted by an appearance on the *Racing Post* list of horses making the longest trip to the racecourse. In truth this was not a sign of our confidence, Paul Webber entered three horses at the meeting so they could keep costs down by sharing a horse box.

We were in London for The Worshipful Company of Pattenmakers' Annual Banquet at the Mansion House – as the Master Pattenmaker there was no way I could make Musselburgh. Instead I watched the race in William Hill at Victoria, which must be one of the shabbier shops in the chain. It was full of regular punters who regarded us with curiosity.

As it was Friday the thirteenth I felt lucky but this was a feeling of false security. Key Cutter failed to fulfil the role of favourite and finished well down the field – perhaps he was tired after travelling from Banbury to Edinburgh.

The following day, after the Banquet, we made an early exit from a lunch where we had entertained a party of Swiss shoemakers, to watch the 2.35 at Sandown – a key race in Safran de Cotte's attempt to qualify for the Pertemps Final at Cheltenham. We were at a Ladbrokes near Oxford Street which was much more comfortable than William Hill, Victoria, but the result was just as disappointing. Safran de Cotte never got near the leaders and finished nearer the back than the front.

2012 had not started well, but I was somewhat cheered the following week when I went to Doncaster with our son Oliver (a race fitted in during a day visiting some of our shops) to see Sixty Something making a late run to get an unlikely 2nd. I was delighted but Jockey Dominic Elsworth was a bit grumpy when he gave his post-race opinion, I think he felt he should have won. It was a costly run, Sixty Something suffered a nasty gash when he hit one of the fences, so I guessed we wouldn't see him on a racecourse again until the season is nearly over.

We had one more entry before going on holiday but we couldn't get to Warwick to watch Arctic Ben as we were at The Goring Hotel enjoying our son James's visit to Buckingham Palace to collect his OBE. On the day before we were due to go to the Caribbean I checked with the Hall Porter who confirmed my fear that the nearest bookie was the shabby William Hill at Victoria where I had lost money on Key Cutter.

The shop was even busier than before and we got a lot of strange looks, but didn't care when Arctic Ben shot into a 20-length lead – nothing got anywhere near and he won by 11 lengths at 17/2. The other customers glared at us when we collected some significant winnings but I ignored them with a smug look on my face. A great start to our holiday.

We timed our trip to Mustique to perfection. It snowed the day after we left and nothing raced until our return. I watched Safran de Cotte come in 6th with another sub-Cheltenham class run at Haydock but the following week we got a new horseracing experience when we went to see Big Sam Bellamy. Big Sam was being viewed as the likely stallion to meet up with our mare Cobbler's Queen, who has a leg that stops her racing but hopefully has everything else in order so she can deliver one of Big Sam's hundreds of foals.

Big Sam lives in Shropshire at Shade Oak Stud, with David and Anne Hockenhull who must like being near horses – they are surrounded by loads of them, young foals penned together waiting until they are old enough to go to the sales.

But the stallions get luxury accommodation, their own stall and their own field in glorious solitude while they wait for the next visitor. I didn't even get close to Big Sam. These animals are dangerous – I just hope he finds the gentle touch when he has his brief meeting with Cobbler's Queen.

Our season seemed to be getting back on track when Miss Tique had a good 2nd at Leicester and Arctic Ben was just 3rd by a neck in a good grade race at Chepstow. So we were optimistic when making our first ever visit to

Towcester to watch Timpo in a fairly competitive chase over 2 miles 4 furlongs.

Towcester was busy (it helps a lot when no one has to pay to go in) so there was a buzzy atmosphere but as a venue it must be near the bottom of the league when it comes to looking after owners. With difficulty, Alex found a seat in the Owners' and Trainers' tent while I queued for a cup of cold tea.

There was a wild horse in Timpo's race who delayed the start and then jumped the first fence at a sharp angle straight into Timpo. Battered and bruised, Timpo ran without enthusiasm – Andrew Tinkler pulled him up after a circuit. It was a long drive home.

It is always exciting going to watch a new horse run for the first time so we were pleased that we could both go to Bangor to see King of Keys in his first bumper. We went across the road with Paul Webber to meet stable lad Charlotte, and watch the saddle being carefully fitted. The bookies quoted King of Keys at 20/1 – it was a hot race so there was little chance of winning but as Alex said to jockey Denis O'Regan, 'Let's hope he enjoys the outing.'

Our race lasted less than 300 yards, which was where King of Keys broke a leg, and we experienced the worst bit of being a racehorse owner. There is nothing much to say when a day at the races ends in tragedy, but it makes you think. We lost a racehorse, but the team in Paul Webber's yard have lost a close friend. We had a bad day but nothing like as bad as it was for Charlotte who travelled back in an empty horse box.

175

Some time ago I realised that racehorse owners are highly unlikely to see any return on their investment but Alex still dreams of saddling a winner at the Cheltenham Festival.

We had three entries for this year's Festival which I followed for several weeks in the ante-post betting market through regular visits to the Oddschecker website. It was a sad and pointless exercise – with all of our horses rated below 130 there was no way they would be there at the start. Sure enough when Festival week arrived they were all balloted out. We therefore enjoyed a stress-free day with a fantastic view from the balcony outside the Weatherbys Box, looking smugly down at the punters pushing and shoving among the record crowd.

We got good news on Cobbler's Queen (she enjoyed her encounter with Big Sam Bellamy) which was followed by a disappointment. Despite showing such pleasure the vet insists she is not pregnant.

Trainers have such a friendly way of bringing bad news. With so little rain in February and March I knew it wouldn't be long before they started grumbling about the ground. ('It would be better to give them a rest now and look forward to some softer going next October.')

But we saw some success in the week after Cheltenham, even though I could only watch in the bookies. I had just left a lunch at the Old Bailey when I popped in to a City branch of Paddy Power to see Arctic Ben easily win a three-horse race at Haydock. The following day it was BetFred in Holyhead who had to pay out my winnings on Miss Tique – a comfortable winner at Chepstow. Alex was hoping to make it three out of three with Sixty Something at Uttoxeter (on the day I preferred golf at Delamere Forest followed by Manchester City v Sunderland at the Etihad Stadium). Sixty Something entertained a big Saturday crowd by misbehaving at the start. His antics in trying to avoid lining up near the tape were so bizarre the on-course screen showed nothing else and 12,000 people had a good laugh at our expense. Despite the energy wasted before the start, Alex assures me Sixty Something would have romped home if he hadn't had an unfortunate fall at the second last.

I had a tense moment at the Grand National. Last year Alex had lunch next to Venetia Williams and within four months she had found us a filly (Miss Tique) which extended Alex's string well over budget. Imagine my concern when I saw that this year Alex was seated next to Willie Mullins – fortunately Alex decided that Ireland is too far from Tarporley.

We did feature at Cheltenham after all – not The Festival but the next meeting where Arctic Ben and Safran de Cotte both started as favourites. Neither horse finished first past the post but Arctic Ben came a creditable 2nd and according to Henry Daly will be 'all the better for that run when he returns in October'.

Another season is ending and Alex considers it has been an unqualified success, her eight wins are a personal best. There is not much point in me highlighting the lack of any financial return. Prize money paid for less than 25 per cent of our expenses and our balance sheet has been battered by an unplanned reduction in our horse power.

We started the season with twelve horses in training and by the middle of March we only had eight. Ordre de Bataille is now living with us in Cheshire hoping to do three-day events. Llama Farmer and Sole Survivor both need to rest until 2013 to recover from leg troubles and King of Keys broke his leg in a Flat race and had to be put down (I wonder whether there are dangerous holes left when the hurdles are removed).

Two of our fit horses (Safran de Cotte and Timpo) are showing signs of fatigue – 'they have run some testing races,' said Henry Daly. 'It is time to give them a break.'

Our two youngest horses have decided to hide their ability until next season. Sixty Something and Upbeat Cobbler are both described as 'babies that run a bit green' and we have been encouraged to think 'they should do well when they step up in distance next season'.

Key Cutter was brought back 'to run races on better ground' but ever since then it has rained so it is now 'difficult to find the right race'.

Currently our future hopes are pinned on Miss Tique and Arctic Ben who both finished the season on a high but I don't expect to see either of them on a racecourse before the end of October.

Most of Alex's horses are now out in the fields eating the grass and costing me less money. We will also take a break from racing during the summer. So our interest over the next few months will be centred on Cobbler's Queen who the vet confirms is now expecting a Big Sam Bellamy baby.

Alex is already optimistic about next season. 'We could win even more races,' said Alex. I was tempted to add, 'And lose a lot more money on the way,' but a long time ago I learnt that it pays to agree with Alex, so I said nothing.

It would have been nice to end the season with a win but sadly we went out with a whimper. Key Cutter, who likes firm ground and had spent weeks incurring full training fees while waiting for the weather to change, should have taken advantage of the drought but after leading for 2 miles finished last in a 3-mile chase.

'Give him a short rest,' said Paul Webber, 'and we'll bring him back early in the season before the races get too hot.' That means we will be racing for modest money, which prompts me to applaud the protesters at Worcester who turned a hurdle with pathetic prizes into a one-horse race. They must, like me, have done the arithmetic – as an owner, you need to win an average of £4,000, every time your horses go racing, simply to break even.

As soon as Key Cutter joined all the others in the field it started to rain – a few more summers like this one and we will have heavy going all year round.

Our only sporting fixture in May was the last game of the football season. Manchester City only had to beat Queens Park Rangers at The Etihad to win the Premiership. Like many City supporters we had watched our team frustratingly stumble from one disappointment to another for over 30 years – now was our chance to enjoy success.

But City gave their supporters a terrible day – 2–1 down with seventeen minutes to go. Alex couldn't take any more and left – missing the two goals that won the game with Sergio Agüero scoring the winner with less than a minute to spare.

With no chance of an entry until October we were free to forget about horses and head for a holiday. We went on an adventure to the USA. After a week in California we flew to Denver and hired an enormous motor home. ('We have to be comfortable and I don't want to hear your snoring,' said Alex.)

When travelling we play to our strengths, I navigate, Alex drives. Alex picked the short straw – driving a 40-foot camper can be extremely stressful.

We went to Wyoming – cowboy country, which meant plenty of horses – but the horse that took our attention came to us in an email from Paul Webber, who had just happened to have 'found the perfect grey at the Doncaster Sales'.

Paul bought the horse on spec and offered him to me with a special deal. 'As Sole Survivor won't see another race-course until autumn 2013 I will keep him for free if you buy this fantastic new boy.'

I fell for it and on our return from the States we dropped in to Cropredy (Paul's yard) to see our latest addition. By then he had an identity. Picking the names is my job, which is why we have horses called Timpo and Upbeat Cobbler, but this time I wanted a way to celebrate Manchester City's win. Someone already has 'Blue Moon'. I was tempted to call him 'Goal Difference' but in the end chose 'Six One Away' – if you don't get the significance ask a Manchester United fan.

We are now heading for the Olympics – a fortnight in London watching a range of events including Weightlifting, Water Polo and the Closing Ceremony. By the time the last Olympic medal has been won most of our horses will be back in training, with promises of 'having a run early in October'.

We are already looking forward to next season.

2011–2012

SEASON 2011–2012

HORSE	DATE	COURSE	RACE	DISTANCE	PRIZE MONEY	JOCKEY	RATING	POSITION	RUNNERS
Ordre de Bataille	9-Nov-11	Bangor-on-Dee	Hand. Chase	2m 4½f	3K	Andrew Tinkler	102	PU	7
	20-Oct-11	Ludlow	Hand. Chase	3m	3K	Mr L.R. Payter	98	6	9
	2-Nov-11	Warwick	Hand. Chase	3m 2f	2K	Jake Greenall	96	2	5
Timpo	20-Nov-11	Towcester	Hand. Chase	3m ½f	2K	Andrew Tinkler	96	1	7
	26-Feb-12	Towcester	Nov. Hand. Chase	2m 5½f	2K	Andrew Tinkler	101	PU	11
	14-Apr-12	Chepstow	Hand. Chase	2m 7½f	2K	Jake Greenall	100	6	12
	16-Oct-11	Kempton	Hand. Chase	3m	3K	Will Kennedy	115	2	7
	7-Dec-11	Leicester	Hand. Chase	2m 6½f	3K	Dominic Elsworth	115	1	5
Key Cutter	13-Jan-12	Musselburgh	Hand. Chase	2m 7f	6K	Dominic Elsworth	125	7	10
	17-Apr-12	Exeter	Hand. Chase	3m 6½f	6K	Dominic Elsworth	123	UR	9
	17-May-12	Ludlow	Hand. Chase	3m 1½f	6K	Dominic Elsworth	121	7	15

(continued)

HORSE	DATE	COURSE	RACE	DISTANCE	PRIZE MONEY	JOCKEY	RATING	POSITION	RUNNERS
Arctic Ben	3-Nov-11	Towcester	Maiden Chase	2m ½f	1K	Richard Johnson	111	3	5
	25-Nov-11	Newbury	Nov. Hand. Chase	2m 2½f	7K	Richard Johnson	108	4	8
	14-Dec-11	Bangor-on-Dee	Hand. Chase	2m 4½f	2K	Jake Greenall	105	4	11
	31-Dec-11	Uttoxeter	Hand. Chase	2m	3K	Andrew Thornton	103	1	6
	26-Jan-12	Warwick	Hand. Chase	2m 4½f	4K	Richard Johnson	108	1	8
	25-Feb-12	Chepstow	Hand. Chase	2m	15K	Andrew Tinkler	118	3	9
	21-Mar-12	Haydock	Nov. Hand. Chase	2m	3K	Andrew Tinkler	118	1	3
	19-Apr-12	Cheltenham	Nov. Hand. Chase	2m 5f	6K	Andrew Tinkler	125	2	6
Llama Farmer	16-Nov-11	Warwick	Nov. Hand. Chase	2m 4½f	3K	Denis O'Regan	105	6	11
Safran de Cotte	5-Nov-11	Sandown	Hand. Hurdle	2m	5K	Andrew Tinkler	120	4	12
	3-Dec-11	Sandown	Hand. Hurdle	2m 6f	9K	Richard Johnson	120	3	19
	17-Dec-11	Haydock	Hand. Hurdle	2m 4f	12K	Jake Greenall	119	1	13
	14-Jan-12	Warwick	Hand. Hurdle	3m 1f	10K	Andrew Tinkler	127	11	16
	18-Feb-12	Haydock	Hand. Hurdle	3m	11K	Andrew Tinkler	127	6	19
	19-Apr-12	Cheltenham	Hand. Hurdle	3m	7K	Richard Johnson	125	7	9

(continued)

HORSE	DATE	COURSE	RACE	DISTANCE	PRIZE MONEY	JOCKEY	RATING	POSITION	RUNNERS
Miss Tique	1-Dec-11	Leicester	3 YO Hurdle	2m	2K	Aidan Coleman	–	5	11
	4-Jan-12	Huntingdon	4 YO Hurdle	1m 7½f	2K	Aidan Coleman	–	6	15
	24-Feb-12	Warwick	4 YO Hurdle	2m	2K	Sam Thomas	–	2	12
	22-Mar-12	Chepstow	Nov. Hurdle	2m	2K	Aidan Coleman	108	1	13
Sixty Something	16-Nov-11	Warwick	Nov. Hurdle	2m 5f	2K	Denis O'Regan	–	9	17
	17-Dec-11	Haydock	Nov. Hurdle	2m 4f	4K	Sam Jones	–	6	9
	11-Jan-12	Doncaster	Nov. Hurdle	2m 3½f	2K	Dominic Elsworth	–	2	14
	31-Mar-12	Uttoxeter	Maiden Hurdle	2m 4f	2K	Dominic Elsworth	113	F	10
	18-Apr-12	Cheltenham	Nov. Hand. Hurdle	3m	6K	Dominic Elsworth	120	PU	17
Upbeat Cobbler	6-Jan-12	Bangor-on-Dee	Nat. Hunt Flat	2m ½f	1K	Andrew Tinkler	–	4	7
	2-Mar-12	Newbury	Nat. Hunt Flat	2m ½f	1K	Andrew Tinkler	–	8	14
King Of Keys	29-Feb-12	Bangor-on-Dee	Nat. Hunt Flat	2m ½f	1K	Denis O'Regan	–	PU	8
Sole Survivor	16-Nov-11	Warwick	Nov. Hurdle	2m	2K	Dominic Elsworth	–	1	15
	3-Dec-11	Sandown	Nov. Hurdle	2m	3K	Dominic Elsworth	–	11	12
	28-Dec-11	Leicester	Nov. Hurdle	2m 4½f	2K	Dominic Elsworth	–	12	15

	RUNS	1ST	2ND	3RD	4TH
Ordre de Bataille	1	0	0	0	0
Timpo	5	1	1	0	0
Key Cutter	5	1	1	0	0
Arctic Ben	8	3	1	2	2
Llama Farmer	1	0	0	0	0
Safran de Cotte	6	1	0	1	1
Sole Survivor	3	1	0	0	0
Miss Tique	4	1	1	0	0
Sixty Something	5	0	1	0	0
Upbeat Cobbler	2	0	0	0	1
King of Keys	1	0	0	0	0
Total	41	8	5	3	4

	TRAIN-ING FEES	ENTRY FEE/ JOCKEY	TOTAL COST	WINNINGS + SPONSORSHIP	NET COST
2011–2012					
Safran de Cotte	19,808	2,140	21,948	14,110	7,838
Arctic Ben	18,875	2,930	21,805	15,590	6,215
Cobbler's Queen	6,725	–	6,725	1,750	4,975
Timpo	18,547	1,155	19,702	4,950	14,752
Ordre de Bataille	8,343	310	8,653	750	7,903
Key Cutter	18,977	2,645	21,622	5,800	15,822
Llama Farmer	13,060	220	13,280	2,500	10,780
Sole Survivor	15,266	1,015	16,281	2,500	13,781
Sixty Something	16,650	1,635	18,285	5,130	13,155
King of Keys	14,002	310	14,312	2,000	12,312
Upbeat Cobbler	15,748	545	16,293	2,500	13,793
Miss Tique	20,613	1,800	22,413	4,880	17,533
					£138,859
Cobbler's Queen (in foal)	5,074				5,074
					£143,933

THE OLYMPICS

With no racing to bother about we signed up for a full-on Olympic experience – at least one event on nearly every day of the Games.

We were at the Sydney Games in 2000 and wondered whether London would get anywhere near to matching the Australian hospitality.

I was amazed: it was just like going back to Sydney twelve years ago. We were greeted by a host of happy and helpful Volunteers wearing their London 2012 uniform. There was another throng of crowd-pleasers guiding us through security and in no time we were walking past the Aquatic Centre where we saw the Park: 'Wow!' This is definitely better than Sydney. The Basketball Arena was a long walk, too long for Alex who spotted the Accessible Buggy and found us a seat. We were driven at walking pace right round the park – our introduction to Olympicland. It is enormous, the arenas are stunning but the great surprise is the gardens. The wild flowers were fantastic – I would love to see a snippet of this display at our home, Sandymere.

We went to a wide range of events. We saw big girls (like, tall) playing basketball, Russians fencing against Romanians, pocket-sized weightlifters with brutal biceps and water polo players trying to drown their opponents, but the highlight for Alex was always going to be athletics.

Athletics started on Friday and we had tickets for the first night. I knew it would be impressive, but still found the first glimpse of the stadium to be a genuine 'Wow!' We were one of the first to arrive but even the empty stadium had a great atmosphere which got even better as the seats filled.

First up was the qualifying round of the women's discus. Three throws to decide who goes into the final – an awful long way to come for only three attempts especially for the big girl who put her first throw into the net.

The crowd got an early chance to go wild when the heptathletes put the shot. All eyes on Jessica Ennis. No pressure! The rowers talk about the home crowd being 'the extra man in our boat'. There must be the danger that the enthusiastic support for our 'bound to win' Jessica would put her off rather than spur her on. It is amazing how top sports stars can cope with the tension. That's why top jockeys tend to get the best rides.

We had a good view of the long jump qualifiers who lined up to have their practice jumps like prep school boys on sports day.

There was a big contrast between the men with ever so thin legs who ran in the 1,500 metre heats and the chaps in the shot-put final at the far side of the stadium. The giant from Poland who won the gold medal could have thrown the fastest runner halfway across the arena.

I had been irritated by the patriotic home crowd in Sydney with their shouts of 'Aussie, Aussie, Aussie' and raucous support for every Australian competitor. We were exactly the same. Just the mention of a GB athlete was enough for most of the crowd to shout support and wave their Union Jacks. But the big roar was reserved for Jessica Ennis who finished the day with a great run over 200 metres and a healthy overnight lead in the Heptathlon.

Saturday was always going to be a big night. Once Jessica Ennis had done well in both long jump and javelin only a sudden injury could deny her the gold medal. 'As

Alex is presented with her first trophy,
Ordre de Bataille having won at Warwick after a stewards' enquiry.
Les Hurley Photography

Alex's
favourite
horse
Thievery;
he still goes
hunting with
the Daly
family.
Racing Post

Llama Farmer at Haydock, winning at 40/1.

Happy with Llama Farmer a 40/1 winner.

Cobbler's Queen and Key Cutter on the way to a Timpson one-two.

Richard Johnson on Cobbler's Queen, winning at Huntingdon in Alex's most successful race.

Safran de Cotte winning at Bangor in his first run over hurdles.

Sole Survivor after his one and only win, ridden by Dominic Elsworth.
Les Hurley Photography

Richard Johnson riding Arctic Ben to his second win in a month at Warwick.
Racing Post

A very cold and muddy day at Chepstow. Jake Greenall and Safran de Cotte won a close race.

Owner Mrs A. Timpson looks good after a win.

Andrew Tinkler on seven-times winner Safran de Cotte at Cheltenham.
Racing Post

Jake Greenall on
Sixty Something, on
the way to winning
a handicap chase at
Doncaster.
Racing Post

AP McCoy on
Arctic Ben – his
only win in
Alex's colours.

Alain Cawley on Royal Palladium, just beaten into 2nd in the Badger Chase at Wincanton.
Racing Post

Transatlantic at Cheltenham – painted purely from imagination.

soon as she has won we'll leave; there are several children at home who need to see us,' said Alex. 'Mo Farah is running as well,' I said in hope. 'If we wait to the end I won't get home until three in the morning, and anyway I don't think he will win the 10,000 metres.'

The atmosphere in the stadium was electric – 80,000 people and most were flag waving, flag wearing Brits looking forward to celebrating victory.

The women had their discus final and 100m semi-finals, the men qualified for the 400m hurdles but everyone was waiting for Jessica, until they saw the standings in the men's Long Jump with GB 1st and 2nd.

Greg Rutherford had jumped into the lead with the chance of a surprise GB gold but nothing was going to divert the crowd's attention away from Jessica. The Heptathlon was pretty much a done deal – she was so far ahead coming into the final event (800 metres) only a catastrophe to eclipse Devon Loch's disaster in the Grand National would have denied her the gold medal.

Jessica was cheered as soon as she appeared and got a rapturous reception when her name was announced. The crowd felt nervous: surely nothing would go wrong now. She set off quickly and kept at the front of the field; the cheers got louder as it became clear the gold medal was a certainty – everyone stood as she crossed the line in 1st place.

It wasn't really a race it was a victory lap. Hardly anyone noticed that during all the excitement Greg Rutherford had increased his lead with a jump of 8.31 metres. The scoreboard, the announcers and the entire crowd were only talking about Jessica's win.

Greg Rutherford was still in the lead with two jumps to go but Jessica had won so Alex said we had to go – we were the only people leaving the stadium.

A screen in the Westfield Centre was showing the early laps of the 10,000 metres. A man on the Javelin Train announced that Rutherford had won gold. We set a record time to Central London and watched the last two laps of the 10,000 metres on the television in our car. Mo's win made it three golds for Britain in the space of an hour.

I was there at The Etihad when City won the Premiership. I watched every ball of the Old Trafford Test when Jim Laker took 19 wickets. And I was there in the Olympic Stadium on the greatest night for British Athletics – I just didn't stay to the end.

We had a great run home, back before 1.00am. There was no one else on the road – they were all watching the Olympics.

I nearly fell asleep watching the synchronised swimming but our morning in the Velodrome was fantastic, only beaten by the day Dame Kathleen came to join us.

Wednesday 8 August was the big one in our diary. Others had pencilled in Usain Bolt or Jessica Ennis but we were going to see my aunt, Dame Kathleen Ollerenshaw.

We had been planning this moment for over seven years, nearly as long as Seb Coe. When London won the Olympic bid I told Kathleen about our trip to Sydney and before the conversation ended I promised she would be sitting in the stadium for 2012. It was a big ask. Dame Kathleen was born on 1 October 1912.

She was in the UK pairs skating championship and played hockey for England at Wembley about 80 years ago.

Apart from her sporting achievements she has an awesome CV. Despite being profoundly deaf from an early age she sparkled at university and became one of the country's leading mathematicians. She was a recognised expert in education, and a local politician who became Lord Mayor of Manchester. She was closely involved in the Northern College of Music and her support for St John Ambulance led to her being appointed a Dame of The Order allowing her to claim the rare distinction of being a double Dame having already been awarded DBE. Kathleen has written several books, including a ground-breaking explanation of magic squares which she wrote in her eighties, by which time she had taken up a keen interest in astronomy.

Kathleen came down by car, driven by driver Martin with our friend Judy in support. She was picked up at 6.00am and driven straight to the disabled car park next to the Westfield Centre. I was watching the women's hammer qualifying competition when Martin rang to say that Dame Kathleen was outside the stadium. I met her, the wheel-chair, Judy and Martin at the entrance. She was amazed to find someone she knew among such a big crowd!

The Volunteers were over the moon, a near-hundred-year-old spectator was just the sort of challenge they signed up for. But the wheelchair viewing area was fully booked so Martin and the strongest-looking 2012 ambassador carried the occupied chair to an aisle seat on our row. Kathleen had made it, she was sitting in a seat in the Olympic Stadium.

With such an interesting and varied life, plus an excellent long-term memory, Kathleen has plenty to talk about, and often does. But sitting in her seat she said nothing. She can hardly hear and sees very little but she took it all in.

Kathleen was there in time for Mo Farah in the 5,000 metre heats. 'Are we winning?' she asked, 'is it time to applaud?' The decathletes did their long jump then moved to the far end of the stadium to throw the shot. Most of the crowd moved but Kathleen stayed, enjoying the atmosphere and savouring another personal achievement – one of the oldest people at the Games.

'Sir Bernard Lovell died today,' she told me talking of someone she knew. 'He was 98, but didn't make 100.' Having been to the Olympics Kathleen is still competitive, her next target is her special birthday on 1 October.

As the crowd left Kathleen got her voice back and the memories started flowing again. Dinner with Lowry, seeing Hitler speaking at a rally and the content of her next book. She walked up the steps, got in her wheelchair and went through the packed crowd enjoying every last bit of her amazing day out.

So Dame Kathleen became one of the outstanding British successes at London 2012 but I am awarding the medals to Christine, my PA, Judy and Martin who made her dream come true.

2012–2013

THE HORSES

After recording eight wins out of only 41 starts last season we feel we are on a bit of a roll. The only thing missing was a runner at the Cheltenham Festival but perhaps this will be the season. With nine horses due to run in Alex's colours we are looking forward to lots of exciting race days and plenty of new additions to our trophy cabinet.

HORSES WITH HENRY DALY:

Timpo age 9 chestnut gelding (rating 100)
Perhaps this steady performer is starting to show his age. He needed a long rest to recover from last season, which was marred by a nasty battering from a wayward horse at Towcester, and may not run again until after Christmas. This could be the next horse to come and live in the fields behind our house, but we reckon it is worth having one more season.

Arctic Ben age 8 grey gelding (rating 125)
Things have suddenly turned a corner and from being one of our most disappointing purchases Arctic Ben must have

been our horse of last season, never out of the first four in eight outings. The switch from hurdles to fences clearly made a big difference but his performance improved as soon as he was allowed to run his own race and make all the running. With a rating now up at 125, a couple more good races could nudge him into contention for Cheltenham.

Safran de Cotte age 6 grey gelding (rating 125)
Despite a big win in the mud at Haydock we were a shade disappointed that Safran didn't fulfil the hopes we had when he was a four-year-old. The plan is to take him over fences this season and his jumping ability should pay dividends.

Upbeat Cobbler age 4 grey mare (novice)
We didn't learn much about this mare from her two bumper appearances, which were predictably reported as being 'a bit green'. The real test will come in the autumn when she starts going over fences. Has shown plenty of ability at home; we will soon see how that translates onto the track.

HORSES WITH PAUL WEBBER:

Key Cutter age 8 bay gelding (rating 117)
Despite some useful performances this long distance chaser has never seemed capable of racing against Class 3 company. We have become accustomed to see him perform on firmer ground towards the beginning and end of each season against modest opposition competing for mediocre prize money. But Key Cutter has shown that he can win races and we are confident that he can win a few more.

Llama Farmer age 7 brown gelding (rating 100)

After a reasonable performance at Warwick last November Llama had a leg problem that had to be fired by the vet and it is unlikely that he will be fit for racing until 2013. After a break of over a year perhaps we will see a rejuvenated horse.

Sixty Something age 6 grey gelding (rating 115)

We have little doubt that this horse has loads of ability but needs to overcome a tricky temperament on race days. Dominic Elsworth certainly spotted his potential when coming a close 2nd at Doncaster and we don't think the facts that Sixty Something fell at Uttoxeter and was pulled up in his last race of the season are anything to worry about. Off a handicap of 115 we expect to pick up some decent prize money.

Six One Away age 3 grey gelding

Our latest addition to Paul's yard will be ready to race after Christmas. We have heard some pretty warm words from head lad Jerry and his team, so we are looking forward to having a fair deal of fun with this horse.

Sole Survivor age 5 grey gelding (novice)

After an unexpectedly poor run at Leicester between Christmas and New Year, Sole Survivor had a wind operation and then suffered one of those inexplicable self-inflicted stable injuries that means he will spend the whole season recovering in a field. Still, if he finally makes the big chaser we are hoping for, it will be worth the wait.

HORSES WITH VENETIA WILLIAMS:

Miss Tique age 4 bay mare (rating 108)

This is another horse that is forced to spend the season convalescing in a field. After finishing her first season with a splendid win in a Novice Hurdle at Chepstow she had a severe, nearly fatal, attack of colic and was only saved by £3,335.56's worth of veterinary treatment. We certainly thought Venetia had found us a good prospect with Miss Tique, but will have to wait another year to see whether she can become a superstar.

Royal Palladium age 4 grey gelding

We were keen to have a second horse with Venetia and she is giving Royal Palladium a confident vote as a long term prospect. We might have to wait until the latter part of the season before he is ready to appear on the track.

THE RACING SEASON

There is a long gap from the last serious racing in April until the next chance that one of our horses will see a racecourse. Our trainers usually talk about the end of September but we now know we are unlikely to be in an Owners' and Trainers' bar until well into October.

Sensitive to this lack of activity and realising that owners are desperate for a bit of action many trainers take the brave decision to hold an Open Day at their stables sometime in September.

The whole yard is on parade, every weed has gone, the

horses have been meticulously groomed, all the stable lads wear the yard logo on their t-shirt and a couple are put on car parking duty.

The trainers go to all this trouble to thank the owners for their support, say 'well done' to their home team, celebrate the successes of last season and demonstrate the promise of more to come. But most of all they want to attract a few new customers and sometimes the trainers have some young horses that they are offering for sale.

For the first half-hour we are encouraged to tour the clearly named horse boxes. Although most owners are really only interested in their own horses some can't resist the occasional caustic comment about others in the yard: 'That's the one that ran so badly at Warwick' or 'I can't believe anyone paid over £70,000 for that!'

The day's major feature is the parade of horses. This is a big test for the trainer who has to pay enough compliments to please each owner without lying about their horse's previous poor performance or being too optimistic about next season's prospects. This difficult task isn't helped by a number of the horses that clearly don't like being led into the arena. The audience probably wonder whether these badly behaved characters are properly trained to enter the paddock at Cheltenham.

Despite the pressure both Paul Webber and Henry Daly are masters in the art of positive talking. They give confidence with their detailed knowledge of every horse in the yard and disguise the odd flaw with a subtle sense of humour:

'He finished the season by winning what was probably the worst handicap hurdle ever run at Towcester.'

'He won two bumpers but has hidden his ability ever
   since.'
'The owner has been very patient. The horse
   struggled with wind problems, had a leg after falling
   when about to win at Folkestone and then cracked a
   pelvis in training, but I'm pleased to see he has made
   it into the arena today.'

The commentary has to be skilfully crafted, especially
when most of the horses are rated 0–110 but the owner
has dreams of Festival success:

'He is almost certainly one of those late developers.'
'We will no doubt benefit from a step up in distance.'
'She shows a lot of ability at home so I'd put a line
   through her disappointing run at Ascot.'

But on one Open Day Paul was brave enough to say: 'We
failed to find a race before Christmas then had two disappointing runs in the spring. To make the frame I do need a
bit more help from the horse.'

It is difficult to placate an owner who has spent over a year
paying training fees for a horse that has never run a race.
Add a possible 20,000-guinea purchase price and at not far
short of £50,000 all they have seen for their money is a view
of the horse on the gallops, followed by a free breakfast.

'Bags of potential but he was just too green to run
   this year.'
'An enthusiastic four-year-old who is still a bit too
   backward but there is plenty of time.'

'With all that rain the ground went too soft, then we
got a dirty scope, I expect a lot better next season.'

The better horses are usually paraded towards the end
(you want the visitors to leave with a feeling of success).
Suddenly the commentary is peppered with performances
at Sandown, Newbury and Cheltenham and even novices
like me notice the difference in physique between real
winners and horses that run in the first race on a card at
Ludlow.

'It could be a big day in December at Haydock.'
'You should be looking at a really good staying chaser
next year.'
'I feel sure he will be a really good hurdler next season
– he is my dark horse to follow.'

The very best is kept to the end. The star of the yard walks
round while the wins at Warwick, Newbury and Aintree
are fondly remembered before the final comment: 'Despite
this great record I still don't think we have seen the best of
this horse.'

After a final 'Thank you to everyone working at the
yard, the generous friends who have advertised in the programme and of course the owners, who trustingly give us
the privilege to look after such a great string of talent', it is
time for lunch.

I think trainers take a risk by encouraging owners to talk
to each other. We are bound to compare notes and before
long the conversation will include the other trainers we
know and use. Owners don't lie, but they can embellish the

truth and it is tempting to think that they are much more successful with another trainer you know nothing about.

The seating plan can be a problem. There is a clear owners' pecking order. At the bottom are members of big syndicates, followed by owners of a leg, then the one horse sole owner and at the top of the tree are those that are paying several training fees at the same time. This should all be recognised in the seating plan and the trainer must pay attention to his top owners while leaving enough time to talk at length to anyone who looks like being a future owner.

It is wise to hold the Open Day early in September – by the time serious racing starts in November everyone will have forgotten the trainer's forecast for the forthcoming season.

A competitive member of my golf club who takes a casual but cynical interest in the Alex Timpson string asked me a challenging question last weekend: 'What does your wife hope to achieve next season?'

I didn't give him an honest answer. The truth is that Alex will be happy as long as Cobbler's Queen successfully delivers the expected foal and all her horses stay fit enough to run plenty of races.

'Hopefully Alex will at least match the eight wins she had last season,' I replied.
'I was really wondering how much money you hope to make?' he asked with a hint of mischief.

'I think you know the answer to that,' I replied.
　'If we have a good season we might get half our
　expenditure back in prize money.'
'So,' he replied as a parting shot, 'you are bound to be
　a loser.'

The conversation made me think. The racing game gives us very little chance of winning big money but perhaps the racecourse owners and The Jockey Club could create a few more ways for owners to enjoy success – after all very few of us are going to get into the Winners' enclosure at the Cheltenham Festival.

All the big fun and the headlines go to owners that can afford to pay a six-figure sum for horses that qualify to join a top trainer's stable. It is time that the owners of honest 0–110 handicap horses had a more competitive programme.

Why not learn a few lessons from football and organise horses in a league system with promotion and relegation at the end of the season. Every horse in each division would make eight appearances each season with points scored according to the finishing position in each race (similar to Formula One). Every week we could see Alex's horses listed in their league table (I guess most would be in the equivalent of The Evo-Stik Northern Premier League).

To make it even more interesting we could have a knock-out cup competition with the first six horses in each race going through to the next round. With 1,500 entrants and eighteen runners in each field there would be four rounds before the final, which could be a way for competitive Class 5 horses to appear at Cheltenham.

Until someone injects a more competitive edge we will

have to go along with the current system. We hope to start our season next Thursday when Key Cutter is entered in the Vera Davies Cup (Handicap Chase) at 3.15 at Ludlow. We won't be competing for a place in the next round or fighting for league points, we will simply be hoping for a share of the modest prize money on offer.

But Alex is not as competitive as me or my friend from the golf club. If Key Cutter comes 3rd and only wins enough money to pay for the horse box from Banbury, Alex will consider it has been a very successful day out.

When Key Cutter failed to make any impression in our first race of the season I began to wonder whether Alex would start to lose interest in the sport, but everything changed at Aintree the following Saturday.

For me, it was the second leg of a three-part sports day. Following a comfortable win at Delamere Golf Club in the morning I was in good time to see Sixty Something be led to the Aintree start by Paul's top guy Jerry (the horse has previous form for bad behaviour).

Sixty Something won and Alex stepped up to collect the prize just in time for us to drive to Eastlands for the kick-off to watch Manchester City beat Aston Villa 5–0. It was a very good day.

Next Thursday we had a runner at Stratford but I had to watch the race in the William Hill branch at Euston Station. Judging by their body language none of my fellow customers had backed Safran de Cotte who romped home at 9/2.

With two wins on the trot we were full of confidence,

could this be the season that an Alex Timpson horse runs at The Festival?

We had a house party of friends staying at the same time as the next meeting at Haydock so, keen to give them a flavour of an owner's day out, we booked a box and persuaded both Paul Webber and Henry Daly to enter one of our horses. They were too polite to point out that neither could find the ideal race on the card.

It was fun introducing our friends to the quaint pageantry of racegoing. On the minibus I gave them a guided tour of the *Racing Post* and once at the course produced a practical demonstration of the difference between betting with a bookie and placing your tenner with the Tote. They were all keen to stand in the paddock where they heard the last-minute discussion between trainer and jockey:

> 'Is anyone keen to make the running?'
> 'There are a couple.'
> 'Just stay handy and if it feels good four from home take it from there.'

It is, however, a pity that they didn't hear Henry Daly's comments by the pre-parade ring.

'If we come last we will have done well,' said Henry as I listened in astonishment. 'Can you say that again?' I asked. 'Perhaps I didn't put that too well,' replied Henry. 'What I meant to say is that 6th would be a fair achievement.' 'But,' I pointed out, 'there are only six runners.'

Henry explained. 'It is an open steeplechase and as Safran de Cotte has already won over the big fences [while I was in William Hill at Euston] he has a 5lb penalty. None of the other five of the novice chasers have won a chase but, based on their hurdles form, they all have a higher rating – one is at 143, we are 128 – so in a handicap we would receive 15lbs but as it is an open race we give 5lb. The chances are that we will be way behind at the finish.'

Safran de Cotte finished 3rd and with our expectations being so perfectly managed we were delighted and celebrated with the rest of our party.

I wonder whether I'm the only owner's husband who thinks the racing industry is incredibly lucky that I abandon all my business instincts and let my wife provide them with runners without any chance of seeing a financial return on the investment.

You would think the racecourse management would show their gratitude by treating every owner like royalty but few do.

One day I hope to publish an owner's guide to UK racecourses to highlight the degree to which each venue shows its gratitude. It might take some time to compile so in the meantime I have decided to give a flavour of what the survey might reveal.

Before race day some venues send information and a parking badge in the post. This can give an indication of how much they value your entry. A few express delight, others take the chance to lay down rules about the limit on free tickets and the need to give 24 hours' notice to qualify for the free carvery. Amazingly some are proud to announce that owners qualify for free tea and biscuits.

The next hint of your relative importance comes in the car park. At Uttoxeter and Bangor-on-Dee (as long as you turn up early) you can put your car pretty close to the turnstiles but at plenty of courses owners are well down the parking pecking order – behind the season badge-holding county set who take pride of place (they are the ones enjoying their champagne picnic as you walk past their prime spot close to the entrance). Newbury issues so many special badges we are relegated to the overflow car park which, on our last visit, was wallowing in mud.

At least since the course has been closed we are now spared the blunt orders barked out by the parking attendant at Hereford who impatiently ordered owners to park prettily at the far end of the field. That wasn't a problem when I went to Towcester where no places are reserved for owners so there is no one to give us any guidance. We had to park in the next parish. Even the otherwise impeccable hosts at Haydock have forgotten the need to provide separate owners' parking. Arrive late, as we often do if our race is down the card, and our complimentary sticker sends us a good stride away from the Owners' entrance.

One of the perks of ownership is to proudly walk up to the Owners' and Trainers' turnstile. Generally a warm welcome awaits from behind the desk but occasionally the person on duty acts more like a security guard than a host. It all depends who is there on the day.

I keep reminding myself that it has cost £4,000 to get our horse to their starting line. In comparison the offer of a free meal isn't a big deal. Haydock usually offers the best lunch, a little tastier than the carvery at Cheltenham which doesn't justify the pain of having to pre-book a table.

Newbury is also a contender for dining course of the year, having recently served Alex with a five-star sausage and mash. Bangor deserves credit for their wholesome comfort food which is hot and served with a smile. Uttoxeter's food voucher doesn't get you much more than a piece of cake – if you want a beef filled bap it will cost you money. You certainly won't get fat on what's on offer at Towcester where I queued for a lukewarm cup of tea in a plastic cup – they had run out of biscuits.

It should feel like a real privilege to enter the Owners' and Trainers' bar but at too many venues it is a total let down. When Hereford was in business we were herded into a tiny shed, Huntingdon is fairly cramped and Uttoxeter should be twice the size. Leicester has a decent bar with a perfect view of the course, but the last time I was there half the area had been let to a private party – the owners hardly had the elbow room to raise a glass to their lips. At Doncaster owners must go to the fourth floor so I didn't bother. By the time we arrived at Aintree (before the first race) all the seats were occupied. Like many courses they let lots of hangers-on enjoy the facilities. True owners and trainers had to take a back seat or got no seat at all.

I keep coming back to that £4,000. It really would not be out of place to treat us like royalty and put us in possession of a universally accepted gold privilege card. Give us a box with the same catering that comes with the top corporate hospitality package. Provide valet parking or a place in the directors' car park. Offer champagne to all owners, not just the winner. Free photographs of every runner (Max Spielmann or Snappy Snaps will do a special deal on the frames!). In short, why not do whatever it takes to show your appreciation and make owners feel special? Courses have Family Days and Ladies' Day, why not have an Owners' Day when every owner gets a bit of the £4,000 back? Come to think of it, why not make every meeting an Owners' Day?

I guess owners have put up with second and third class standards for far too long and even if I produce my Owners' Guide it will make little difference.

Owners live for that magic moment when their horse is led into the Winners' enclosure, before we are taken to a dingy room to watch the DVD while celebrating the win with a glass of cheap champagne for which we all appear pathetically grateful.

I made a mistake – it is something that men occasionally do! A few months ago I claimed that on average it costs an owner £4,000 to get a horse to the starting line. It costs much more. In making this calculation I assumed our horses would run an average of six times a year but failed to include those that don't run at all because they 'have a leg', are recovering from colic or find some other veterinary reason to spend the whole season in a field instead of in training.

As we approach the end of another season I analysed the results from the Alex Timpson stable that now numbers twelve horses and provides a reasonable sample to show what other owners can expect.

'We've had another good year,' said Alex. 'Eight wins equals our best season.' But as she never glances at her

Weatherbys account she is unaware that the 'successful season' has come at a record cost. Her horses appeared 32 times and achieved eight 1sts, two 2nds and five 3rds. Not a bad strike rate but a pity we had so few runners.

Her horses fall into four categories – winners, losers, on probation and on sick leave. The four winners have, as I predicted, had an average of six outings and with eight wins between them produced a success rate of one in three – a lot better than most but the prize money was still nowhere near big enough to cover more than half the training costs.

Safran de Cotte and Sixty Something both won three times. Dennis O'Regan said, after a good performance at Aintree, that Sixty Something will be 'a good prospect over fences next season'. Richard Johnson said something similar about Upbeat Cobbler after her win at Ffos Las (it helped having only three other horses in the race). Alex's other winner Arctic Ben finished the season by competing in the Topham Chase over the Grand National fences at Aintree on Ladies' Day (a day not to be missed). We didn't win a prize but Alex was relieved to see Jake Greenall complete the course.

So we have plenty of success to remember and a few hideous trophies to put on display but our season has also had a few strands of disappointment.

Paul Webber was very excited about our newly acquired and well-named four-year-old Six One Away but expectation turned to disbelief when he was last of thirteen in a bumper at Huntingdon. Tests suggested he was suffering from cramp – 'never seen it for at least six years,' said Paul. Despite receiving reports from Venetia Williams that the yard was very pleased with Royal Palladium, two bumpers only produced one 3rd place. Both yards expect the true potential to be revealed over hurdles next season.

Two of Alex's horses have done nothing but eat and meet the vet. Sole Survivor and Miss Tique both needed a year away from racing to recover from a catalogue of injuries and vets' bills. We are assured that our faith in their future will be fully justified next season.

The three other horses have been on probation. We now realise that horses rated 0–90 aren't much fun unless they win the odd race. It is soul destroying to see your colours trail in behind a mediocre field competing for a first prize of £1,650. The trainer and jockey get paid the same whether the horse is rated 135 or 74 so it seems sensible to stop spending money on poor performers.

Llama Farmer, following a depressing effort at Leicester (which isn't Alex's favourite racecourse), was given a few excuses by the vet and is heading to the fields behind our house. Timpo (rated 97) and Key Cutter (overrated 115) are both in the last chance saloon and may not feature in our plans for 2014.

Some time ago we realised that to guarantee an active season you need to have a decent sized squad (a bit like Manchester City), so more purchases will soon be on the agenda but don't expect me to be bidding six-figure sums at the sales. There is no pleasure in paying so much for a horse if you are only happy if it qualifies for The Festival.

Our season has ended on a high. We have an addition to the Timpson stable – Cobbler's Queen has produced a foal, which after four years of keep, training and vets' fees will hopefully appear in the Winners' enclosure. Alex says the picture of our new arrival proves that the pleasure racing brings is well worth the money whether we win or lose.

April and May are important months for football teams at the bottom of the table – with one or two bad results liable to lead to relegation. Although, I suspect, the victims were unaware of their situation, the same two months have also decided the fate of three poor performers in the Alex Timpson stable.

As Alex's financial advisor I am delighted to report she has started to take a tougher line on the prospective return produced on the money I invest on her behalf. A few seasons ago she would have been persuaded by a trainer's promise 'I am sure I can find a race it will win next season' but paying out the total annual cost of £24,000 to secure an outside chance of winning a £2,000 race is, thankfully, no longer seen as satisfactory.

Ten years of experience have taught Alex to recognise the difference between a horse rated 95 and one on 130. Her ambitions are no longer satisfied by Tuesday trips to Towcester to watch a Class 5 race. Alex wants Saturday horses that can step up in class through Newbury, Haydock and Sandown on the way to the Cheltenham Festival. It would be nice to have a horse so famous that it is featured on Channel 4's *Morning Line* – although Alex still insists she won't be interviewed.

When Alex started her interest in racing I was surprised to discover it costs nearly as much to run a Grade 5 plodder as you pay to support horses heading to Cheltenham.

The trainer and the jockey fees are the same and it takes no more diesel to drive a good horse to the starting line.

After ten years of weak cash control during which the number of horses wearing the Timpson colours has been growing every year, I have introduced a budget – expressed in simple terms, so there can be no misunderstanding. We now have a limit to the number of horses Alex has in training. From now on she will have no more than twelve.

I am beginning to realise this may not be the economy measure I anticipated. Alex's urge to land the Cheltenham Gold Cup has led to the early retirement of any horse that has no chance of being seen racing on a Saturday. I might be saved the cost of training horses to win small prizes at low profile courses but now face the prospect of regular and more expensive trips to the Doncaster Sales to keep Alex's string up to my nominated number.

By the middle of March it was clear that three horses were in danger of relegation: Llama Farmer, who won a race at Haydock and a lot of money for our friends who backed him at 66/1 (I only got 40/1!) but for the next three years has shown why the odds were so high; Timpo, who despite paying a fancy price is only rated at 95; and Key Cutter, who is overrated at 113 because the handicapper has failed to keep up with his loss of form.

We ran a sort of eliminator on a miserable day at Leicester (it usually is!) where we entered Timpo and Llama Farmer in the same race. Timpo surprised us by finishing 3rd but Llama finished a depressing last. We decided to give them both another go. Timpo to check this sudden improvement in form and Llama Farmer to see if blinkers and firmer ground will make any difference, but before we could try the blinkers Llama got a leg and a big vets' bill. After a year of training fees to get him fit again to race he had that one hopeless run in the pouring rain at Leicester and we could only look forward to another year of training fees and no racing. It was an easy decision Llama was loaded into a horse box that headed to a field at the back of our house.

Timpo ran at Towcester in a pathetic handicap where the worst horse was off a mark of 64. The punters decided it was a two-horse race and amazed me by picking Timpo as one of the two. He started second favourite, finished 2nd and booked his place in Henry Daly's yard for another season.

While all this was going on Key Cutter was waiting for firm ground and found it at Wincanton on 9 May. With only four horses in the race his 2nd place probably wasn't much to shout about, so we needed another run to decide his fate.

Key Cutter could be described as fickle – it is fine as long as he is on a right-handed track with blinkers, firm ground and he arrives at the course in a positive frame of mind. We went to see his final run at Uttoxeter – the ground was firm but it was a left-handed course and Key Cutter didn't like it. Jake Greenall pulled him up with a mile left to go.

Key Cutter arrived at our house last Wednesday to join Llama Farmer in a field with Transatlantic and Ordre de Bataille who have been retired some time.

'We are going to have to get some new horses soon,' said Alex when she thought I was in a good mood, 'but first I think we need to buy a few more acres at the back of our house.'

I am writing this update looking across the beautiful blue Caribbean Sea to the island of Bequia, sitting by the pool outside the highest house on Mustique. The only blot on my idyllic holiday is the knowledge that the weather is just as good back home.

Apart from some sunshine we are not missing much – no racing until nearly November and Manchester City don't play their first Premiership match until mid-August.

Both Manchester City's new manager Manuel Pellegrini and Alex Timpson Racing have been busy in the transfer market to strengthen their squads for next season. Man City have spent over £80 million on four new players while we have invested less than £60,000 on a four-year-old to be called Rubber Sole and a three-year-old who will probably be Pretty Mobile (Cute Key Girl, Heel Bar Baby and Watch Ticker are also being considered). Fortunately we will not have to find the £150,000 a week that City pay out in wages to an average player even when he is unfit to play. But there is every chance that on top of the £20,000 a year training fees we will find the vets' bills are much bigger than the prize money.

Man City are investing £400 million in a new training facility but I am proud to say that when it comes to youth policy Alex Timpson Racing is several steps ahead. Cobbler's Queen's foal (Cobbler's Son) is growing fast and looking good – bookies watch out in 2017 and mum is now expecting foal number two. That makes three keep fees to fund without the chance of any prize money for four years.

In the same way City have 'let some players go' we have said goodbye to Llama Farmer and Key Cutter. Unlike Man City we didn't receive a transfer fee.

Key Cutter has cost more with the vet since he came to live with us than I was paying in training fees. He has been having physiotherapy for a severely strained back, is lame in three legs (no doubt when they are fixed the fourth will go), and while I am in luxury in the Caribbean, Key Cutter will be having a more expensive day than us going for an MRI scan at £1,200 (no doubt plus VAT!).

Llama Farmer is also involved with a vet but thankfully this vet is going to take him off our hands in the hope that he, personally, can ride him in endurance events.

We have more holidays to come before the National Hunt season gets serious. During most of September we will be in New Zealand on the next stage of our geriatric gap year, a long term project that for a month at a time makes up for the fact that our children all went travelling. Now it is our turn, at ten times the price.

We will be back before the beginning of October, in time to hear the reasons why our trainers feel we shouldn't run until November:

'The going is too firm (or too soft).'
'The race is too hot.'
'He needs another three weeks.'
'Little bit of a niggle in one of her hind legs.'
'Can't find the right race.'
'Everyone wants to enter and we've been balloted out.'

By the time we return from New Zealand we will be full of optimistic anticipation for a winning season with the diary clear to see our entries run at the Cheltenham Festival, prior to watching Man City win the Champions League.

SEASON 2012–2013

HORSE	DATE	COURSE	RACE	DISTANCE	PRIZE MONEY	JOCKEY	RATING	POSITION	RUNNERS
	20-Feb-13	Ludlow	Hand. Chase	3m	4K	Jake Greenall	97	F	13
Timpo	8-Mar-13	Leicester	Hand. Chase	2m 6½f	4K	Andrew Tinkler	97	3	10
	26-Apr-13	Chepstow	Hand. Chase	3m 2f	2K	Richard Johnson	95	2	8
	25-Oct-12	Ludlow	Hand. Chase	3m	3K	Dominic Elsworth	117	PU	12
Key Cutter	2-Dec-12	Leicester	Hand. Chase	2m 6½f	3K	Denis O'Regan	115	2	6
	9-May-13	Wincanton	Hand. Chase	3m 1f	6K	Liam Treadwell	115	2	4
	26-May-13	Uttoxeter	Hand. Chase	3m	3K	Jake Greenall	113	PU	10
	16-Nov-12	Cheltenham	Hand. Chase	2m	28K	Richard Johnson	125	11	14
	8-Dec-12	Chepstow	Hand. Chase	2m 3½f	7K	Andrew Tinkler	125	6	10
Arctic Ben	27-Dec-12	Haydock	Hand. Chase	2m	9K	Jake Greenall	122	5	8
	11-Feb-13	Catterick	Hand. Chase	2m 3f	7K	Jake Greenall	119	4	9
	1-Mar-13	Newbury	Hand. Chase	2m 4f	3K	Jake Greenall	119	1	8
	5-Apr-13	Aintree	Hand. Chase Grade 3	2m 5f	67K	Jake Greenall	126	14	29
Llama Farmer	8-Mar-13	Leicester	Hand. Chase	2m 6½f	4K	Liam Treadwell	100	PU	10

(continued)

HORSE	DATE	COURSE	RACE	DISTANCE	PRIZE MONEY	JOCKEY	RATING	POSITION	RUNNERS
	1-Nov-12	Stratford	Chase	2m 6½f	5K	Richard Johnson	122	1	11
	23-Nov-12	Haydock	Nov. Chase	2m 6f	16K	Andrew Tinkler	128	3	6
Safran de Cotte	29-Dec-12	Doncaster	Hand. Chase	3m	8K	Andrew Tinkler	126	4	11
	30-Jan-13	Leicester	Nov. Chase	2m 6½f	3K	Jake Greenall	124	1	6
	23-Feb-13	Chepstow	Nov. Chase	2m 7½f	3K	Jake Greenall	125	1	7
	20-Mar-13	Haydock	Hand. Chase	2m 4f	12K	Jake Greenall	130	PU	7
	27-Oct-12	Aintree	Nov. Hand. Hurdle	3m ½f	3K	Dominic Elsworth	115	1	12
	23-Nov-12	Haydock	Nov. Hurdle	2m 4f	4K	Denis O'Regan	124	5	7
	14-Dec-12	Bangor-on-Dee	Hand. Hurdle	2m 7f	4K	Dominic Elsworth	124	1	8
Sixty Something	29-Dec-12	Doncaster	Hand. Hurdle	3m ½f	11K	Dominic Elsworth	129	5	8
	16-Feb-13	Haydock	Hand. Hurdle	3m	12K	Denis O'Regan	128	4	9
	10-Mar-13	Market Rasen	Hand. Hurdle	2m 7f	7K	Dominic Elsworth	127	1	9
	4-Apr-13	Aintree	Hand. Hurdle Grade 3	3m ½f	28K	Denis O'Regan	135	6	21

(continued)

214

HORSE	DATE	COURSE	RACE	DISTANCE	PRIZE MONEY	JOCKEY	RATING	POSITION	RUNNERS
Upbeat Cobbler	8-Nov-12	Towcester	Maiden Hurdle	2m	1K	Jake Greenall	–	F	14
	31-Jan-13	Towcester	Maiden Hurdle	2m 3f	1K	Andrew Tinkler	–	3	13
	21-Feb-13	Huntingdon	Nov. Hurdle	2m 4½f	3K	Richard Johnson	–	3	13
	20-Mar-13	Warwick	Hand. Hurdle	2m 5f	3K	Paddy Brennan	98	2	4
	23-Apr-13	Ffos Las	Hand. Hurdle	2m 6f	3K	Richard Johnson	98	1	4
Royal Palladium	9-Feb-13	Warwick	Nat. Hunt Flat	1m 6f	1K	Aidan Coleman	–	3	8
	11-Mar-13	Taunton	Nat. Hunt Flat	2m ½f	2K	Aidan Coleman	–	4	7
Six One Away	3-Mar-13	Huntingdon	Nat. Hunt Flat	1m 7½f	1K	Denis O'Regan	–	13	13

	RUNS	1ST	2ND	3RD	4TH
Timpo	3	0	1	1	0
Key Cutter	4	0	2	0	0
Arctic Ben	6	1	0	0	1
Llama Farmer	1	0	0	0	0
Safran de Cotte	6	3	0	1	1
Sixty Something	7	3	0	0	1
Upbeat Cobbler	5	1	1	2	0
Royal Palladium	2	0	0	1	1
Six One Away	1	0	0	0	0
Total	35	8	4	5	4

	TRAINING FEES	ENTRY FEE/ JOCKEY	TOTAL COST	WINNINGS + SPONSORSHIP	NET COST
2012–2013					
Safran de Cotte	17,534	2,475	20,009	10,940	9,069
Arctic Ben	17,538	2,730	20,268	6,065	14,203
Timpo	16,796	1,160	17,956	4,270	13,686
Key Cutter	18,121	1,370	19,491	5,475	14,016
Llama Farmer	14,145	465	14,610	2,280	12,330
Sixty Something	17,397	3,780	21,177	16,540	4,637
Upbeat Cobbler	18,719	1,140	19,859	6,315	13,544
Miss Tique	12,605	–	12,605	2,500	10,105
Royal Palladium	12,169	585	12,754	2,745	10,009
					£101,599
Cobbler's Queen	9,327				9,327
Incl. £3,000 for Big Sam Bellamy					£110,926

OUR GERIATRIC
GAP YEAR – 2013

We bought Transatlantic, Alex's first horse, in 2002. Since then we've been talking about horses nearly every day, and receiving updates from trainers every week. We have watched all of our horses run 228 races and enjoyed 34 wins. We were ready for a break – nearly a month, mainly in New Zealand, with no horses on the itinerary. This was part of what we call our geriatric gap year – spread over several years and at many times the price paid by our children between school and university.

BANGKOK

We stopped for two nights in Bangkok where, not for the first time, Alex made a smart move. She booked a guide to take us sightseeing. He was waiting for us in the foyer surrounded by at least 60 smart officials, mostly in uniform, all wearing a badge 'ROYAL ENTOURAGE'. A letter in our room (Dear Esteemed Guest) had warned us that the hotel was about to be taken over by the King and Queen of Malaysia and their entourage during a state visit, and even the most esteemed guest had to use the back door and was banned from the elevator between 11.00am and noon.

Kistic was small and thin, even for a Thai, with a camp walk and a big handbag. At first I had to listen carefully to catch his English, but as the tour progressed I got the drift.

We set off by boat, one of the Bangkok gondola types with an outboard motor – not easy for pensioners to climb into from the jetty but there were plenty of respectful hands to help.

After ploughing through weeds for half a mile we turned left from the river into a side canal lined by rickety homes built on stilts. Kistic kept pointing at temples (there were plenty) but our eyes were drawn to the shacks over-hanging the canal. They all had a balcony, most covered with clothes hanging out to dry, but inside seemed to be little more than one big room, cluttered with all the family possessions. Saucepans hanging outside, rubbish thrown in the canal and the structures look unlikely to be still stand-ing in twenty years' time. The tourist route took in plenty of temples, but provided a grandstand view of poverty in the process.

With difficulty, we clambered out of the boat by the Temple of the Dawn, an ornate tall temple which we could have climbed, to get a panoramic view of Bangkok, but it was getting hot so we didn't bother.

We struggled back on board for a short trip across the river where a couple of respectful boatmen hauled us ashore so we could walk through a market where coconuts, pas-sion fruit and banana fritters all looked appetising and cost next to nothing but we only bought two bottles of water. It was hot and humid at 10.00am. We could only have taken 800 steps to reach The Grand Palace but that was enough for us to be covered in sweat and to have drunk half the water.

In April we went to the Vatican, queued for 90 minutes (the Pope was a new boy) and, frankly, wondered whether it was worth it. Bangkok beats the Vatican in every department. No queues and loads to look at. Buddhas, bonsai, gold leaf snakes, temples decorated with porcelain, providing the well-mannered crowd with a feast of colour. All this was in sharp contrast to the shacks we saw earlier in the morning. A succession of kings and their monks, with unlimited funds and plenty of space, had kept building to produce a village of multi-coloured temples liberally covered in gold.

No one can, will or even wants to argue with the extravagance. Everyone is given respect but the ultimate in respect is reserved for Buddha and the King. We could only look through the gate at the King's Palace but we saw the Coronation Chair and the building where monarchs lie in state when they die – for nine months standing up inside their coffin, so the respectful Thai people can pay their respects. But it can't be a happy time for the family.

Perhaps we should have looked at more treasures, taken more steps, and taken our shoes off more than once to go inside the temples but, frankly, it was too hot so we were grateful to get into an air conditioned car.

Although Alex was ready to head back to the Mandarin Oriental, Kistic was determined we should see Wat Pho, where we took our shoes off to examine an enormous horizontal Buddha from every angle, then returned to the car via a long line of exotic Buddhas, who, thankfully, were in the shade.

Alex had had enough and, although I didn't admit it, so had I. There is a limit to how much culture you can take in 35 degrees of humid heat.

We arrived at our hotel just as the King and Queen of Malaysia were preparing to leave to meet the King and Queen of Thailand. We slipped in the side door and sat down, to settle up with Kistic, behind a crowd of uniformed officials all wearing 'ROYAL ENTOURAGE' security badges and showing respect. We only waited two minutes before the Royal Party appeared and gracefully walked to their car.

Abdul Halim of Kedah is unique – the most rare of kings. In Malaysia kings are elected for a five-year term (if they live that long, and some haven't) then someone else is elected to wear the crown. Each state takes it in turn to pick the king. The system started when Malaysia gained independence in 1950 and Abdul is the first king to get a second go. He was born in 1927 so was only 43 when first elected in 1970. And having been so young first time around, he was still going strong when it was his state's turn to pick again. He must have made a decent fist of the job to be asked again 40 years later, but you do wonder why the electorate couldn't find someone younger with kingly credentials. Abdul is still a keen golfer and a Frank Sinatra fan – good for him, perhaps that swayed the vote in his favour. He is now 86 but the younger King of Thailand expects Abdul to travel 200 miles to see him at his residential palace.

King Bhumibol Adulyadej of Thailand is also a bit of a record holder. He came to the throne in 1946 at the tender age of seventeen. It took them four years to get round to a coronation (in 1950) but he still got there before our Queen. He is the longest-ruling monarch worldwide

– 67 years – but the last few years have been tough. Both King and Queen have spent a lot of time in hospital (in the King's case four years until his recent discharge). With the prospect of spending nine months stood up in a coffin I can understand his determination to live a bit longer. We found all this background fascinating. Alex has become much more interested in history since we did some research into her family tree and discovered that her maternal grandmother was Jewish. The search is now on for distant cousins she has never met.

EDENHOUSE

We spent our first few days in Auckland, Keri Keri and Wellington before heading to South Island for our first taste of Kiwi lodge hospitality.

We hadn't expected to be met at Nelson, but a tubby and talkative guy approached and asked if I was Mr Timpson. At first I thought he was a rep doing a bit of helpful greeting; even when he introduced himself as Peter it took some time for me to twig that he and his wife Bobbie own the lodge where we were staying for the next two nights.

Before our bags were in the boot of the hire car Peter was trying to organise our itinerary. 'It looks like rain tomorrow so, with such a great day today, I have a helicopter standing by. You simply don't want to miss the view.' We explained that Alex doesn't like helicopters and we were keen to go for a drive. Peter took some persuading but eventually let us find our own way to his lodge via a drive round the town of Nelson (much smarter than North Island) and lunch in a small place called Motueka (crisps, chocolate and mini donuts bought at the local Countdown supermarket).

When I finally found Edenhouse, the lodge, at 3.00pm Peter was standing in the drive to greet us.

It is a great spot – looking at mountains in every direction and set in about 40 acres of grass, much of it forming a somewhat neglected garden.

Peter, an Aussie financial trader, and Bobbie, a Kiwi interior designer, built the house in about 2004 after having lived for several years in London. They said the initial plan was simply to entertain friends, then they started taking in paying guests.

We, the only people staying, had the two-bedroom cottage in the garden and although we were given the run of the large house, with a choice of rooms where we could sit and relax, we were very happy to keep ourselves in the cottage and walk round the garden.

Being a paying guest in someone's house is very different from staying in a hotel. I was much happier in the cottage. It didn't have all the trappings interior designer Bobbie had chosen for the main house, which was full of Bobbie's character. Every chair looked too good to sit on.

The four of us met for drinks in the drawing room before we dined, widely distributed round a large dining room table. The food and wine matched the spectacular views and we didn't find conversation too difficult. They talked about their life in Knightsbridge, the famous neighbours near their country house on the Surrey/Sussex border (Ringo Starr is a mate), their recent visit to Sydney and the furniture they brought over from England.

We all found plenty to talk about but our cook (a young girl from down the road) was the star of the evening – the food was almost as good as our first dinner at the Mandarin Oriental.

Our breakfast, served in 'The Studio', another designer room, was cooked by a humourless woman with a German, Swiss or Dutch accent. We ate alone but both Peter and Bobbie were on hand to give advice on how to plan our day. At first Peter was keen that we should charter a boat – 'It's the only way to see Abel Tasman National Park' – but fortunately Peter's friend, Rod Stewart, the boat owner, said the sea would be rough and Alex quickly confirmed she is a bad sailor.

We were allowed to do what we had already planned and set off over the mountains towards Takaka and Golden Bay, but not before Peter insisted on drawing a detailed itinerary and Bobbie gave us a number of things we could do on the way.

It is strange to see lambs, blossom, magnificent magnolia, daffodils and 'rhodos' at the beginning of September. We drove past miles of fields full of regimented fruit trees – all bark and no blossom so we could only guess which were apples, pears or kiwi fruit. Easier to identify the trees in many gardens, bulging with oranges and lemons. I said to Alex that if we lived in New Zealand the jump racing season would be coming to a close and, as if by magic, within minutes of my remark I received an email from Paul Webber with pictures of Sixty Something out on the gallops getting fully fit for the first fixtures in October.

There were stunning views as Alex took our 4×4 twisting and turning over the mountains – green valleys below and sea in the distance. We took a ten-minute walk to the Hawke's observation platform where we looked down on a complete rainbow in the bottom of the valley.

Golden Bay was disappointing. We enjoyed the mountains much more than the coast, although it was a pity pylons blighted many of the best views. Our destination was so remote we had to retrace our steps to get back to Edenhouse but despite being in the middle of nowhere I received plenty of emails, including a further update from Paul Webber. I got much better reception than is ever available on my regular route from Tarporley to our office in Wythenshawe.

CHRISTCHURCH

We got our first glimpse of what the earthquakes did to Christchurch when we found our hotel, which I thought was standing in a dull and fairly desolate suburb. I later discovered it was close to the city centre.

There was nothing wrong with The George Hotel, it was busy. A lot of women, smarter than any we had seen elsewhere in New Zealand, were waiting in the lobby for the appearance of a local celebrity dietician. We were rescued from the chattering women of Christchurch society by Mark, the concierge, who answered all Alex's questions, took us up to our rooms, then fixed us up with Wi-Fi, lunch and a tour of the city.

We went in a double decker London bus driven by Steve, who did a great job entertaining us and our seven fellow passengers (apart from a Chinese student who couldn't understand English) with a three-hour commentary, even though the earthquakes have left precious little to talk about.

The founding fathers who came to Christchurch from England in 1850 made a big mistake by building the city on marshland. When the big earthquakes came in 2010 and 2011 foundations failed and a large number of buildings either collapsed or were declared unsafe for habitation. A lot of the timber buildings survived but a brick building needed foundations set several metres down into the ground to be safe.

After a time you realise that a lot of the buildings still standing are actually waiting to be demolished. Much of the city is fenced off by safety barriers, the buildings shored up to stop them collapsing, before their turn comes to join the deconstruction programme. Towers of metal containers were set up to prevent debris falling on pedestrians or passing traffic.

Some significant places still await their fate – both Church of England and Roman Catholic Cathedrals suffered so much damage that you wonder whether they ought to be knocked down and completely rebuilt. While clergymen continue to negotiate with their insurance companies the council have decided to save the County Hall at a cost of about $150 million (£75 million). One of the saddest sites is the rugby stadium, built for the World Cup in 2011 but the earthquake got there first and no game has ever been played on the ground and probably never will be – the playing surface is overgrown and the stands have been deemed unsafe.

The city centre has lots of waste land where demolition has been completed and a small amount of construction has started. Steve was enthusiastic about the new plans for his city but it could be a long time before Christchurch regains its character. The centre reminded me of urban areas in post-war UK where the Blitz and slum clearance left little standing apart from run-down churches and pubs.

Other than the construction workers there wasn't much reason for anyone else to come to town. There were some temporary shops and a small new precinct with about twenty small stores. We saw sculptures created as a memorial to the 185 people who lost their lives, but apart from the odd tourist no one went near them. All the accountants, lawyers and bankers had found a new home out of town. You wonder whether they will ever return, having tasted the convenience of working closer to home.

Steve talked throughout the tour – there was little to see but he had plenty to say. We had signed on for the full three-hour trip that took us out to the suburbs and up into the hills.

Christchurch has spacious parks which, with the sun out and the blossom in full bloom, had attracted lots of joggers. All over New Zealand there are rugby posts – every school seems to specialise in sport, all Kiwis are sports fans and it is politically correct to play to win.

At first I thought all the devastation was in the city centre, but our trip into the suburbs took us past boarded-up houses with official warning notices at the entrance, empty plots where houses had been demolished and a few buildings that were being renovated. I looked up from the bus and saw half a house left stranded on the edge of a crumbling cliff.

Back in The George Hotel you were not aware of the

life-changing destruction that had taken place. The bar was buzzing with several celebrations – a very smart black tie dinner function was happening upstairs while we sat in the dining room below near an office party. Bar one bloke, it was an all-female affair – I suspect he was married to the middle aged boss who displayed a big proportion of her bosom with confidence while fussing round the late arrivals and changing the seating plan.

They filled the room with their upbeat chatter, betraying no hint of the traumatic time many must have experienced since the earthquakes changed the face of Christchurch.

QUEENSTOWN

Top location on our trip was the Matakauri Lodge at Queenstown, where we woke to see a stunning view across the blue lake in glorious sunshine. It seemed a pity to leave such a perfect location, but we had booked a day trip to Milford Sound. We weren't sure what to expect but our itinerary said we had to be ready to go by 7.30am. We had made a 600-mile detour to make sure we didn't miss this part of the Kiwi experience, so it must be good.

Malcolm, our driver for the day, arrived while we were having breakfast (dish of the day – poached eggs, mushrooms, spinach and caramelised onions).

Throughout the day Malcolm gave a commentary: 'The mountain range is called The Remarkables and the lake is Wakatipu.' Then he stunned me by saying, 'We will stop in about two-and-a-half hours. Will you be all right until then?' I got the drift when I saw a sign 'Milford Sound 278 km'. It clouded over and started to rain. My mind went back to the sunny lake we had left behind.

Malcolm was a careful driver. He and Alex talked non-stop for over two hours about gold mining (Malcolm pans for gold), deer farming (deer are aggressive animals), fencing, irrigation, the climate, his grandchildren, our grandchildren and where Malcolm goes on holiday. I sat in the back working out a few answers for my column in *The Daily Telegraph*, and writing a new blog about our racing experience.

Malcolm promised something special, 'Rudyard Kipling called Milford Sound the eighth Wonder of the World.'

We were back to blue sky by the time we reached Te Anau, our scheduled stop. We left the shores of an attractive lake to venture down a dull street in search of a café which Malcolm claimed 'has excellent facilities'. The drivers of six tour buses were clearly of the same opinion. We were expected to buy a coffee and jostle with 100 Chinese trippers to buy the odd souvenir and give Malcolm the 25 minutes he needed to complete his log.

With only 120 km to go, the sun was beating down and the scenery got more interesting. We went round hairy hairpin turns, through a big gorge and a scary tunnel that was built in 1940 and still doesn't look finished.

It wasn't easy to get to Milford Sound; a few days before it would have been impossible because the road was blocked by a landslide. But we were lucky: the road was clear and so was the sky, rare for a place where it rains 200 days a year.

Milford Sound is a fjord, much easier to get to by sea, but Captain Cook sailed straight past and failed to spot it, so its discovery was left to a Welshman, John Grono, who named it after his birthplace Milford Haven – also placed at the end of a long road as we have discovered since opening a shop in nearby Haverfordwest.

Rudyard Kipling had a point. 'Eighth Wonder of the World' might be a bit of an exaggeration but Milford Sound is awesome. It was like going through Yosemite on a boat. We floated below sheer cliffs topped with snow, and dramatic waterfalls to entertain us.

Despite the long journey Milford Sound is not to be missed and I had the comforting thought that journeys never seem as far on the way back. Malcolm speeded up, not enough to break the law, but by cutting out the comfort stop we took 45 minutes less on the way home. That still gave Malcolm plenty of time to talk about the tricky tours he has had with Arab and Russian clients, his days as a rally driver and the day he met the lady who is Mayor of Queenstown. Alex says I missed the rest of his life story when I fell asleep.

SINGAPORE

On the plane to Singapore Alex came up with an unexpected comment, 'Do you realise that it's over a week since we last talked about our horses? I wonder when we will first see one on a racecourse.'

It had been nearly a fortnight since we had had an email from Paul Webber but as we were now close to the end of September we should soon be given a list of possible dates to put in our racing diary.

From several thousand miles away it was easy to feel optimistic – at the very least we expected to have more than the eight winners we have had for each of the last two seasons.

'Which one do you think has the best chance of going to Cheltenham?' asked Alex. 'Safran de Cotte,' I replied without hesitation. 'I can even see you picking up the prize.'

The trip to New Zealand had taken us a long way away from reality.

I was reading a book about Raffles on my Kindle and was keen to finish before we reached Singapore, the city he founded. I was making good progress: with five hours to Changi Airport, the Kindle said I only had 29 per cent of the book left.

I'd read about Raffles' amazing career with the East India Company. Starting as a clerk in London, he was given a roving role and spent most of his career in the Far East where he was regularly promoted, despite a habit of ignoring orders. Either by negotiating with local rulers, or with the help of a few thousand men, he took control of several islands by agreement or force.

He made a name for himself in Java before turning his attention to Singapore. His 'upside down' style of management was helped by slow communication with head office. With all messages sent by ship it could take well over a year before he had a response from his boss.

Although he threw some fantastic parties, Raffles wasn't always as popular as you might think, particularly with a Scottish guy called William Farquhar, who he put in charge of Singapore, but subsequently sacked with the speed of an unsuccessful Premiership manager. Farquhar was guilty of using his own initiative and ignoring Raffles' master development plan for the town. Raffles didn't practise upside down management if he was the boss.

When these two men first landed in Singapore it was a village. But they realised it was in the perfect place to become a major port. It wasn't long before they created a fast growing community, quickly rising to over 5,000 inhabitants.

Farquhar always claimed that it was he, not Raffles, who founded Singapore. He was one of the enemies Raffles acquired among his many friends. But Raffles was lucky – a lot of those that disliked him died. Someone perished every few pages, including Raffles' first wife and all his children (so many I lost count) and most of his friends.

Java and Singapore don't seem to have been healthy places to live and Raffles decided to up sticks and return to England with his second wife and all the possessions he could fit on a decent sized boat. He collected a lot of big bits of furniture, paintings, a library of books and manuscripts, plus lots of animals, most stuffed but many alive. Unfortunately, shortly after setting sail for home, one of the crew went below to get some brandy. His candle lit the liquor, the boat was completely destroyed by fire and Raffles' life collection of enormous nick nacks was sunk without trace (or, in the case of the menagerie, drowned).

Back in England Raffles tried to get some compensation for his loss from the East India Company and a decent pension (at the age of 43), but he scored an own goal. They claimed even more from him, for salary he had received while taking a couple of years off and the personal gain he made when trading on the company's account. He suffered in the stock market crash of 1825 and ran out of money. Despite his debts Raffles still purchased two expensive houses, 'did the season' and was President of a newly formed Zoological Society keen to put a collection of rare animals into Regent's Park.

With my Kindle saying I'd read 76 per cent of the book, I expected Raffles to return to Singapore for a triumphant tour of duty, when to my amazement he died. The Kindle misled me, I'd finished the book ten pages later and still had five hours to go before we landed in Singapore.

Raffles would be very surprised and pretty pleased with how Singapore has turned out. Within three hours we saw the city from the Singapore Flyer (like the London Eye but bigger), a river boat, and our room on the sixteenth floor which gave a fascinating panoramic view of boats, cars and joggers, constantly on the move, and up to 50 very big container ships at anchor, waiting their turn to dock at the world's second busiest port.

The Singapore Flyer took us above the F1 starting line that had been the centre of attention twelve hours earlier. The river boat went past the busy restaurants and cafés that lined the waterfront. Singapore works – there is a relaxed air of simple efficiency.

Everyone we met was friendly and helpful, the place seemed confident and optimistic. The taxi drivers quite rightly complained about all the road closures for the Grand Prix, but there are no complaints about the strict regulations that mean no graffiti, no litter and no chewing gum. Different from Cotebrook where I expect a couple of Coca-Cola cans and a McDonald's Happy Meal were thrown on our grass verge last night.

Next week will be different, the emails will be closer to home and Alex will be back at the kitchen table, on the phone talking to Paul, Henry and Venetia about the going at Warwick and Uttoxeter. It's been great to escape but now is the time to return to reality. I will be watching City at The Etihad instead of in a hotel in Singapore. We will be following Alex's horses instead of the America's Cup. Alex will be back helping Home Start and I will be visiting our shops. I have a number of speaking engagements and Alex will continue to find out about her family tree.

Alex, who now knows she has Jewish blood, will continue to trace descendants of her great grandfather, the father of Edith Leon. While we were in Singapore, she had some positive news – one of her relations has been found.

She lives in Auckland, New Zealand.

2013–2014

THE HORSES

We are hoping to build on another successful season when, despite being plagued by various injuries, we yet again had eight winners but from a very modest number of 35 starts. We have to be happy with a better than one in five strike rate. With the prospect of more horses fit and ready to run we confidently predict that this will be the first season when our number of winners reaches double figures.

HORSES WITH HENRY DALY:

Timpo age 10 chestnut gelding (rating 98)
Close to retirement at the end of last season Timpo, when racing in Class 5 company with horses rated as low as 64, suddenly seemed to have turned a corner and is ready for another year of chasing. His handicap of 98 gives him every chance of scoring another win before retirement.

Arctic Ben age 9 grey gelding (rating 125)
Now that we allow him to race into an early lead Arctic Ben always gives us a run for our money. He loves being up

front and will fight hard to stop being overtaken, but once back in the field he starts to lose his jumping form and often fades out of the picture. I used to think that any horse with a 20-length lead is bound to be hauled in by the rest of the field but Arctic Ben has shown that a front runner can be a winner. No doubt he will give us more fun this season.

Safran de Cotte age 7 grey gelding (rating 126)

Performed really well after going chasing last season with three wins in five outings before getting end of season weariness when being pulled up in a competitive Handicap Chase at Warwick. A plucky performer who thrives on sticky ground. He showed a lot of stamina and determination to see off strong opposition to land his third win of the season on a wet and windy day at Chepstow. Our best bet for a place at the Cheltenham Festival.

Upbeat Cobbler age 5 grey mare (rating 101)

Got steadily better over hurdles and a modest handicap mark of 98 gave her the chance to land a first win over 2 miles 6 furlongs at Ffos Las. We hope to continue to pick up some decent prize money from mares-only handicap hurdles before going chasing next season.

 WITH PAUL WEBBER:

Sole Survivor age 6 grey gelding (rating 100)

After a year out with a tendon injury, we hope this big horse will be able to put in some big performances. If the handicapper had been to the yard and seen how impressive he looks he certainly wouldn't have put him off a mark of 100. We have every reason to hope that our patience with this horse will soon be rewarded. So far his winnings have been matched by the vets' fees.

Sixty Something age 7 grey gelding (rating 135)

With three wins last season from seven starts, a handicap of 135 and a decent performance in the Topham Chase at Aintree on Ladies' Day (which would have been better if the starter hadn't recalled the field for a second go) Sixty Something can now claim to be our best horse in training. All the experts suggest that he will produce his best performances over fences so will make a move to Novice Chasing from the start. Apparently he has 'developed well over the summer' so we are looking forward to an exciting season.

Six One Away age 4 grey gelding

We have yet to see what this horse can do. He waited all of last season to run in a bumper and then finished last and was found to be suffering from cramp. We sincerely hope there are no further fitness worries when he starts running in handicap hurdles in the autumn. The yard describes him as 'bold, with plenty of scope'.

Rubber Sole age 4 grey gelding

A new horse that we saw being schooled indoors shortly after arriving at Cropredy from Ireland. Certainly looked full of life and, I am told, is the perfect build for chasing, but will start over hurdles. Has developed and strengthened during the summer and should make his debut before Christmas.

Pretty Mobile age 2 grey filly

This young horse has been bought with the idea of running on the Flat before going hurdling in France, where there is much bigger prize money and a good choice of restaurants. Will spend most of the winter out in the fields before training in earnest from February onwards.

 WITH VENETIA WILLIAMS:

Miss Tique age 5 bay mare (rating 108)

Missed the whole of last season due to an expensive colic operation, which we hope won't set back a career that certainly seemed to be heading in the right direction. We are told she 'looks terrific' and off a modest rating of 108 should have every chance of adding more wins to her tally.

Royal Palladium age 5 grey gelding (novice)

Given the confidence that came from the yard we expected much better results last season than finishing 3rd and 4th, but it is unwise to read too much into the way a horse performs in a Flat race when it has been bred for jumping. We look forward to seeing him perform over hurdles which should be a true test of his ability.

THE RACING SEASON

I now find it best to pour a large gin and tonic before reading the monthly Weatherbys statement which charts the inevitable cash outflow of Alex's racing finances. The report

I received in October was particularly gloomy – none of the training fees and vets' bills were offset by prize money so we were heading into the red. It needed a substantial cheque to tide us over until the season gets going and we start to pick up some winnings.

With eleven horses in training Alex says plenty of top prizes are sure to roll in. But even Alex agrees our season has got off to a pretty slow start. Five out of the eleven have yet to see a racecourse. Sole Survivor and Miss Tique are still 'recovering from a year off, and we must ease him/her in gradually'; our two new additions Rubber Sole and Pretty Mobile will not run until after Christmas and Safran de Cotte is waiting for heavy ground.

The other six horses have appeared eight times between them but I have only been to the races twice. Alex couldn't support Arctic Ben at Stratford so I fitted the race into a trip when I was visiting some of our shops. By the time I turned up the Owners' and Trainers' car park was full, so no change there – another season with the owners getting a second rate service. It isn't easy to find the Stratford Owners' and Trainers' bar which is stuck up two flights of stairs. When I got there I wished I hadn't bothered. Rubbing shoulders with all the people who manage to obtain a badge may be fun for the local county set but not if you are on your own. Sadly we finished 5th – out of the prize money.

Nor did we pick up a penny when I went to Uttoxeter. It was my shortest racecourse visit ever. In the morning I was at Uppingham School chairing a finance meeting, which I finished just in time to get to Uttoxeter for the 1.40. Due to some heavy lorries and a crash on the Leicester ring road, by the time I arrived the horses were already at the start.

Royal Palladium came 5th before I met up with Alex and our jockey Liam Treadwell who told us, 'jumped beautifully but there was the hint of a wind problem'. We left Uttoxeter eighteen minutes after I had arrived.

I watched both of Six One Away's races in Ladbrokes, Wythenshawe – who don't pay out for 5th and 6th. I was also in Ladbrokes (Didsbury) to see Timpo come 5th.

Despite discarding my jacket and trying to look casual I usually feel pretty conspicuous in a high street bookmaker, but the other punters are so engrossed in their own bet or one of the cash guzzling fruit machines they hardly notice I am there. I always place a bet, it seems unfair to watch their television without being a customer, so I feel entitled to use their loo (useful to remember if you are caught short while shopping) and take away a few of their handy looking biros.

I saw our other three runners at home on the television including Upbeat Cobbler's win at Uttoxeter. The following day we settled down in our drawing room ready to watch Sixty Something help to make history. We were odds-on favourite in the first race of a good quality card at Wetherby. For the first time A.P. McCoy was riding for Alex Timpson and the morning papers all agreed that Sixty Something would be the first of the ten winners he needed to reach a career mark of 4,000.

Sixty Something slipped on landing over the second fence but A.P. stayed on board and was back with the leading pack when Sixty Something slipped again at the ninth fence and they parted company. No win for McCoy and a first prize of £4,500 that didn't go into my Weatherbys account.

Between races our trainers have supplied a steady

stream of pictures showing fit looking horses and a plentiful collection of warm words:

'He's done everything right at home.'
'He will have really come on for the run.'
'I am sure we will find a race he can win.'
'Plenty of character there, he's a good sort.'
'He jumps really well.'
'Let's see how we go when he gets a handicap.'
'He's a big boy, just made for chasing next season.'

I've discovered you pay the same training fees for losers as well as winners, so we definitely need a few horses that do everything right on the racecourse as well as being perfect back at the yard.

Last year we had eight winners and the prize money covered less than 25 per cent of our costs. I am beginning to think the 2013/2014 season will be even worse.

Alex, however, is more relaxed. 'We are bound to have the odd difficult year after our success over the last few seasons.'

When watching her horses race, Alex wants to be left in solitude. It isn't simply superstition, she likes to experience the joy or disappointment all on her own. However, Alex had to share her experience, when Sixty Something ran at Haydock towards the end of November because we were invited to lunch. Although pretty pleased to have two horses running on a Saturday (Upbeat Cobbler was at

Ascot) we didn't want to boast to fellow guests about being proud owners, at least until after we'd won the big race.

We watched Upbeat Cobbler, on television, take the lead at Ascot but, as all owners know, things often change 6 furlongs from home. The pace quickened, we didn't, and Upbeat Cobbler finished a lacklustre 7th out of ten runners.

At 25/1 it would have been a surprise to pick up a prize in Sixty Something's bid to win big money in his first Class 1 start, but that didn't stop us heading for the parade ring full of optimism.

We started at the back and stayed there, finishing 13th out of seventeen. No prize money and nothing to brag about to the other lunch guests. But, apart from one irritating guest in a tweed suit, who tried to console us by smugly remarking, 'Horses are like that', no one else seemed to notice our disappointment. As an owner, you are desperate to win but, unless they back your horse, no one else cares.

I had greater hopes of Arctic Ben at Doncaster. Alex didn't go, so I fitted the race in between visiting some of our Yorkshire shops. Perhaps Doncaster is quite buzzy on a big race day but, on this wet November Friday, it totally lacked atmosphere.

Of all of Alex's horses I think I have got to know Arctic Ben better than any other. Early in his career he suffered by being held up. He didn't like a steady pace or even being 'handy'. Arctic Ben is a front runner, who gave us a great win when I was in the grotty William Hill by Victoria Station and he shot into a 20-length lead and was never overtaken.

Nick Scholfield hadn't ridden for us before and Henry Daly was elsewhere so I took the initiative on the pre-race briefing. 'Whatever happens let him take the lead.' 'But four others also want to set the pace,' was the response.

We set off at the front but not for long. By the time the field passed the grandstand for the first time he was in 4th place, jumping inaccurately and losing interest. Arctic Ben finished 8th out of eleven runners and I waited for the usual inquest after a losing run. 'They went off so quickly I pulled him back a bit,' said the jockey. I said nothing until I rang Henry Daly on my mobile. 'I don't know much about horses,' I said, 'but if we had kept the lead we could have had a much better chance.' Henry had seen the race on television and shared my irritation. I have learnt that it helps to use a jockey who knows you and knows the horse.

Our statements from Weatherbys were still full of expenditure on training fees with precious little income from prize money to compensate. It doesn't help when some horses in training don't go near a racecourse. Our new horses, Rubber Sole and Pretty Mobile, hope to run in the spring, Miss Tique is reportedly 'tied up', Sole Survivor is looking for the right race and Safran de Cotte was waiting for heavy going ahead of the Tommy Whittle Chase at Haydock.

On 1 December, although the going wasn't heavy, we went to Carlisle to see Safran de Cotte. It was our first visit to the Carlisle course and we were pleasantly surprised. They give owners a friendly welcome and there are great views of the surrounding countryside. The food isn't bad, but we had to fight our way through the crowd to hand over our luncheon vouchers in the Owners' and Trainers' lounge. The room was just big enough to cater for owners and trainers but unfortunately they also let in a lot of non-owning racegoers who clearly thought it was the place to be.

The way things had been going, we feared the worst. On form, Safran de Cotte was certainly one of the three contenders but it was soon clear that on fairly good ground the other two were too quick for him. Still, 3rd won enough money to pay for the trip up the M6 and as Jake Greenall told us 'he will have come on for the run'.

The race was at 1.55 and by 2.15 we were heading south to the Etihad Stadium, arriving just in time to see Alvaro Negredo score the first of Manchester City's goals in a 3–0 defeat of Swansea City. Alex has a theory that if our horses do well our football team will struggle and vice versa. The way her horses are going this season City should win the Premiership.

The following week, Sixty Something nearly changed our fortunes at Uttoxeter in a 3-mile chase. Another furlong would have made all the difference – we lost by a neck.

Last season we had eight winners, so far this year there has been just one. After a time you get used to receiving the jockey's report well away from the Winners' enclosure. This year we have heard many reasons why a poor run could still give hope for future success.

We went to Bangor knowing that our two horses, running in the same race, would both struggle to reach the front. The only trophy we were likely to hold that day was a mounted pair of silver spurs won by Sixty Something at the same meeting in 2012. It had pride of place in my snooker room – I never realised we were only allowed to keep it for a year. On arrival at Bangor we handed back the trophy, in the sure knowledge we would leave empty handed.

Royal Palladium (40/1) was heading for a wind operation but needed to run in one more Novice Hurdle to get a handicap. Six One Away started at 100/1, a fair reflection of past performance, so we were pleased when he finished 5th out of fifteen. Royal Palladium was 8th. It was an unsuccessful wet day at Bangor, where you have to arrive early to claim a spot in the Owners' and Trainers' car park but once through the gate you get the best complimentary lunch on the circuit.

We didn't go to Southwell to watch Timpo run in a Handicap Chase against competitors rated as low as 58. We watched on a wet Sunday with five other customers at a bookies in Newport Pagnell. Thanks to the leader falling three from home, Timpo came a poor 3rd (64 lengths behind the winner) but won just enough money to pay for the horse box.

21 December promised to be the biggest day of Alex's racing career. Oddschecker and Timeform were both backing Arctic Ben and Safran de Cotte to do well. It was the Tommy Whittle Day at Haydock and we not only had two runners, but Safran was favourite to win the Tommy Whittle Chase – to put on more pressure we were invited to join several pretty posh other guests for lunch.

We didn't have a great day. Lunch was fine, apart from me failing to follow the dress code (I left my jacket on a chair in our kitchen). Arctic Ben came 4th out of six and Safran de Cotte never looked happy, soon fell back through the field and was pulled up half a mile from home. We got some sympathetic looks from our fellow racegoers when we returned from our ordeal for tea, but we left before the last race both muttering 'I can't believe that horse ran so badly.'

I shared my misery with a keen owner whom I meet in Mustique. He gave me some advice: 'Horses are like that. They get you all excited about their potential, then wham, they disappoint. Bit like family, colleagues, politicians, governments and football teams. But when things go well it's great to be involved.'

Surely things are bound to get better but it is probably unwise to suggest the second half of our season can't be as bad as the first.

With plenty of spare time between Christmas and New Year we were looking forward to seeing some of Alex's horses in action. We were even happy to go to Leicester, a miserable place on a sunny day and pretty forlorn on 27 December in driving rain. The weather was so bad that, when hot favourite Sixty Something was in the parade ring, we watched from the shelter of a horse box. After a disappointing run he was lucky to be 3rd, and we felt ashamed going to the Winners' enclosure – there were only four horses in the race. 'Trainer's error,' said Paul Webber. 'I ran him too soon after his last race.'

Two days later we were at Haydock. With runners in the second and sixth races we were in for a long day, so booked a place in the Owners' and Trainers' where the service is cheerful and the unimaginative food is free. We were hopeful that Upbeat Cobbler, our only winner of the season on 1 November, would come good again. She finished 7th out of nine. 'Just don't know what to say,' said Jake Greenall. 'Didn't feel the same horse as I rode at home.'

Later we watched Sole Survivor in the parade ring for the first time since he had a wind operation then tendon problems after running two years and two days ago at the same lacklustre Leicester fixture where we had just seen Sixty Something's sub-par performance. We didn't expect much so were surprised to see Sole Survivor contesting the lead but two years is a long lay-off and he tired in the last 2 furlongs to finish 5th out of a field of seven.

We couldn't get to the Saturday meeting at Warwick to watch Safran de Cotte in the big race of the day. The race was analysed in depth on Channel 4's *Morning Line* but our horse never got a mention. However, they did talk about us during the race with Safran prominent throughout and finishing 6th in a field full of Cheltenham hopefuls. Perhaps things are looking up.

Persistent rain turned the going at most courses to 'heavy' so we didn't expect to see a lot more racing. In some ways it was a relief that we were spared watching further attempts finish in disappointment – less stress and no anguish.

The next time any of our horses ran we were in the air, en route for Mustique. It took some time to get an internet connection after we landed in Barbados and when I finally got online wondered why I'd bothered. The quick results confirmed that neither horse had finished in the first three, and the details showed that Miss Tique was 6th out of seven and Sole Survivor was pulled up ('just too sticky' emailed Paul).

Before going away, Christine at the office had succeeded in setting up *Racing Post* coverage on my iPad so we were able to watch Arctic Ben at Catterick while we sat by the pool at our rented house, Toucan Hill, overlooking the Caribbean. We won ... the best turned out! – but had no success on the course; Arctic Ben, although starting at 5/1, was hardly mentioned in the commentary and finished way back at 6th out of 7. Henry Daly emailed: 'He needed the run, but the ground was never going to be to his liking.'

Back from Mustique, on 12 February we returned to Haydock to watch Sixty Something in the 4.35 race. As Manchester City were kicking off an FA Cup game against Chelsea at 5.15pm the timing wasn't great. With 6 furlongs to go Sixty Something lost touch with the leaders and I got ready to race off to The Etihad. But Paul Webber suddenly sounded more positive as Sixty Something found another gear and came back from nowhere to finish 2nd. Paul was relieved. For weeks a virus had caused many horses from his yard to lack pace in the last half mile so this was a sign of recovery. We spent some precious minutes in the Winners' enclosure before politely refusing a champagne invitation and set off for the football. We reached our seats 35 minutes after leaving the racecourse, just in time to see City's first goal. A much better day.

I viewed our next race in a betting shop. Alex watched Miss Tique at Ludlow while I was in Coral at Chichester. Another disappointment – she finished last of seven. 'Wrong ground,' said Alex when I rang her on her mobile.

Safran de Cotte might not be winning but he is certainly running in good company – a true Saturday horse. His next big race was at Newcastle and yet again we couldn't go, this time due to a wedding. But the wedding went well, a very pretty 1,000-year-old church where the service finished at the perfect time to visit a betting shop in Gerrards Cross on the way to the reception. For most of the race we were at the front, only being beaten by better horses on the run-in – 4th and over £2,000 in prize money. It almost felt like a win.

Five days later Alex was back at Ludlow and I was in Betfred, Holyhead, watching Upbeat Cobbler finishing a tired looking 6th out of ten runners. 'I thought that was better,' said Richard Johnson. 'She will certainly win more races … one day. I would take her over fences next season.'

More bad news, Sole Survivor has a hole in his tendon. After two years recovering from injury and two races (5th out of seven, then pulled up) this big horse that looked a certain candidate for Cheltenham is going to retire with career winnings of £3,596.64 at an estimated cost to the owner's financial advisor of £135,000. Who said that racing doesn't pay? With Sole Survivor soon to arrive and Timpo to follow at the end of the season the fields behind our house are being extended to provide proper accommodation.

We went on a three-night trip to Las Vegas, not to gamble (we lost £10 on a one armed bandit through complete ignorance and gave up), but to chill out and see Celine Dion. The trip meant we missed City's next Cup tie against a woeful Wigan whose only real success was beating us in last year's Cup final. A surprisingly friendly US Border Guard checked the score while he checked our passports. More bad news – City lost 1–2. But Alex has this theory that when City do badly her horses do well so perhaps we would strike lucky the following day when Miss Tique was running at Plumpton. We followed the race thanks to Paddy Power who have a text commentary alongside a cartoon of the first three horses moving across the screen. For 2 miles we neither read a word nor saw a picture of our horse, then, approaching the last fence, Miss Tique appeared on the screen, challenged for the lead, jumped the last and went on to win. Fantastic. Five seconds later the names changed and Miss Tique was no longer mentioned. I guess it was a case of mistaken identity, the true winner had similar light blue silks that must have fooled the commentator. We later discovered that Miss Tique fell three from home, the only horse that failed to finish.

Our Las Vegas trip coincided with the Cheltenham Festival. Three months ago Alex chastised me for choosing a week when we should have been enjoying Owners' hospitality at the big event. But as the holiday got closer it became clear that none of our horses were good enough. Their lack of ability got me off the hook.

Thanks to Racing UK we were able to watch The Festival and, while having breakfast at the Mandarin Oriental, saw Henry Daly's horse Hot Totti come in a creditable 4th ridden by Jake Greenall. We are Jake's sponsor, so Jake was proudly displaying the Timpson logo on his thighs. That is probably as near as we will ever get to competing at Cheltenham.

Our Weatherbys bank statement was waiting for me when I got home from Vegas – a consistent tale of negative cash flow. But Alex remains positive. Alex feels we need a more focussed strategy to find the winner of The Gold Cup.

Once the season is over Alex is planning a thorough review. Alex says we should take a keener look at cash flow but I expect the new policy will be just as costly as the old one.

After a succession of disappointments so far this season, we came back from our short break in Vegas well prepared for further failure, so it came as a pleasant surprise on the day of our return when we watched Royal Palladium, on television, fresh from his wind operation, coming 2nd in a modest hurdle race at Towcester. Our joy was short lived, Royal Palladium returned to form nine days later finishing 7th out of seventeen in a somewhat more competitive race at Newbury.

The following day's meeting at Bangor clashed with a trustee meeting at Uppingham so I couldn't get to the course in time to watch Sixty Something. I stopped in a housing estate fifteen miles away and, thanks to Racing UK, watched him on my iPad as he romped home as the easy winner. I arrived at the course in time to see Arctic Ben being saddled up, with thoughts of our first double. Arctic Ben seems to sulk if he isn't in front. I was hopeful when Jake Greenall took him into a healthy lead, but this isn't the season for fairy stories and we finished 2nd. There were only four runners but at least we won enough money to pay for a week's training fees.

With both our main trainers Henry Daly and Paul Webber present at Bangor Alex asked them back home for tea and a chat about how we could find more success. Horseracing isn't like running a chain of shoe repair shops. When I open a new shop I have a pretty good idea how much profit we will make; with horses the result is impossible to guess, but it is almost certain you will always lose money.

'After ten years as an owner,' said Alex, as Henry and Paul listened with nervous anticipation, 'I am not so keen on going to Leicester on a Monday to watch an outsider running in a 0–95 handicap. I am not saying the Cheltenham Gold Cup is essential but I do want horses that appear on Channel 4's coverage of Saturday racing.' I could see Paul and Henry thinking that's exactly what they want too, but my mind was considering the return (or loss) on investment.

I have come to the conclusion that the way to enjoy racing is …

1) Forget how much you have paid for the horses.
2) Look at the detail of each monthly training account to check you are not picking up someone else's vets' fees (but don't look at the total bill).
3) Remember it costs no less to train a dobbin than a trainer is paid to produce the winner of the Grand National.
4) A day at Sandown costs owners no more than Thursday at Southwell.
5) Don't pay a lot of money for a horse. Most of us get our pleasure by beating one of the big spenders who pay over £150,000 with a horse that cost less than £15,000.
6) Follow your instinct. You might think you are a novice but after five years as an owner you know a lot more than you realise.
7) Cut your losses. Horses rated 93 seldom improve enough to run at the Cheltenham Festival.
8) Beware of Jockey and Trainer talk that can lead you to fund another season for a no hoper – 'he's still green', 'bred to be a chaser', 'will come into her own over big fences next season'.

The meeting with Henry and Paul was more expensive than I expected. Our new 'Saturday horses policy' means that we are likely to retire our poorest performers and already have plans to buy five new additions to our stable.

Our clear positive strategy for success made no difference to our horses in training. We went to Uttoxeter to watch Six One Away who showed so little interest in racing Denis O'Regan pulled him up with nearly a mile to go. 'If you ask me the horse is no good,' said Denis in the unsaddling area, but back home they discovered a painful shoulder so we decided to give the horse another go.

We were pleased we couldn't go to a disappointing day at Towcester, where we would have seen Upbeat Cobbler come 5th out of twelve (just good enough to earn the chance to run again next season). In the same race Miss Tique finished next to last and has run her last race.

It got worse. Timpo was running at Stratford on the same day Manchester City had a crucial away game against Liverpool. The pub I picked with Sky Sports was friendly but pretty rough and full of Liverpool supporters. City lost 3–2 but did a lot better than Timpo who was not the slightest bit interested in running round the course, so he ended his career with PU ('pulled up') against his name.

'Still,' said Alex, 'that's racing. They don't run for ever. But we can look forward to Cobbler's Queen's second foal which is due in May and at least we've got our new horses Rubber Sole and Pretty Mobile to enjoy when they run in a few weeks' time. Paul is very pleased with their progress.'

Safran de Cotte had been balloted out of the Midlands Grand National at Uttoxeter but we were counting the days to our first visit to Ayr where he was entered to run in the Scottish Grand National. 'We must go,' said Alex. 'Big Saturday races are what it's all about.'

I visited most of our shops in Edinburgh ten days before the race and discovered that some Timpson colleagues know lots more about our horses than we do: 'Should suit the soft going', '33/1 looks a fair price to me' … but despite their knowledge they still asked me 'What are the chances?' In fact he had no chance. We were balloted out again and still haven't watched racing at Ayr. With the weather forecasters promising sunshine there was no chance of any racecourse having heavy going so Safran de Cotte won't have another run until next November.

A lot of our shop colleagues have a keen interest in racing but it hasn't always done them much good. When I was visiting some shops in Oldham in 1974, with Stuart Lyons who was the managing director of John Collier, we popped into the John Collier shop to find the manager on the phone to his bookie, with a copy of the *Racing Post* spread out on the shop counter. He was lucky not to lose his job.

More recently a Timpson colleague tried to solve his debt problem by going to the betting shop next door and putting £1,000 from the till on the nose of a racing certainty – it didn't win so he tried another hot favourite the following day before admitting defeat and confessing to his crime.

We had better news of Sixty Something, who came 2nd in a reasonable race at Cheltenham where we were able to go into the Winners' enclosure to the applause of about ten spectators in driving rain. I wonder how long we will have to wait before we are there after winning The Gold Cup.

Is there a training course that gives trainers a few tips on how to break bad news? Paul had a tricky task when he rang Alex to tell her that Rubber Sole had rolled over in his stall and done enough damage to have written off any chances of running this season.

At least Paul also had some good news. Pretty Mobile has been entered at Newmarket on the Flat before running over hurdles at Deauville towards the end of June. This is part of a cunning plan to avoid bumpers and take advantage of the more generous prize money in France. Great excitement – our first experience on the Flat and our debut in France. We booked the plane and started to check out restaurants near Deauville.

I was in Ladbrokes, Wythenshawe, when Arctic Ben came 3rd in a chase at Southwell. I got the usual strange looks from my fellow punters but a smile from the manager behind the counter who no doubt knows I usually lose. This time I got exactly my money back on £10 each way.

It was Henry's turn to give Alex bad news when he called about Cobbler's Queen. The foal was born the wrong way round, was severely disabled and had to be put down. Mum recovered after several days of intensive care, which sounds quite expensive.

Two days later it was Paul on the telephone: 'We will have to put Deauville on hold I'm afraid. Pretty Mobile has tweaked a muscle and won't be doing any work for a couple of weeks.'

At last May arrived, Man City were Premiership Champions and we could almost forget about racing for a few months. But Alex raised another problem: 'we're running out of room; a few more retired horses and our fields will be full'. She has a point. At the start of the year we only had Transatlantic and Ordre de Bataille, but they have already been joined by Sole Survivor, with Timpo and possibly Miss Tique on the way here soon. Six One Away is sitting on the naughty step and is only one race away from possible retirement. I am beginning to wonder if there is money to be made as a tourist attraction. The Shire Horse Centre down the road in Cotebrook gets a lot of visitors – perhaps retired racehorses would have a similar appeal.

There was one piece of unfinished business before we could forget racing. Nearly all our horses are enjoying a rest, having been put out to grass, and I am enjoying the lower training fees but Six One Away had one more run in the last race on a Sunday at Uttoxeter. We had decided this was his last chance – a poor result and that would be the end of his racing career. I feel a bit guilty that we didn't go to the meeting, but it clashed with a planned mini-break so we watched At The Races in our cottage in North Wales.

His performance summed up our season: it was hopeless, we finished 7th out of eight runners. At no point in the race did I think we would win any money. But Alex gave Six One Away another chance. 'He might be better over fences next season.' I hope she's right, otherwise I really will have to buy some more fields behind our house.

SEASON 2013–2014

HORSE	DATE	COURSE	RACE	DISTANCE	PRIZE MONEY	JOCKEY	RATING	POSITION	RUNNERS
Timpo	24-May-13	Towcester	Hand. Chase	3m ½f	2K	Richard Johnson	95	2	12
	6-Nov-13	Warwick	Hand. Chase	3m 2f	3K	Jake Greenall	98	5	9
	15-Dec-13	Southwell	Hand. Chase	3m 1½f	2K	Jake Greenall	94	3	8
	13-Apr-14	Stratford	Hand. Chase	3m 3½f	3K	Tom O'Brien	91	PU	11
Arctic Ben	31-Oct-13	Stratford	Hand. Chase	2m 3½f	6K	Jake Greenall	125	5	9
	29-Nov-13	Doncaster	Hand. Chase	2m 3f	6K	Nick Scholfield	124	8	11
	21-Dec-13	Haydock	Hand. Chase	2m	9K	Jake Greenall	122	4	6
	31-Jan-14	Catterick	Hand. Chase	2m 3f	7K	Richard Johnson	120	6	7
	22-Mar-14	Bangor-on-Dee	Hand. Chase	2m 4½f	3K	Jake Greenall	117	2	4
	23-Apr-14	Southwell	Hand. Chase	2m 4½f	3K	Jake Greenall	117	3	8
Safran de Cotte	1-Dec-13	Carlisle	Hand. Chase	3m 2f	8K	Jake Greenall	130	3	7
	21-Dec-13	Haydock	Hand. Chase	3m ½f	21K	Jake Greenall	129	PU	12
	11-Jan-14	Warwick	Hand. Chase Grade 3	3m 5f	34K	Jake Greenall	126	6	15
	22-Feb-14	Newcastle	Hand. Chase	4m ½f	37K	Jake Greenall	122	4	16

(continued)

HORSE	DATE	COURSE	RACE	DISTANCE	PRIZE MONEY	JOCKEY	RATING	POSITION	RUNNERS
Miss Tique	24-Jan-14	Huntingdon	Hand. Hurdle	2m 4½f	3K	Aidan Coleman	119	6	7
	19-Feb-14	Ludlow	Hand. Hurdle	2m	9K	Aidan Coleman	117	7	7
	10-Mar-14	Plumpton	Hand. Hurdle	2m 1½f	6K	Aidan Coleman	110	F	7
	10-Apr-14	Towcester	Nov. Hand. Chase	2m 4f	3K	Robert Dunne	105	8	12
Sole Survivor	30-Dec-13	Haydock	Hand. Hurdle	2m 4f	3K	Jake Greenall	100	5	7
	24-Jan-14	Doncaster	Nov. Hand. Chase	2m 3f	2K	Denis O'Regan	100	PU	12
	2-Nov-13	Wetherby	Nov. Chase	3m 1f	4K	A.P. McCoy	135	F	6
	23-Nov-13	Haydock	Hand. Hurdle Grade 3	3m	45K	Jake Greenall	135	13	17
Sixty Something	10-Dec-13	Uttoxeter	Nov. Chase	3m	5K	Jake Greenall	132	2	8
	27-Dec-13	Leicester	Nov. Chase	2m 6½f	6K	Jake Greenall	132	3	4
	15-Feb-14	Haydock	Nov. Hand. Chase	2m 5½f	8K	Jake Greenall	132	2	6
	22-Mar-14	Bangor-on-Dee	Nov. Chase	3m	3K	Jake Greenall	129	1	7
	17-Apr-14	Cheltenham	Nov. Hand. Chase	3m 1f	6K	Jake Greenall	129	2	10

(continued)

HORSE	DATE	COURSE	RACE	DISTANCE	PRIZE MONEY	JOCKEY	RATING	POSITION	RUNNERS
Upbeat Cobbler	1-Nov-13	Uttoxeter	Hand. Hurdle	3m	3K	Tom O'Brien	101	1	7
	23-Nov-13	Ascot	Hand. Hurdle	2m 5½f	5K	Richard Johnson	107	7	10
	30-Dec-13	Haydock	Hand. Hurdle	3m	3K	Jake Greenall	107	7	9
	27-Feb-14	Ludlow	Hand. Hurdle	3m	5K	Richard Johnson	105	6	10
	10-Apr-14	Towcester	Nov. Hand. Chase	2m 4f	3K	Jake Greenall	103	5	12
	1-Nov-13	Uttoxeter	Nov. Hurdle	2m 4f	3K	Liam Treadwell	–	4	12
	16-Nov-13	Uttoxeter	Maiden Hurdle	2m 4f	2K	Liam Treadwell	–	5	11
Royal Palladium	30-Nov-13	Bangor-on-Dee	Nov. Hurdle	2m 3½f	3K	Harry Challoner	–	4	7
	13-Dec-13	Bangor-on-Dee	Nov. Hurdle	2m ½f	3K	Robert Dunne	–	8	15
	12-Mar-14	Huntingdon	Maiden Hurdle	3m 1f	3K	Liam Treadwell	104	2	7
	21-Mar-14	Newbury	Hand. Hurdle	3m ½f	3K	Aidan Coleman	104	7	17
	24-Oct-13	Ludlow	Nov. Hurdle	2m	3K	Jake Greenall	–	6	14
Six One Away	13-Nov-13	Bangor-on-Dee	Nov. Hurdle	2m ½f	3K	Denis O'Regan	–	5	7
	13-Dec-13	Bangor-on-Dee	Nov. Hurdle	2m ½f	3K	Liam Heard	–	5	15
	29-Mar-14	Uttoxeter	Hand. Hurdle	2m 4f	3K	Denis O'Regan	106	PU	9
	25-May-14	Uttoxeter	Nov. Hand. Hurdle	2m 4f	2K	Denis O'Regan	100	7	8

	RUNS	1ST	2ND	3RD	4TH
Timpo	4	0	1	1	0
Arctic Ben	6	0	1	1	1
Safran de Cotte	4	0	0	1	1
Miss Tique	4	0	0	0	0
Sole Survivor	2	0	0	0	0
Sixty Something	7	1	3	1	0
Upbeat Cobbler	5	1	0	0	0
Royal Palladium	6	0	1	0	2
Six One Away	5	0	0	0	0
Total	43	2	6	4	4

	TRAIN-ING FEES	ENTRY FEE/ JOCKEY	TOTAL COST	WINNINGS + SPONSORSHIP	NET COST
2013–2014					
Safran de Cotte	18,889	2,160	21,049	6,085	14,964
Arctic Ben	18,758	2,165	20,923	5,070	15,853
Timpo	17,824	880	18,704	3,588	15,116
Sixty Something	19,236	2,205	21,441	10,790	10,651
Upbeat Cobbler	18,687	1,250	19,937	6,590	13,347
Miss Tique	20,446	1,315	21,761	3,000	18,761
Royal Palladium	21,537	1,725	23,262	4,230	19,032
Pretty Mobile	14,159	–	14,159	3,000	11,159
Sole Survivor	14,435	570	15,005	3,000	12,005
Rubber Sole	15,942	–	15,942	3,000	12,942
Six One Away	19,149	1,370	20,519	3,000	17,519
					£161,349
Cobbler's Queen	8,305				
Cobbler's Son	3,257				£11,562
					£172,911

2014–2015

THE HORSES

Last season was a desperate disappointment. We went weeks without seeing any of our runners picking up any prize money and finished a miserable season with only two winners out of 43 attempts.

In June when we discovered that Alex had biliary cancer, racing quickly slipped down our list of priorities. But, although we were less likely to get to the usual number of race meetings, we could follow the action on television and I still wanted Alex to get her winning day at the Cheltenham Festival. All three trainers were looking out for new potential Saturday horses with a view to qualifying for The Festival in four years' time. So we start the season with four new horses plus a couple more that have yet to see a racecourse.

It is bound to be a different sort of season but we still have the hope that we will both be at Cheltenham to watch a horse running in Alex's colours.

WITH HENRY DALY:

Arctic Ben age 10 (rating 115)
Last season Arctic Ben slipped down the ratings which

suggests we might have seen the best of this front running chaser. Can perform on any ground from good to soft, but on heavy ground he is unlikely to stay for more than 2 miles.

Despite being our oldest horse in training there are no thoughts of retirement.

Safran de Cotte age 8 grey gelding (rating 121)

Could be past his best but still puts in some excellent performances in very good company. His performance at Newcastle over 4 miles in the top race of the day ended the season on a high. We can expect him to have plenty of chances to be mentioned on Channel 4's *Morning Line*. One day we expect him to win a big race.

Upbeat Cobbler age 6 grey mare (rating 101)

When Upbeat Cobbler won at Uttoxeter at the beginning of November we thought it was a good omen for her season and for ours. Little did we realise this was one of the few highlights. In her four other races she was never in contention. Switching to fences in April seemed to suit her better so we hope a full season of chasing will give her the chance to prove her potential.

Another Cobbler age 4 grey mare

New to Downton Stables in the summer but likely to run in a bumper before Christmas. So far the noises coming from the yard are non-committal, but trainers are often careful to control their owners' expectations. So far phrases like 'a lot to learn', 'a bit green' and 'hopefully we will see plenty of progress' all suggest that we might have to be patient.

The Artful Cobbler age 3 grey gelding
Another new addition, The Artful Cobbler has attracted a lot of praise for his attitude and physique. We have been encouraged by some of these remarks but one rarely sees any true evidence until the first bumper early in the New Year.

WITH PAUL WEBBER:

Sixty Something age 8 grey gelding (rating 129)
No doubt Sixty Something was the one shining light in our season of despair. With five consecutive finishes in the first three there is no doubt this is our best prospect for a run at the Cheltenham Festival.

Despite parting company with A.P. McCoy on his first run of the season in a chase he was expected to win at Wetherby. Sixty Something is proving to be a bold and accurate jumper. This is definitely a horse to watch.

Six One Away age 5 grey gelding (rating 95)
One wonders why, after such a poor record, the handicapper has rated him as high as 95. We need to see a miraculous change in form for Six One Away to remain in training.

Oddly he performs really well on the gallops, runs happily for the first mile or so round a racecourse but fails to respond as soon as the pace quickens. Seems he lacks any competitive streak. The only hope is to try fences and pray for an amazing change of form.

Pretty Mobile age 3 grey mare

The idea of a trip to France to run for better prize money collapsed when Pretty Mobile had an irritating niggle. We even missed out on our gourmet lunch. We are now expecting to start in the early autumn with a Flat race – perhaps we will be going to Ascot or Newmarket.

Pretty Mobile is a small, fairly fragile looking mare who needs to grow a bit if she is, one day, going to tackle big fences.

Rubber Sole age 5 grey gelding

It's been a catalogue of injury and very little training for this fine looking grey that looks every inch a competitive chaser. Over twelve months of training fees and the odd bill from the vet haven't got Rubber Sole fit enough to enter a chase, a hurdle or a bumper.

Let's hope we can get the show on the road next season.

The Venerable Bede age 3 grey gelding

With lots of positive comments about this big horse which everyone seems to agree will, given time, make a great chaser, we are looking forward to seeing Bede on a racecourse. The sooner the better.

 WITH VENETIA WILLIAMS:

Royal Palladium age 6 grey gelding (rating 104)

A modest year over hurdles, interrupted by a wind operation, has produced a modest handicap of 104. We are told not to worry, this horse will make his mark over fences, and everything so far has been no more than preparation for the real thing. This coming season should show whether we have a true winner.

Super Sam age 4 grey gelding
Already placed in both bumpers under previous ownership Super Sam has plenty of appeal. He may only have one season over hurdles before going chasing but this is clearly a quality horse that promises to rise rapidly through the handicaps.

Could be one of our future stars to follow.

THE RACING SEASON

I'd always planned to produce a comprehensive financial account of Alex's National Hunt career to date, but before writing this book decided that knowing the truth would take away some of the enjoyment. I have, however, gained a lot of satisfaction from looking at some of the statistics that chart the performance of other owners. If you can't succeed yourself at least you can get pleasure from finding out that the failure of others can be far worse. Even the best-known owners who bid the big prices at the Doncaster Sales have plenty of horses that win nothing. The statistics seem to show that like us they are lucky if their horses run six times a year and through injury and the wrong ground they all have some that don't run at all. With many more horses they probably lose a lot more money than us but they do own a few that are rated over 150, so are guaranteed plenty of big race Saturdays and some runners at the Cheltenham

Festival. A significant trading loss is the price you pay for the ultimate prize.

Part of the problem is the conventional way of measuring financial success. The benchmark for owners isn't 'break even'. On average racehorse owners can only expect to recover about 20 per cent of their costs in prize money so anything better should be celebrated. On that basis Alex has beaten the benchmark in two out of the last three years and although 2013/2014 failed to hit the target, her record suggests that she has hit on a winning formula.

With this track record in mind we are following the strategy of retiring any non-Saturday horses that can't even pick up prize money off their modest handicap and replacing them with three-year-olds, full of promise, that have been handpicked by Henry, Paul and Venetia with Cheltenham in mind. As a result we head for a new season with six horses that hope to appear on a racecourse for the first time. Rubber Sole, Pretty Mobile, The Artful Cobbler, Super Sam, Another Cobbler and The Venerable Bede. Cobbler's Son will have another season growing up in the fields before we discover if our first foal has star quality.

We are keeping the Cheltenham Festival week free in our diary.

After a break of over four months we are back. Pretty Mobile, the filly that spent last season being prepared for a debut at Deauville only to be foiled by an injury in training, got her first outing in the less exotic surroundings of Wolverhampton. It wasn't the day trip we had dreamt about but the evening meeting was both our first Flat race and the first time we had run under floodlights. The *Racing Post* had little to say other than telling the world we had paid €22,000 for a horse that had such a slim chance of winning it was 'best watched'.

I had a lunch commitment in London so neither of us could go to Wolverhampton, but I called at Coral in Tarporley on my way home who generously offered 40/1 despite three non-runners reducing the field to nine. I worked out that a win would pay out over £1,000 for my £20 each way and with the £2,850 first prize we would collect a total of over £4,000. Not a bad start to the season.

We watched the event on At The Races. There weren't many people at Wolverhampton which, with its all-weather surface and glaring lights, looked more like a dog track than a racecourse. We turned on the television in time for the 7.20 (the race before ours), an anonymous affair with horses that could have been mistaken for the virtual runners that you can bet on down at the bookies. The only excitement was watching whether a particularly stubborn four-year-old would agree to enter the starting stalls.

When our race came at 7.50 Pretty Mobile went happily into the stalls but didn't like them, and as a result she was agitated and jumped off at the back of the field which is where she stayed. 'Pretty Mobile is running a bit green,' said the commentator but she settled down towards the end and finished 6th, which was better than the heavily backed odds-on favourite who was well in the lead coming into the final straight when he moved to the right, got an unwelcome reminder from the jockey who then fell off. I would have been interested to hear how he explained the incident to the owner and trainer, when, battered and bruised, he returned to the paddock.

We got our explanation over the phone: 'She was a bit green, but will have gained a lot from the experience.'

Our season really started at Exeter where we had entries in consecutive races. We couldn't go because Alex is undergoing a course of chemotherapy, but we looked forward to a full afternoon of sport as the two races were quickly followed by Manchester City's European Cup game in Moscow. It promised to be an enjoyable afternoon in front of the television.

I popped out from the office at lunchtime to place my bets. It was fortunate timing – they had a special offer for people having a punt between noon and 1.00pm, I got the odds currently quoted or the starting price, whichever gave me the bigger payout.

Sixty Something led the field for the first 2½ miles of a 3-mile chase and was still contesting at the second last when he tripped and sent Jake Greenall to the ground. It was little consolation to hear the commentator say that he had run a good race up to that point and should win races sometime this season.

In the next race Royal Palladium never got into the lead. Despite being quite handy until the last half mile it was a disappointing performance and we finished well down the field. Inevitably we were told that 'He will have come on for the run'.

The football seemed to be going better with City 2–0 up at half time, but a combination of a bitterly cold Moscow night and an outrageous penalty decision caused our team to concede two goals in the second half and complete a disappointing afternoon. Still I can't complain – if either of our horses had been in the frame Ladbrokes would have paid out on generous odds.

Two days later I couldn't even see our runners on television. When Upbeat Cobbler ran in the 1.30 at Southwell I was at a presentation in the House of Lords where the only thing shown on screen is details of the current debate. Good news greeted me when I got out and checked my iPad. Upbeat Cobbler came in 2nd, 5 lengths behind the winner, and we collect £1,107 – the first bit of positive cash flow for five months.

We didn't have as much luck with Six One Away in the 4.10, a 2-mile handicap hurdle. I missed that race because I was on the train back to Crewe but the *Racing Post* told me nearly all I needed to know: 'Went left at first, chased leader until after three out, weakened rapidly, tailed off and pulled up before next.' I later discovered that tests after the race showed an infection that is likely to lead to a little lay-off and a biggish vets' fee.

After our first five races we have produced one 2nd, two mediocre placings, a faller and one who failed to finish. However our trainers report that 'they all should be better next time out' and those yet to appear 'look really good and full of running'.

With Cheltenham still five months away we don't want to peak too early.

We hit a landmark on 31 October when not only was Arctic Ben starting a new season at Uttoxeter, but it was the first time Alex has been able to go to a racecourse since she was diagnosed with biliary cancer during the summer. That made only four courses – Haydock, Bangor, Aintree and Uttoxeter – practical propositions for Alex to appear at in person. I made a quick exit from the golf course and we got to Uttoxeter in time to place a bet on the grey in the 1.15 – it won and I put the £20 return on an each way bet following Alex's tip for the next race – it only came 2nd but I still won enough to put £20 each way on Arctic Ben in the next race. The bookies clearly thought I was taking a big chance – the odds were 12/1. Alex, on her most ambitious adventure for three months, got to the saddling up stables and the paddock before watching Arctic Ben leading the field for most of the race before being overtaken by the favourite at the last fence. We won a bit of money and I beat the Tote but, most important of all, Alex had a great day.

Our next runner clashed with Manchester United's league visit to Manchester City, so I watched Pretty Mobile's race at Huntingdon on my iPad in The Etihad car park before going in to watch the match. This horse, trained by Paul Webber and named to mark the launch of our mobile phone repairs, is certainly pretty but has yet to prove if she is mobile. The jury is still out after she finished 6th out of eleven in a modest field. But it didn't really matter because City beat United.

We were keenly anticipating the reappearance of Alex's best horse, Safran de Cotte, who, despite preferring even heavier ground, was entered on the Saturday of Cheltenham's Open Meeting. We got an encouraging mention on Channel 4's *Morning Line* and I made the mistake of bragging about it to my mates at the golf club who promised to watch the race. I hope they weren't tempted to put on a bet because, after being in contention for most of the way, Safran lost contact with the leaders and was pulled up. Tests showed the problem was a burst blood vessel, something that will be easily cured by a few good bills from the vet and a little lay-off on full training fees.

I confess that when I bought four new additions to Alex's string during the summer it was all done in a bit of a daze. Before Alex discovered about the cancer she had devised this new strategy to give us horses with the ability to compete at the highest level. We retired a few that didn't even have an outside chance of running at the Cheltenham Festival and planned to bring in new blood with the promise of going up the grades and running regularly on a Saturday.

Following our guidelines Venetia Williams bought Super Sam (with a grandson called Sam the name sold the deal) but in my keenness to keep Alex's racing hobby up to date I hadn't realised Super Sam had already run in two competitive bumpers. That experience made a vital difference when Super Sam became our first winner of the season, a hurdle race that he always looked like winning, at Chepstow. I watched at a bookies in Epsom with Martin our driver. We both put £20 to win – Martin took the odds when placing his bet while I went for the starting price that eased just before the off – to 11/8 from 5/4 – so I had the satisfaction of walking out with more winnings than Martin.

Unfortunately it was another day when success on the racecourse caused disaster for our football team – City had a horrendous home loss to Moscow.

I was with Martin when Royal Palladium ran in his first chase at Lingfield. I was talking to a conference in Bridgend but if the audience didn't ask too many questions I would get to a bookies to watch the race. I jumped out of the car and just made it to Ladbrokes in time to hand over my £20 – indeed by the time Martin had parked the car the race had started and it was too late for him to place a bet – I took his £10 and shared my £20 on the nose.

There were only four runners and Royal Palladium took the last just behind the leader who fell leaving us well clear of the only other finisher – our two horses with Venetia Williams have both started the season with a win.

Sixty Something, following the unfortunate fall at Exeter, was entered in a 3½-mile chase on soft ground at Haydock, the perfect opportunity to re-establish his credentials. We were already committed to take our Swansea City-supporting friends to watch their team play at The Etihad so we watched the 12.45 race on Racing UK before leaving home for the match. It didn't go well. Sixty Something settled down after a couple of awkward jumps then three from home was spooked by another horse. He finished a comfortable 3rd but unfortunately Jake Greenall wasn't on board when he crossed the line. At least City beat Swansea later that afternoon.

The following Saturday we had two runners at Bangor-on-Dee. With the first not until 2.00pm I had time for golf before taking Alex for her second day's racing since starting chemotherapy. Super Sam just didn't have the bounce that had brought him the win at Chepstow and finished 3rd out of five. Another Cobbler, still with a baby face, was seeing a racecourse for the first time in the bumper at the end of the card. He was quite composed but ran out of steam with half a mile to go and finished 6th out of seven.

'Got some ability,' said Jake back in the paddock, 'but not a bumper horse.' I asked Henry about future plans. 'I think another bumper after Christmas before going over hurdles.' There was only one winner at Bangor that day, it was Alex, who, despite being totally exhausted by the time we got home, thoroughly enjoyed being back at the races.

I have had a few triumphant trips to our local betting shop but wasn't so bumptious after watching Six One Away hand Ladbrokes my money after his first trip over fences in a low grade race at Ludlow. When I named this horse I envisaged a fanatical following of Manchester City fans going to Cheltenham both to remember our famous 6–1 win at Old Trafford and to celebrate the first of his wins at The Festival. Sadly Six One Away is destined to be a mid-week horse looking for a low class win at Leicester on a Monday. He was 4th out of nine runners at Ludlow without a City supporter in sight. 'That's the best we've seen so far,' said Paul Webber after the race. 'Perhaps we might just have a chance over fences.'

The following day Royal Palladium was out again and despite a big jump in his rating still started 5/4 favourite. It was chemotherapy day for Alex so I was visiting local Timpson shops while our daughter Victoria spent the day in Christie Hospital with her mother. They watched Racing UK on an iPad while I saw the race in David Pluck's betting shop in Cheadle. It was a comfortable win, the third in a row for Royal Palladium who proved Venetia Williams right when she said, earlier in the year, he could be much better when he goes chasing. I telephoned Venetia while I was still in the bookies – a couple of regular customers looked up from their *Racing Post*s when they could clearly hear

Venetia shrieking with delight down the phone. Although there wasn't quite the same excitement back at the Christie Hospital, Alex was delighted to record another win and I'm pretty pleased that she has a horse that looks as if it might pay its way this season.

On the Sunday that Upbeat Cobbler ran at Huntingdon we were invited for lunch near Wolverhampton so found ourselves watching the race on my iPad in a lay-by on the way home. We thought we had picked a spot with good reception but during our race the coverage kept cutting out. After a mile and a half the picture froze with our horse handily placed but 30 seconds later when action resumed we were a good 10 lengths off the pace. We rang Henry to find out what happened and found him surprisingly cheerful. 'Not a bad run,' he said, 'but maybe 3 miles is too far on that sort of ground. Perhaps drop down in distance next time out.'

I was busy on the day Sixty Something was entered to run at Bangor or Doncaster (I suppose it must be worth paying two entry fees to give yourself the chance to pick the right race at the last minute). Despite it being a day after chemotherapy Alex planned to go to Bangor with her friend Annie. But the race at Bangor was too hot and Sixty Something was declared to run at Doncaster in the same meeting as Arctic Ben. I persuaded Alex and Annie not to risk the trip across the Pennines (Doncaster might be buzzy for the big meetings but in December it is soulless, cold and uncomfortable). We watched the meeting in our drawing room in front of a roaring fire. Sixty Something, after failing to finish in his last two races, needed to prove Paul Webber's claim that he has 'plenty of ability'. It helped having only five horses in the race and helped even more when the biggest threat fell and the only other decent looking horse jumped the second last poorly and was pulled up. We won by 50 lengths. An hour later Arctic Ben looked as if he was going to give Alex a double until Jake Greenall asked him to take off too soon four from home and Arctic Ben finished a comfortable 3rd without the rider. Still we now have five winners and it isn't even Christmas. With lots of possible runners over the holiday period things are starting to look good.

Like last year we entered Safran de Cotte in the Tommy Whittle Chase at Haydock. It's his sort of race, we know the Whittle family well and with Haydock just down the road there was a good chance Alex could go, especially as we had been invited to lunch.

It was unfortunate, but Alex had a bad day and didn't feel well enough to get out of bed, never mind spend three hours at Haydock, so I went on my own. It didn't go well. I lost every bet I placed, including my £20 each way on Safran de Cotte who looked quite handy for the first circuit but steadily fell back and was last of the finishers, providing some modest prize money for 6th place. 'Just not quick enough,' said Jake, perhaps stating the obvious but at least giving a frank assessment. Henry agreed. 'The handicapper should treat him kindly after that performance, so we can drop down in class and enjoy ourselves being the top weight in a 0–120 Handicap Chase.' Doesn't sound as if Safran will be going to Cheltenham this year.

The following day we sat in front of the fire at home watching racing from Fakenham. Six One Away, our least likely prospect, seemed to enjoy jumping the first circuit in the lead. He was still in contention with three to go when the only two other likely winners both fell leaving Six One

Away in front all on his own, almost. The only other horse in camera shot suddenly quickened just as we lost momentum and a certain win became runner up by 16 lengths. 'I was pleased with the jumping,' said Paul Webber, 'but perhaps he needs better ground.'

Our next meeting was going to be on 27 December with Royal Palladium hoping to make it four out of four at Chepstow but on Boxing Day Venetia decided that Haydock on 30 December was a better option with Super Sam running at the same meeting. Alex was still not keen to go out but persuaded me to organise a party. Lunch was booked for myself, three grandchildren, my son James, his father-in-law and Venetia. With 24 hours to go both our horses were quoted as clear favourites. That was before I went to Sainsbury's. I was just trying to work out which aisle was most likely to stock the maple syrup when I got an email. Haydock inspection – abandoned.

Super Sam had another option for New Year's Eve at Warwick and again was the favourite to win but that meeting was cancelled after an 8.00am inspection bringing our racing to an end for 2014.

Not a great year but with Royal Palladium showing real potential and three horses (The Artful Cobbler, The Venerable Bede and Rubber Sole) due to make their debuts in the spring we remain optimistic. Our main hope is that Alex will soon be feeling well enough to travel to Cheltenham.

When, in spring 2014, we agreed to concentrate on

Saturday horses, with the hope of running in big races for top prize money, we knew it would take time for our new policy to produce a string of winners. But we did expect that, during January and February, we would be drawing up careful plans to prepare most of our horses for their appearance at Cheltenham.

As it happened, we had other things on our minds. Alex spent the second week of January in hospital for three precautionary procedures to help prevent infection from the side effects of her cancer and the chemotherapy. It was going to be a close call for Alex to be fit enough to travel to Mustique on 23 January for a fortnight's holiday.

I broke off from a trip round some of our shops in North Wales to be at Bangor to watch Upbeat Cobbler run in a modest Novice Handicap Chase. I was hopeful after Simon who saddled her up said, 'She's been in great form at home. I've never seen any better jumping from a novice.' She misjudged two of the first four obstacles and unseated her jockey at the last fence of the first circuit.

Later in the week I slipped out of the office to Ladbrokes where I watched Pretty Mobile finish way down a mediocre field at Ludlow.

Our Saturday racing policy showed some sign of success on the day before Alex went back into hospital. Sixty Something was in the Classic Chase at Warwick – the big race of the day. We watched the build-up on Channel 4's *Morning Line* but although our horse got a mention no one tipped it to win.

We had two runners that Saturday. Arctic Ben was at Wetherby, ridden by A.P. McCoy (only his second ride in our colours, having fallen on Sixty Something a year earlier). Henry Daly had given A.P. strict instructions to go off at a good gallop, and that's what he did. His lead stretched to over 30 lengths before the field started closing the gap but they were never going to catch us. Arctic Ben won by 6 lengths and A.P. McCoy was so pleased he'd achieved his ultimate aim, a win for Alex Timpson, that he announced his retirement.

In the Classic Chase at Warwick, Sixty Something was in contention until the last bend before the leaders showed too much pace and we finished 4th (but won over £3,000 – much more than the £121 we could have won for coming 4th at most meetings on a Monday).

While Alex was in hospital I was in William Hill watching Royal Palladium at Ludlow trying to make it four wins out of four. He never looked fluent and fell with a few fences left to jump. I gave Ladbrokes the pleasure of my company when I watched another hugely disappointing attempt from Six One Away. He was pulled up at Plumpton after sharing the lead for a circuit and, like a 1,500m pacemaker, quickly dropped back through the field. Paul Webber is so perplexed and so certain the horse has ability, he is keeping Six One Away for free until he shows some proper form at the beginning of next season.

Alex was determined to get to Mustique and was back home from hospital with five days to go, just in time to watch Super Sam come a disappointing 3rd out of nine runners in a Class 3 Handicap Hurdle at Taunton, where 2nd place was taken by the cleverly named 'Italian Yob' owned by Mustique managing director Roger Pritchard and House Owner David Morgan. They are certain to mention the race when we arrive on the island.

Although we could have called at Warwick to see Safran de Cotte's race on our way down to Gatwick we watched it in a bookies outside Bicester. He came a poor 3rd.

When we were away Upbeat Cobbler was pulled up in a Novice Handicap Chase at Taunton. Just after our return from holiday our two Cheltenham entries both had a last chance to secure qualification. Royal Palladium came 4th out of five in a hot race on a cold Monday at Leicester and Sixty Something came 3rd out of seven over 4 gruelling miles at Catterick, when a win would have put Cheltenham beyond doubt.

While waiting for the Cheltenham declaration dates we had three more disappointing performances. Arctic Ben could not repeat the win at Wetherby. With a young apprentice on board instead of A.P. McCoy, Arctic Ben was not given the enormous lead he needs and finished 5th out of eight. Safran de Cotte came in for some stick from the Racing UK commentator who simply couldn't believe how our horse had become the bookies' favourite to win a Class 3 Handicap Chase at Exeter. He was right: although Safran was in contention for the first mile-and-a-half he then faded and was pulled up well before the finish. Five days later Upbeat Cobbler did exactly the same thing and we began to wonder whether Henry Daly's horses are suffering from a virus in the yard.

Despite our business plan, no new Cheltenham hopefuls have emerged during the season. Another Cobbler, after a poor bumper at Bangor before Christmas, is still waiting for better ground before making another appearance. We are told The Artful Cobbler looks promising at home but this potential is yet to be tested on a racecourse.

The Venerable Bede who 'looks every bit a racehorse' was two weeks away from his debut when he 'threw a splint' and sent me searching through Wikipedia for an explanation, which left me none the wiser. All I know is that the horse won't be going racing this season and I'm facing a few more vets' bills.

None of this bad news matched the disappointment concerning Rubber Sole who, after eighteen months of careful preparation, has spine problems and will 'never be right'. Like Manchester City, there might have to be a major change to our team during the close season.

With only two horses good enough for us to even think about entering them for Cheltenham, 2015 looked like another year without the Timpson colours appearing at The Festival. But we still paid the fee for Royal Palladium and Sixty Something to enter two of the less prestigious races, just in case enough of the better horses pulled out to pursue the bigger races or better prizes on offer elsewhere.

With four weeks to go things didn't look hopeful, but I still kept counting the number of entries with a higher rating. With a maximum of 24 runners in the Kim Muir Handicap I counted over 30 horses that had a higher handicap than Sixty Something, with Royal Palladium's entry for the National Hunt Chase 29 places away from a guaranteed start. No wonder I was pessimistic.

Unexpectedly, a padded envelope arrived in our post a week before The Festival with badges, tickets and all we needed for ourselves and two friends to watch Royal

Palladium run in the 4-mile Toby Balding National Hunt Chase on the first day of The Festival. I don't know how Venetia Williams secured the entry off a handicap of 122 but when I checked my iPad, Alex's horse was listed as one of 24 starters.

Two weeks earlier Alex had clearly stated that if we had an entry she would be watching the race on the television in the comfort of her own home. After five months of chemotherapy she felt that walking to the paddock and coping with the crowds would be too exhausting.

When the possibility of an entry turned to reality with the arrival of that envelope Alex changed her mind. She decided to go. We acquired a wheelchair, which, after two successful test attempts at assembly, I folded neatly and put in the boot of the car.

We got to the racecourse just as the first race finished and headed for a table in the Owners' and Trainers' marquee. This was not the usual owners' and trainers' scrum that takes place at most courses where owners have to share their privilege with lots of members, members' friends and others who think they deserve to be there. This marquee was only for those owners with runners on the day. At last I was able to enjoy the sort of hospitality owners deserve. There were plenty of tables and chairs and the food was so much better than I've been offered at any other course I had difficulty believing that this was racecourse catering and that the food was free. At last The Jockey Club has recognised that they won't have a sport without the owners, who deserve all the pampering possible.

My only problem was the disabled ramp. As a learner wheelchair driver I didn't see the raised metal fixing at the bottom of the slope. The chair got stuck, so I reversed a couple of yards and had a run at it, nearly tipping Alex out of the chair. We ignored all the helpful advice of fellow racegoers who suggested I should pull Alex backwards and, while holding up a queue of twenty tweed-clad owners and their friends, Alex got out of the chair, I lifted it over the obstacle, then Alex resumed her seat. By the end of the day, after negotiating several more similar obstacles, we perfected this procedure into a pretty slick manoeuvre.

After an excellent lunch that included crab and smoked salmon, I left Alex in the marquee, watching the racing on television, while I went to survey the disabled access and the wheelchair viewing areas. I did such a thorough job I joined the Tote queue too late to bet on the next race (I saved £20 by not backing two greys that finished well down the field).

As a trial run I wheeled Alex about 250 yards so she could watch the next race on a big screen by the paddock. Within a few strides I discovered how difficult it is to push a wheelchair through a throng of racegoers who are so keen on talking on their phone, looking at their BlackBerry or chatting to girls with enormous feathers in their hair, they don't look where they are going and certainly won't see a wheelchair.

The biggest bugbear are the stoppers and blockers. The stoppers suddenly stop moving to answer a phone call or consult their race card while the blockers stand in groups of three or four upsetting the pedestrian flow while they continue an irrelevant conversation that started over three pints of Guinness.

The crowd took so little notice of Alex in the wheelchair I started muttering to myself, 'Will they ever move!' 'Hello! We're here!' 'This is a nightmare.'

As we watched the race a couple of absent-minded men with check suits and bright ties didn't realise that they were blocking Alex's view of the big screen so we had to keep changing position.

I decided that for the big race, the Champion Hurdle, Alex would see the action from the wheelchair viewing area. It was a bold move. I had to push the wheelchair uphill. I thought everyone was going to totally ignore this 72-year-old man, sweat pouring down his face, struggling up a gradient that felt like 45 degrees. Halfway up the hill it suddenly got easier and I picked up speed. Just near the top I realised that a kind punter had taken pity on me and was doing most of the pushing.

The wheelchair area gave Alex a great view of Willie Mullins-trained favourite Faugheen fly past us up the finishing hill to win for jockey Ruby Walsh. I now had to get Alex back to the marquee for tea.

Guiding a wheelchair downhill brings a different set of challenges, especially at Cheltenham on a slope that veers to the right. It all happens so much quicker than the uphill trip. There seemed to be just as many people to whom the chair was invisible, but the biggest problem was still the stoppers and blockers. To avoid one group of celebrating Irishmen I steered to the right and, almost too late, realised that the camber was causing the chair to tilt and Alex looked likely to take a tumble. It was then that I realised why the chair is fitted with a safety belt.

Safely back in the upmarket Owners' and Trainers' marquee for tea, scones and eclairs, I placed a losing bet on the next race before going to the pre-parade ring to meet Venetia Williams and her team. Alex kept well clear in case the wheelchair scared the horses as much as it was scaring me, but it didn't stop her entering the parade ring with two fellow owners helping me to push the chair across the grass.

It was an amateurs' race with most horses ridden by jockeys who were unknown to both trainer and horse. Our rider Mr T. Hamilton looked about twelve years old but assured us he is nineteen. He had been around enough to make the right jockey type comments – 'I'll get him handy, pop over a few and see how we go.'

There was no way we were going to get the wheelchair across the paddock, up the hill and to the viewing area in time for the start, so we stayed in the middle of the paddock and watched the race on the big screen, which showed that Royal Palladium was bottom of the betting at 100/1.

At least our jockey was handy enough in the first mile to be mentioned by the course commentator, but he dropped towards the back halfway through the race, with 2 miles still to go. For the last mile the big screen wasn't big enough to show the stragglers and Royal Palladium didn't get another mention. We saw eight horses go past the winning post then the camera cut away to picture the joy of the winning jockey.

Five minutes after the race we discovered that Royal Palladium finished the course in 13th place but was not accompanied by the jockey who was unseated at the last fence.

With no horse to pat and no jockey to tell us how much better we would have done on softer ground, I pushed Alex and the wheelchair to the exit for the long drive back to Cheshire.

The following day we were faced with an important decision. Despite my pessimistic calculations it seemed likely that Sixty Something would make the cut to compete in the Kim Muir Chase on Festival Thursday. We had to decide whether to run in the Kim Muir or go for the more valuable and probably more competitive Midlands Grand National on Saturday. We bravely made our usual decision by telling Paul Webber 'It's up to you Paul', adding that Alex won't be going back to Cheltenham but could get to Uttoxeter, I wondered how easy it would be to push the wheelchair through the gravel in Uttoxeter's car park. Paul was decisive: 'We should go for the Kim Muir.' So having waited for years to get a runner at Cheltenham we have two in a week.

I scrubbed my plans to visit our shops on Humberside and substituted a route that took in Redditch, Bromsgrove, Worcester, Evesham and Tewkesbury. I was anticipating parking problems – our entry was secured so late in the day Cheltenham didn't have time to send the usual badges and tickets; I simply had an email to show to the parking attendant. I needn't have bothered. There was no one supervising the car parking – we must have hit their lunch hour.

I got into the racecourse at 2.00pm, just in time to lose £20 on the two slowest horses in the second race.

Following my experience on Tuesday, I had avoided the temptation of a Greggs sausage roll in Evesham and kept my appetite for a second bite of the Owners' and Trainers' buffet. More crab and smoked salmon washed down with a pint of Guinness.

While waiting for the Kim Muir at 4.40pm I lost a lot less money than on Tuesday. I didn't pick a winner but three minor places meant I will not have to return to a cash machine to fund the weekend.

It was so easy to move around compared with Tuesday; without the wheelchair people were less irritating but I was more conscious of being courteous to wheelchair users myself.

The Kim Muir is another amateur riders' race and once again our jockey Mr J.P. McKeown had yet to meet our horse, although our regular jockey, Jake Greenall, had given him a briefing on the telephone.

If everyone in the paddock before that race was an owner or trainer they must have been part of some enormous syndicate – by the time we arrived there was hardly any space for us to form the pre-race huddle; I would have been really struggling with a wheelchair.

Sixty Something's odds weren't shown on the big screen (we were included in the group of also-rans labelled 25/1 bar), though my hopes were raised when our jockey appeared and filled me full of confidence. He, inevitably, talked about being handy at the start but stressed the importance of being positive. I hoped that Sixty Something, for the first time running with blinkers, would approach the race with the same strength of mind and singleness of purpose, but it was difficult to tell what the horse was thinking as he walked round and round the paddock. Perhaps he was trying to work out what these blinkers were all about.

It must be a tense type of torture for the trainer to watch the race standing next to an owner who is only happy if the horse is at the front of the field. Conversation tends to be brief, and awkward questions are avoided by the trainer looking through his binoculars. On this occasion we were extremely quiet.

Sixty Something was more than handy – he was in the first three when the field passed the grandstand for the first time and a circuit later he was lying second. There were a couple of worrying jumps that caused Paul to raise his binoculars but with four fences to go our horse took a 4-length lead and was going away from the field.

I said nothing, but thought a lot. We were in the lead at the Cheltenham Festival, looking better with every stride and heading for the final bend. It was a magic moment. I thought about Alex watching at home and Paul standing beside me, both of whom were due for a big slice of good fortune. Alex got enormous pleasure from having two of her horses running at The Festival, we had a leg in Pressgang that came 2nd in the bumper six years ago but to have a winner in the Alex Timpson colours would be fantastic. I felt a tension similar to the times when Manchester City is one goal up with five minutes to go. I was willing the finishing post to come as quickly as possible. There could only be about 30 seconds between now and Alex's dream of a Cheltenham Festival winner.

Sixty Something looked amazing, going away from the field with every stride approaching the next fence. He flew into the jump and fell on landing, there was a groan from the small part of the crowd that had backed a 25/1 outsider, then the race carried on. But our day came to a full stop and it looked like getting worse.

'I can't see them,' said Paul, raising his binoculars with serious concern. 'And,' he continued, 'they are putting the screens up. I fear the worst, John.' I can't think of a time when my emotions changed so quickly.

The race had finished and the racegoers had already

forgotten the horse that fell when racing for home. They knew the result of the race but we didn't.

Paul set off in search of both horse and jockey, but found neither. Sixty Something suddenly appeared in front of the grandstand walking fairly normally but with his hind legs covered in blood. The vets loaded him into a horse ambulance just as our jockey reappeared a bit shaken and with the prospect of a splitting headache the following morning. 'He went fantastic,' he said. 'I hardly moved and there was still a load left in the tank.'

I had some veterinary bulletins from Paul during the drive home – nothing broken but Sixty Something is extremely sore.

When I got home I watched the replay on Racing UK. I was hoping that I had been dreaming and we had won the race after all. But Racing UK saw what I saw. Sixty Something was well in the lead going away from the field when he fell three from home.

Perhaps Alex will get her first Festival winner next year.

SEASON 2014–2015

HORSE	DATE	COURSE	RACE	DISTANCE	PRIZE MONEY	JOCKEY	RATING	POSITION	RUNNERS
Arctic Ben	31-Oct-14	Uttoxeter	Hand. Chase	2m 4f	3K	Jake Greenall	115	2	10
	12-Dec-14	Doncaster	Hand. Chase	2m 3f	3K	Jake Greenall	119	F	7
	10-Jan-15	Wetherby	Hand. Chase	2m 4½f	3K	A.P. McCoy	119	1	8
	13-Feb-15	Fakenham	Hand. Chase	2m 5f	7K	Mr James Jeavons	125	5	8
	24-Apr-15	Chepstow	Hand. Chase	2m 3½f	6K	Tom O'Brien	125	4	5
Safran de Cotte	15-Nov-14	Cheltenham	Hand. Chase	3m 3½f	28K	Andrew Tinkler	121	PU	14
	20-Dec-14	Haydock	Hand. Chase	3m	18K	Jake Greenall	121	6	8
	22-Jan-15	Warwick	Hand. Chase	3m 2f	4K	Richard Johnson	114	3	8
	3-Mar-15	Exeter	Hand. Chase	3m 6½f	11K	Jake Greenall	112	PU	13
Sixty Something	21-Oct-14	Exeter	Hand. Chase	3m	7K	Jake Greenall	129	F	10
	22-Nov-14	Haydock	Hand. Chase	3m 5f	16K	Jake Greenall	129	UR	8
	12-Dec-14	Doncaster	Hand. Chase	3m 2f	6K	Jake Greenall	129	1	5
	10-Jan-15	Warwick	Hand. Chase Grade 3	3m 5f	34K	Jake Greenall	132	4	14
	9-Feb-15	Catterick	Hand. Chase	3m 1f	7K	Jake Greenall	132	3	7
	12-Mar-15	Cheltenham	Hand. Chase	3m 2f	35K	Mr J.P. McKeown	131	F	24

(continued)

HORSE	DATE	COURSE	RACE	DISTANCE	PRIZE MONEY	JOCKEY	RATING	POSITION	RUNNERS
Upbeat Cobbler	23-Oct-14	Southwell	Nov. Hand. Chase	3m	3K	Tom O'Brien	101	2	7
	7-Dec-14	Huntingdon	Nov. Hand. Chase	2m 7½f	4K	Tom O'Brien	99	5	9
	6-Jan-15	Bangor-on-Dee	Nov. Hand. Chase	3m	4K	Tom O'Brien	97	UR	7
	5-Feb-15	Taunton	Nov. Hand. Chase	3m 2½f	4K	Tom O'Brien	97	PU	12
	8-Mar-15	Market Rasen	Hand. Hurdle	2m 7f	3K	Andrew Tinkler	101	REF	5
	21-Oct-14	Exeter	Hand. Hurdle	2m 2½f	3K	Aidan Coleman	104	7	12
	11-Nov-14	Lincoln	Nov. Hand. Chase	2m 4f	4K	Aidan Coleman	100	1	4
	24-Nov-14	Ludlow	Nov. Hand. Chase	3m	6K	Liam Treadwell	105	1	8
Royal Palladium	4-Dec-14	Market Rasen	Nov. Hand. Chase	3m	7K	Aidan Coleman	112	1	6
	15-Jan-15	Ludlow	Hand. Chase	3m	9K	Mr W. Biddick	124	F	7
	12-Feb-15	Leicester	Nov. Hand. Chase	2m 6½f	6K	Aidan Coleman	124	4	5
	10-Mar-15	Cheltenham	Nov. Chase	4m	50K	Mr T. Hamilton	122	UR	17
	23-Oct-14	Southwell	Hand. Hurdle	1m 7½f	3K	Charlie Poste	95	PU	14
Six One Away	3-Dec-14	Ludlow	Nov. Hand. Chase	2m 4f	5K	Jake Greenall	90	4	9
	21-Dec-14	Fakenham	Nov. Hand. Chase	2m ½f	3K	Jake Greenall	87	2	5
	12-Jan-15	Plumpton	Hand. Chase	2m 1f	2K	Jake Greenall	87	PU	6

(continued)

HORSE	DATE	COURSE	RACE	DISTANCE	PRIZE MONEY	JOCKEY	RATING	POSITION	RUNNERS
Pretty Mobile	3-Oct-14	Wolverhampton	Nat. Hunt Flat	2m ½f	1K	Denis O'Regan	–	PU	8
	2-Nov-14	Huntingdon	3 YO Hurdle	1m 7½f	3K	Jake Greenall	–	6	11
	7-Jan-15	Ludlow	Maiden Hurdle	2m	2K	Jake Greenall	–	10	14
	2-Apr-15	Ludlow	Nov. Hurdle	2m 5½f	4K	Jake Greenall	–	4	5
	5-Nov-14	Chepstow	Maiden Hurdle	2m 3½f	1K	Aidan Coleman	–	1	11
Super Sam	29-Nov-14	Bangor-on-Dee	Nov. Hurdle	2m 3½f	3K	Liam Treadwell	–	3	5
	17-Jan-15	Taunton	Hand. Hurdle	3m	6K	Callum Whillans	111	3	9
Another Cobbler	29-Nov-14	Bangor-on-Dee	Nat. Hunt Flat	2m ½f	2K	Jake Greenall	–	5	6
	12-Apr-15	Market Rasen	Maiden Nat. Hunt Flat	2m ½f	2K	Jake Greenall	–	9	12
The Artful Cobbler	9-May-15	Warwick	Nat. Hunt Flat	2m	1K	Tom O'Brien	–	10	16

2014–2015

	RUNS	1ST	2ND	3RD	4TH
Arctic Ben	5	1	1	0	1
Safran de Cotte	4	0	0	1	0
Sixty Something	6	1	0	1	1
Upbeat Cobbler	5	0	1	0	0
Royal Palladium	7	3	0	0	1
Six One Away	4	0	1	0	1
Pretty Mobile	4	0	0	0	1
Super Sam	3	1	0	2	0
Another Cobbler	2	0	0	0	0
The Artful Cobbler	1	0	0	0	0
Total	41	6	3	4	5

	TRAIN-ING FEES	ENTRY FEE/ JOCKEY	TOTAL COST	WINNINGS + SPONSOR-SHIP	NET COST
2014–2015					
Safran de Cotte	18,304	1,835	20,139	3,885	16,254
Arctic Ben	19,514	1,225	20,739	7,260	13,479
Timpo	2,847	–	2,847	1,500	1,347
Sixty Something	19,924	3,175	23,099	10,900	12,199
Upbeat Cobbler	18,348	1,075	19,423	4,385	15,038
Miss Tique	924	–	924	500	424
Royal Palladium	20,302	1,275	21,577	17,150	4,427
Pretty Mobile	17,180	1,625	18,805	3,385	15,420
Rubber Sole	12,752	–	12,752	3,000	9,752
Six One Away	12,752	1,095	13,847	4,100	9,747
Super Sam	18,390	1,255	19,645	5,530	14,115
Another Cobbler	17,822	485	18,307	3,100	15,207
The Artful Cobbler	15,559	228	15,784	3,000	12,784
The Venerable Bede	12,287	–	12,287	3,000	9,287
					£149,480
Cobbler's Queen	2,436				£2,436
Cobbler's Son	5,781				£5,781
					£157,697

2015–2016

ALEX'S LAST SEASON

It was May last year when Alex first became ill and since then she has spent a lot of time in hospital, both as an out-patient for chemotherapy and in several spells as an inpatient following some nasty infections caused by the tumour. Consequently I've spent more time at home (perhaps I am finally getting near retirement) and among the cooking and caring I started writing this book.

Not much happens during the summer. We haven't had any horses at a racecourse and we didn't go to the Doncaster Sales, but Venetia Williams contacted me with a plausible proposition: a handy grey horse that had already shown some form in France was available at less than £30,000 – and would be ready to run over hurdles within months of purchase. I wasn't tempted until Venetia told me that the name, Un Prophete, when put into a search engine was translated as 'In Profit'. That settled it: at last I had found a horse that promised to make money.

We certainly haven't made anything out of Rubber Sole, a horse we bought two years ago. Paul Webber has had the difficult job of keeping us up to date with a catalogue of injuries that started with 'He seems to have tweaked a muscle so it will be another three weeks before we can make an entry'. After the three weeks became three months Paul said, 'We will have to wait until next season. Hopefully a restful summer is just what he needs.' But another visit to the vet revealed a severe back problem that ruled him out of racing for ever. Rubber Sole now lives in the fields behind our house, having never appeared on a racetrack.

Our chances of success in this new campaign were dented before the season even started when Venetia Willliams reported that Super Sam has a nasty tendon problem and will be taking a year off. Our first runner was Six One Away, who, despite a reduction in handicap from 106 to 82, has failed to win a race (his 2nd at Fakenham last season was in a five-horse race where only three finished). This was his last chance and he fluffed it, coming 5th out of eight runners in a poor race at Sedgefield. He has followed Rubber Sole in the horse box to the fields behind our house.

Pretty Mobile, another horse that has a lot to prove, having failed to get in the first three in four outings, did herself no favours when we watched her on television being pulled up at Worcester. Both jockey and trainer took a positive view of the performance which was hampered by breathing problems. She is having a wind operation before getting back into training. I can't see any of the wins we need coming from Pretty Mobile, but will be happy if the experts prove me wrong.

Our season has started with one retirement, a wind operation, a tendon that needs to take a year out, a modest novice finishing 12th, plenty of training fees and no prize money. I wasn't optimistic when our next runner Upbeat Cobbler ran at Ludlow, after failing to finish her last three races last season. Alex was hoping to go to the meeting but

I was pleased she decided to stay at home. I was in Newbury visiting some of our shops and watched the race in Coral. It was so foggy it was difficult to make out the horses on the in-store screen. The spectators at Ludlow could only see the horses jump two fences. When the field disappeared on the second circuit Upbeat Cobbler was lying 5th; when we saw them again she was in the lead. We recorded our first win of the season.

Another Cobbler who has had a restful summer following two mediocre bumper performances last season came up to expectations when finishing his first hurdle race 12th in a field of sixteen. But, I'm told, 'you never know with a young horse' … 'they all have to start somewhere' … 'she's still got a lot of growing to do' … 'she'll come on leaps and bounds for the experience' … and, 'pity that such a green horse found herself in a hot race'.

Another Cobbler is one of many novice hurdlers that are really running to get a handicap. That doesn't mean we aren't trying – we would love to win, but the rules require three qualifying races before the handicapper can match you on equal terms with the other runners. Novice horses face the same challenge as new golfers, who have to mark three cards before the committee will allocate a handicap. But, although competitors with a generous handicap can win the occasional competition, poorer players will never win the club championship. Owners like their horses to win but we all want to win the Cheltenham Gold Cup.

Venetia Williams knows we are keen to run in big Saturday races and she followed our wishes when she entered Royal Palladium into a Listed Race, the Badger Chase at Wincanton, with a first prize of over £34,000.

We didn't even get a mention on Channel 4's *Morning Line* and started at 20/1. But we were in the lead over the last fence and heading for Alex's biggest ever win when Royal Palladium was caught with less than a furlong to go and lost by half a length.

But it wasn't a bad week. I did the sums and with winnings of over £16,000 I'm pretty sure we made a profit.

By the time we got to Bangor to watch The Artful Cobbler run in a novice hurdle, there were no disabled spaces left in the Owners' and Trainers' car park, but we had a bit of luck. The guy on the gate, who we discovered has a wheelchair-bound daughter, took sympathy and moved some of the tape that was reserving a prime spot for the imminent arrival of the Princess Royal and her party. It gave me only a short distance to push Alex to the Owners' and Trainers' entrance and across to the bar for our free lunch. Fortunately there was enough hard ground to use inside the paddock so I didn't have to push the wheelchair over the grass. Alex was able to give Jake Greenall her usual advice about not using the whip and wished him a safe ride. To Alex, the welfare of both horse and jockey was far more important than winning, which on this occasion wasn't even in my mind having seen the odds of 100/1. As expected, The Artful Cobbler failed to get in the frame but 6th out of nine runners was good enough for Jake to say that he wasn't disappointed and that 'he will be all the better for the run'.

Before leaving Bangor I had a chat with Jake's father Peter (Lord Daresbury) who was himself an amateur jockey and has more recently had the courage to be involved in racecourse management committees. Whenever he attends a race meeting Peter must run the risk of being berated by belligerent owners with their own personal axe to grind so he was clearly pleased to hear my praise for the hospitality owners received during The Festival at Cheltenham, where Peter chairs the catering committee.

Ten days later we took the wheelchair to Haydock where Royal Palladium was performing on the day of the Betfair Chase. We were following the feature race so arrived in time for a late lunch. The Owners' and Trainers' car park was full of press and Betfair bigwigs and there wasn't a single disabled parking space left. I had to drop Alex off in her wheelchair just by the entrance while I abandoned the car in a muddy field. Fortunately one of the first people I met in the Owners' and Trainers' restaurant was Peter Daresbury who includes Chairman of Haydock among his racing responsibilities. I hope I didn't ruin Peter's day but it was the perfect opportunity to press the case on behalf of disabled access. You don't realise what is entailed until you become a wheelchair pusher.

It was a bitterly cold day and Alex was wrapped in a thick rug and her Manchester City scarf as we saw Royal Palladium finish a disappointing 5th ('we were not helped by the handicapper who took too much notice of our performance in the Badger Chase at Wincanton'). It was time to leave, so I somehow pushed the wheelchair through the mud and we went home wondering when our luck was going to change.

Royal Palladium's new stable mate Un Prophete made his first appearance in Alex's colours the following Monday at Ludlow and failed to impress, coming 10th in a field of fourteen. 'It was a useful run,' said Venetia. 'He's still a bit of a baby and will have come on a lot for the run.'

December was filled with disappointment. With Alex paying frequent visits to the Christie Hospital there was no chance of getting to a racecourse so we watched a succession of failures on the television. Pretty Mobile was 10th out of thirteen in a Novice Hurdle at Leicester then The Artful Cobbler went all the way to Exeter to finish a respectable 8th out of seventeen runners. Upbeat Cobbler came next to last at Huntingdon and Royal Palladium simply didn't like the heavy ground in a 3-mile chase at Ffos Las and was pulled up.

By the time we reached Christmas Alex was becoming more tired as the daily dose of strong antibiotics fought the infections in her liver but on Boxing Day she came down-stairs to watch two of her horses perform at Huntingdon. Upbeat Cobbler didn't repeat the early season form she had shown at Ludlow, finishing 5th in a field of ten. Further down the card Safran de Cotte, reverting to hurdles in an attempt to rebuild confidence, struggled to keep up with the pace, despite the benefit of a career handicap low of 105. He was the last horse to finish by a distance.

When Alex came downstairs on 30 December to watch Another Cobbler in a Novice Chase on very heavy ground at Haydock, the odds of 100/1 managed our expectations so we were encouraged when he finished 7th out of ten runners.

In the last seven weeks we have had ten runners and none of them has picked up any prize money. This is by far the worst performance in the thirteen years since Alex got Transatlantic, her first racehorse, in 2002. I now know that this spectacularly unsuccessful sequence also marked the end of Alex's racing career. On New Year's Eve we went back to the Christie Hospital, where our consultant Prof Juan Valle very gently told us that Alex had suffered enough prodding, poking and procedures and that from now on we should simply concentrate on treatment to relieve pain.

Alex never saw The Artful Cobbler win our first prize money in eight weeks when he came a creditable 4th in a Novice Chase at Huntingdon at 100/1. An upbeat Henry Daly rang me from the course and I had to tell him that Alex had died the day before. Ten days later a piece appeared in the *Racing Post* …

DALY PAYS TRIBUTE TO 'REMARKABLE' OWNER

Henry Daly yesterday paid tribute to owner Alex Timpson, who died aged 69 this month, saying it had been an honour to have known her.

Timpson, whose husband John owns the Timpson chain of shoe repair and key-cutting shops, had horses in training with Daly, as well as Venetia Williams and Paul Webber.

She had more than 40 winners, having had her interest in ownership sparked by taking a share in Pressgang, who found only Hairy Molly a head too good in the 2006 Champion Bumper at Cheltenham.

Arguably her finest hour as an owner came when she provided the one-two in a handicap hurdle at Huntingdon in January 2010 courtesy of Cobbler's Queen and Key Cutter, and her colours were carried to second by the Williams-trained Royal Palladium in the Badger Ales Trophy at Wincanton in November.

Outside of racing, Timpson provided foster care for 90 children, adopted two and had three of her own, including Edward Timpson, now the MP for Crewe and Nantwich and minister for children and families.

Before Timpson's memorial service yesterday, Daly said: 'I consider it an honour to have known her. She really was a truly remarkable person and what she did in providing foster care to so many children was unbelievable.'

Venetia Williams, Paul Webber and Henry Daly were among the 1,000 or so people who attended Alex's Thanksgiving Service. The congregation was drawn from all parts of Alex's varied and colourful life, but there was a common theme: Alex was always a giver not a taker; she got most of her pleasure through helping other people. The majority of those present had first-hand experience of her generosity.

For the last thirteen years Alex put part of her personality into the racing world and it was my privilege to provide the financial support needed to fund her favourite hobby. Originally the title of this book was going to be *How to Lose Money*, and doing the required research has indeed confirmed that racing isn't cheap. I might have lost money but, thanks to Alex's enthusiasm and interest in other people, I have learnt a lot about the racing scene and made lots of new friends along the way.

Lots of racing connections will miss Alex and I will miss her most of all. But I'm the really lucky one, I have spent two-thirds of my 73 years with Alex and am therefore the person who benefitted most from her love of life. When we got married I could never have guessed that it would involve 90 foster children and 20 racehorses. Life with Alex was never dull.

CONCLUSIONS

Writing this book has brought back some of the happiest memories of my life with Alex and has finally made me face the financial facts of funding a racehorse owner. I always knew it was going to be an expensive game but didn't realise just how much money we were almost certain to lose.

At the end of this chapter I reveal the sombre statistics that chart thirteen years of an uninterrupted drain on my cash. We have lost money every season and no horse has got anywhere near making a profit. The figures would look even worse if we weren't able to reclaim the VAT and didn't benefit from some modest sponsorship.

Despite the lessons, we have learnt from experience our losses have increased over the years. We reckoned if we had more horses we would win more races. This theory has worked out in practice but we missed the obvious fact that the more horses you own the more money you lose.

We will never be able to compete with the top owners who pay the biggest prices at the Doncaster Sales, but I take comfort in the fact that if they have twenty times as many horses as us they will probably be losing twenty times the money. Although the top owners pay the biggest prices at auction we have no proof that the more expensive horses are certain to jump better or run quicker.

Our highest-rated horse is Sixty Something who reached a high mark of 135; our most successful is Safran de Cotte with seven wins and racecourse earnings of over £45,000; and I still have special admiration for Ordre de Bataille who was our first winner.

I pushed the boat out when we bought Arctic Ben, a horse that is rated in our top five performers but has yet to find enough form to qualify for the Cheltenham Festival. Our next most expensive purchase, Sole Survivor, had a disappointing career that was cut short due to injury. He has now recorded his first win as a team chaser and is costing me much less money.

Despite losing me more money than most, Alex's favourite was Thievery, an honest trier with a rating that seldom rose above 90. Thievery still lives at Downton Stables enjoying regular hacks and occasional days out hunting.

I lost least money on The Crafty Cobbler who, sadly, died of a heart attack on the gallops after I had paid for a few months' training. Next cheapest was King of Keys who broke a leg and had to be put down after only 300 yards in his first and only race. Rubber Sole is our most unproductive purchase – after nearly two years' training he was diagnosed with severe back problems and was retired without ever seeing a racecourse.

In preparing the statistics for this book I was intrigued by the items that appeared on my training bills. Regular extras were 'wormer', 'attention to teeth', 'farrier', 'clipping', 'chiropractor' and of course 'vets' fees', which included

£1,569.37 for treating a fetlock injury and £3,335.56 for dealing with Miss Tique's colic.

We paid £3,000 for the services of Big Sam Bellamy when his successful meeting with Cobbler's Queen led to Cobbler's Son. Something that can't be matched by Transatlantic, whose castration cost me £220.32.

It costs less than £20 to transport a horse from Henry Daly's yard to run down the road at Ludlow, but a trip to Carlisle cost £451 and Newcastle was a whopping £600.60. The £335.80 I paid for Key Cutter to be taken on 'Horse box to home' produced an excellent financial return. The trip took him to a new life in the fields behind our house where the keep fees are considerably cheaper.

Most trips to the racecourse cost about £600 after you have paid the entry fee, the jockey, a contribution to the Professional Riders' Insurance Scheme, stable expenses and the cost of the horse box, but it can be much more. Key Cutter had a particularly expensive trip to Kempton, which included 'transport to vet', 'X-rays' and 'vet' which put the total cost up to £1,426.

I have produced a lot of statistics that show that owning a racehorse inevitably costs you money, but a pessimistic friend, who is an accountant, pointed out that I don't list the initial cost of investment. As I told him, you will enjoy racing much more if you forget what you paid for the horse.

I count myself lucky having the money to 'invest' in racing. It could have been worse. Alex might have wanted to fund a football club, go grouse shooting, have a big yacht or back a Formula One racing team.

Business criteria don't apply to racing. At times we are able to find acquisitions that give a two-year return on our investment. In racing you can expect the investment in a horse to be matched by what you lose over the next two years.

My advice to any new owner who wants to enjoy the sport is to go in with your eyes wide open and keep them closed when you open the bills.

By keeping the costs well and truly in the back of my mind I have thoroughly enjoyed the experience. Alex loved the whole racing scene and, secretly, so do I. Without experiencing all the ups and downs, meeting lots of racing characters and doing loads of people watching at lots of different racecourses I would never have been able to write this book.

We have had plenty of good days, our 44 winners could be said to have cost us about £40,000 each but it is silly to regard racing as simply a financial exercise.

We not only have the memories of past successes; I still have the hope of that big win at Cheltenham or glory in the Grand National.

The whole experience has been enhanced by the support of our trainers, Henry, Paul and Venetia, who have all become good friends and shared the emotion of each success and disappointment. If any of my comments in the book appear critical of their training fees or the way trainers have to manage our expectations, let me make it quite clear that we have been very happy customers. Their presence is an asset to the world of racing.

Most of all I enjoyed watching Alex gaining more knowledge with each successive season. When she was a young girl Alex often went to Haydock as the guest of her uncle John Hughes who was the Clerk of the Course. He lit a spark of interest in the sport that was flickering for over 40 years before Alex achieved her ambition of being a racehorse owner. I might have lost a lot of money but I have no doubt that it was worth it. I would recommend the experience to anyone – as long as they are prepared to spend plenty of money with little or no prospect of any return on their investment.

It is perhaps fitting that Alex's last race day was at Haydock, one of the courses that kindled her interest in racing as a teenager. To be honest, it wasn't our greatest day: no spaces in the disabled car park, cold driving rain, Alex wrapped up in a thick rug with me pushing the wheelchair across rough, muddy turf to watch Royal Palladium finishing a pretty poor fifth. But Alex was determined to be there. She showed brave determination in her fight against cancer but, looking back, I think she knew it might be her last chance to hear the jockey reporting why we might be better tackling a shorter distance on better ground on more of a galloping track.

That could also have been the end of my involvement in racing, but I still had three trainers, ten horses and a foal to think about. The foal made me think most of all. With Cobbler's Son due to run next season there was no way I was going to give up – Alex would never have let me – so I continue to be under orders as the husband of a racehorse owner who got an enormous amount of pleasure from the sport she loved.

STATISTICS

The figures that follow reveal almost all you need to know about our racing experience. They show that we have been reasonably lucky. Some owners never get a winner, we have had over 40, a strike rate of once in every eight outings. The 2012/2013 season was probably our best, with nearly half the runners coming in the first three and over a fifth recording a win. Statistically our best horses are Safran de Cotte and Sixty Something.

I am told that if a punter put a pound on the nose of every one of Alex's runners they would be sitting on a modest profit, but as the owner, Alex did somewhat worse, proving that if you want to make a small fortune start with a bigger one and buy a few racehorses.

EARLY SEASONS
2002–2008

SEASON 2002–2003

HORSE	DATE	COURSE	RACE	DISTANCE	PRIZE MONEY	JOCKEY	RATING	POSITION	RUNNERS
	27-Feb-03	Ludlow	Nov. Hurdle	2m	4K	Richard Johnson	–	15	18
	16-Mar-03	Ludlow	Maiden Hurdle	2m	3K	Warren Marston	–	14	17
Transatlantic	23-Mar-03	Huntingdon	Maiden Hurdle	2m	3K	R. Forristal	–	10	17
	21-Apr-03	Hereford	Nov. Hurdle	2m	3K	R. Forristal	81	PU	9

RUNS	1ST	2ND	3RD	4TH
4	0	0	0	0

SEASON 2003–2004

HORSE	DATE	COURSE	RACE	DISTANCE	PRIZE MONEY	JOCKEY	RATING	POSITION	RUNNERS
	7-Jun-03	Worcester	Maiden Hurdle	2m 4f	3K	Mark Bradburne	78	6	10
Transatlantic	4-Dec-03	Leicester	Hand. Hurdle	2m	3K	Mark Bradburne	80	2	12
	17-Dec-03	Bangor-on-Dee	Hand. Hurdle	2m ½f	2K	Josh Byrne	83	PU	12

RUNS	1ST	2ND	3RD	4TH
3	0	1	0	0

SEASON 2004–2005

HORSE	DATE	COURSE	RACE	DISTANCE	PRIZE MONEY	JOCKEY	RATING	POSITION	RUNNERS
Transatlantic	14-Mar-05	Taunton	Nov. Hand. Hurdle	2m ½f	4K	John McNamara	80	6	13
Thievery	24-Feb-05	Haydock	Nat. Hunt Flat	2m	1K	Josh Byrne	–	2	10
	30-Apr-05	Uttoxeter	Nat. Hunt Flat	2m	2K	Josh Byrne	–	14	16

	RUNS	1ST	2ND	3RD	4TH
Transatlantic	1	0	0	0	0
Thievery	2	0	1	0	0
Total	3	0	1	0	0

SEASON 2005–2006

HORSE	DATE	COURSE	RACE	DISTANCE	PRIZE MONEY	JOCKEY	RATING	POSITION	RUNNERS
Transatlantic	8-Jun-05	Hereford	Nov. Hand. Hurdle	2m 1f	3K	Richard Johnson	80	8	11
	17-Jun-05	Stratford	Nov. Hand. Hurdle	2m 2½f	4K	Richard Johnson	80	7	14
	17-Nov-05	Market Rasen	Nov. Hurdle	2m 3½f	3K	Mark Bradburne	–	F	16
Thievery	3-Dec-05	Haydock	Nov. Hurdle	2m 4f	5K	Andrew Thornton	–	9	14
	16-Dec-05	Uttoxeter	Nov. Hurdle	2m 4f	3K	Mark Bradburne	–	7	14
	3-Mar-06	Newbury	Nov. Hand. Hurdle	2m 3f	3K	C.D. Thompson	89	12	16
Ordre de Bataille	9-Mar-06	Towcester	Nat. Hunt Flat	2m	2K	Mark Bradburne	–	2	11
	15-Apr-06	Haydock	Nat. Hunt Flat	2m	1K	Mark Bradburne	–	12	20

	RUNS	1ST	2ND	3RD	4TH
Transatlantic	2	0	0	0	0
Thievery	4	0	0	0	0
Ordre de Bataille	2	0	1	0	0
Total	8	0	1	0	0

SEASON 2006–2007

HORSE	DATE	COURSE	RACE	DISTANCE	PRIZE MONEY	JOCKEY	RATING	POSITION	RUNNERS
Thievery	5-Nov-06	Hereford	Hand. Hurdle	3m 2f	2K	Sam Thomas	85	PU	10
	22-Nov-06	Chepstow	Hand. Chase	2m 3½f	4K	Mark Bradburne	85	5	8
	22-Dec-06	Hereford	Hand. Chase	2m 3f	3K	Richard Johnson	80	11	17
	11-Jan-07	Hereford	Hand. Chase	2m	2K	Richard Johnson	77	PU	9
	1-Feb-07	Towcester	Hand. Chase	2m ½f	2K	Richard Johnson	72	6	8
	26-Feb-07	Hereford	Hand. Chase	2m	2K	Richard Johnson	69	2	10
	31-Mar-07	Uttoxeter	Hand. Chase	2m	3K	Mark Bradburne	71	5	8
Ordre de Bataille	26-Oct-06	Stratford	Nov. Hurdle	2m ½f	6K	Mark Bradburne	–	2	12
	15-Nov-06	Warwick	Nov. Hurdle	2m 5f	3K	Mark Bradburne	–	1	18
	30-Dec-06	Haydock	Nov. Hurdle	2m 4f	4K	Mark Bradburne	–	6	10
	3-Feb-07	Sandown	Nov. Hand. Hurdle	2m 4f	5K	Richard Johnson	110	10	17
	22-Mar-07	Ludlow	Hand. Hurdle	2m 5f	4K	Mark Bradburne	108	1	17
	18-Apr-07	Cheltenham	Nov. Hand. Hurdle	3m	8K	Mark Bradburne	116	9	14
Timpo	3-Mar-07	Newbury	Nat. Hunt Flat	2m ½f	34K	Mark Bradburne	–	6	21

	RUNS	1ST	2ND	3RD	4TH
Thievery	7	0	1	0	0
Ordre de Bataille	6	2	1	0	0
Timpo	1	0	0	0	0
Total	14	2	2	0	0

Statistics

SEASON 2007–2008

HORSE	DATE	COURSE	RACE	DISTANCE	PRIZE MONEY	JOCKEY	RATING	POSITION	RUNNERS
Thievery	22-Nov-07	Hereford	Nov. Hand. Chase	2m	2K	Mark Bradburne	69	1	14
	26-Dec-07	Huntingdon	Hand. Chase	2m ½f	3K	Paul Callaghan	84	3	12
	14-Feb-08	Chepstow	Hand. Chase	2m	2K	Richard Johnson	78	3	11
	6-Mar-08	Lingfield	Hand. Chase	2m	2K	Mark Bradburne	78	2	9
	18-Apr-08	Taunton	Hand. Chase	2m	2K	Andrew Tinkler	79	4	8
Ordre de Bataille	2-Nov-07	Uttoxeter	Chase	3m	4K	Richard Johnson	–	3	10
	29-Dec-07	Bangor-on-Dee	Chase	2m 4½f	4K	Mark Bradburne	116	3	10
Timpo	21-Nov-07	Warwick	Nov. Hurdle	2m 5f	3K	Mark Bradburne	–	1	15
	5-Jan-08	Wincanton	Nov. Hurdle	2m 5½f	2K	Andrew Tinkler	111	4	11
	29-Feb-08	Newbury	Nov. Hurdle	2m 4½f	3K	Mark Bradburne	112	1	18
Cobbler's Queen	8-Mar-08	Sandown	Nat. Hunt Flat	2m	14K	Richard Johnson	–	7	19
	4-Apr-08	Aintree	Nat. Hunt Flat	2m 1f	19K	Mark Bradburne	100	13	20

	RUNS	1ST	2ND	3RD	4TH
Thievery	5	1	1	2	1
Ordre de Bataille	2	0	0	2	0
Timpo	3	2	0	0	1
Cobbler's Queen	2	0	0	0	0
Total	12	3	1	4	2

	TRAINING FEES	RACE FEES	TOTAL	WINNINGS	COST
2002–2003					
Transatlantic	7,284	525	7,809	1,600	6,209
2003–2004					
Transatlantic	8,762	445	9,207	1,735	7,472
2004–2005					
Transatlantic	11,328	165	11,493	1,000	10,493
Thievery	12,218	355	12,573	1,490	11,083
					£21,576
2005–2006					
Transatlantic	3,796	165	3,961	1,225	2,736
Thievery	15,139	970	16,109	1,000	15,109
Ordre de Bataille	13,927	215	14,142	1,000	13,142
					£30,987
2006–2007					
Thievery	15,610	1,058	16,668	2,558	14,110
Ordre de Bataille	16,240	1,570	17,810	9,285	8,525
Timpo	5,818	727	6,545	1,975	4,570
					£27,205
2007–2008					
Thievery	17,446	1,045	18,491	5,415	13,076
Ordre de Bataille	14,682	758	15,440	2,715	12,725
Timpo	16,340	942	17,282	4,035	13,247
Cobbler's Queen	14,131	694	14,825	1,500	13,325
Key Cutter	9,990	–	9,990	1,500	8,490
Llama Farmer	227	–	227	100	127
					£60,990

TOTAL TO DATE

	HORSES	RUNS	WINS	2ND	3RD	4TH	TOTAL COSTS (AFTER WINNINGS)
2002–2003	1	4	0	0	0	0	6,209
2003–2004	1	3	0	1	0	0	7,472
2004–2005	2	4	0	1	0	0	21,576
2005–2006	3	7	0	1	0	0	30,987
2006–2007	3	14	2	2	0	0	27,205
2007–2008	6	12	3	1	4	2	60,990
		44	5	6	4	2	£154,439

RECORDS BY HORSE

HORSE	DATE	COURSE	RACE	DISTANCE	PRIZE MONEY	JOCKEY	RATING	POSITION	RUNNERS
	27-Feb-03	Ludlow	Nov. Hurdle	2m	4K	Richard Johnson	–	15	18
	16-Mar-03	Ludlow	Maiden Hurdle	2m	3K	Warren Marston	–	14	17
	23-Mar-03	Huntingdon	Maiden Hurdle	2m	3K	R. Forristal	–	10	17
	21-Apr-03	Hereford	Nov. Hurdle	2m	3K	R. Forristal	81	PU	9
	7-Jun-03	Worcester	Maiden Hurdle	2m 4f	3K	Mark Bradburne	78	6	10
Transatlantic									
	4-Dec-03	Leicester	Hand. Hurdle	2m	3K	Mark Bradburne	80	2	12
	17-Dec-03	Bangor-on-Dee	Hand. Hurdle	2m ½f	2K	Josh Byrne	83	PU	12
	14-Mar-05	Taunton	Nov. Hand. Hurdle	2m ½f	4K	John McNamara	80	6	13
	8-Jun-05	Hereford	Nov. Hand. Hurdle	2m 1f	3K	Richard Johnson	80	8	11
	17-Jun-05	Stratford	Nov. Hand. Hurdle	2m 2½f	4K	Richard Johnson	80	7	14

RUNS	1ST	2ND	3RD	4TH
10	0	1	0	0

HORSE	DATE	COURSE	RACE	DISTANCE	PRIZE MONEY	JOCKEY	RATING	POSITION	RUNNERS
	24-Feb-05	Haydock	Nat. Hunt Flat	2m	1K	Josh Byrne	–	2	10
	30-Apr-05	Uttoxeter	Nat. Hunt Flat	2m	2K	Josh Byrne	–	14	16
	17-Nov-05	Market Rasen	Nov. Hurdle	2m 3½f	3K	Mark Bradburne	–	F	16
	3-Dec-05	Haydock	Nov. Hurdle	2m 4f	5K	Andrew Thornton	–	9	14
	16-Dec-05	Uttoxeter	Nov. Hurdle	2m 4f	3K	Mark Bradburne	–	7	14
	3-Mar-06	Newbury	Nov. Hand. Hurdle	2m 3f	3K	C.D. Thompson	89	12	16
Thievery	5-Nov-06	Hereford	Hand. Hurdle	3m 2f	2K	Sam Thomas	85	PU	10
	22-Nov-06	Chepstow	Hand. Chase	2m 3½f	4K	Mark Bradburne	85	5	8
	22-Dec-06	Hereford	Hand. Chase	2m 3f	3K	Richard Johnson	80	11	17
	11-Jan-07	Hereford	Hand. Chase	2m	2K	Richard Johnson	77	PU	9
	1-Feb-07	Towcester	Hand. Chase	2m ½f	2K	Richard Johnson	72	6	8
	26-Feb-07	Hereford	Hand. Chase	2m	2K	Richard Johnson	69	2	10
	31-Mar-07	Uttoxeter	Hand. Chase	2m	3K	Mark Bradburne	71	5	8
	22-Nov-07	Hereford	Nov. Hand. Chase	2m	2K	Mark Bradburne	69	1	14

(continued)

HORSE	DATE	COURSE	RACE	DISTANCE	PRIZE MONEY	JOCKEY	RATING	POSITION	RUNNERS
	26-Dec-07	Huntingdon	Hand. Chase	2m ½f	3K	Paul Callaghan	84	3	12
	14-Feb-08	Chepstow	Hand. Chase	2m	2K	Richard Johnson	78	3	11
	6-Mar-08	Lingfield	Hand. Chase	2m	2K	Mark Bradburne	78	2	9
	18-Apr-08	Taunton	Hand. Chase	2m	2K	Andrew Tinkler	79	4	8
Thievery	3-Nov-08	Warwick	Hand. Chase	2m	3K	Andrew Tinkler	79	1	11
	9-Nov-08	Hereford	Hand. Chase	2m	6K	Richard Johnson	85	1	8
	26-Dec-08	Huntingdon	Hand. Chase	2m ½f	3K	Mark Bradburne	91	4	12
	18-Jan-09	Towcester	Hand. Chase	2m ½f	3K	Richard Johnson	91	2	11
	5-Mar-09	Carlisle	Hand. Chase	2m	3K	Andrew Tinkler	94	8	12
	21-Apr-09	Towcester	Hand. Chase	2m ½f	5K	Richard Johnson	94	6	9
	22-Oct-09	Ludlow	Hand. Chase	2m	5K	Richard Johnson	92	2	9
	14-Feb-10	Hereford	Hand. Chase	2m	1K	Richard Johnson	92	8	14
	12-Mar-10	Wincanton	Hand. Chase	1m 7½f	3K	Richard Johnson	92	5	6
	28-Apr-10	Southwell	Hand. Chase	1m 7½f	2K	Richard Johnson	89	UR	7

(continued)

Statistics

HORSE	DATE	COURSE	RACE	DISTANCE	PRIZE MONEY	JOCKEY	RATING	POSITION	RUNNERS
Thievery	21-Oct-10	Ludlow	Hand. Chase	2m	3K	Richard Johnson	85	6	8
	11-Nov-10	Taunton	Hand. Chase	2m	2K	Andrew Tinkler	78	UR	10
	21-Nov-10	Towcester	Hand. Chase	2m ½f	1K	Michael Murphy	78	F	6
	13-Jan-11	Hereford	Hand. Hurdle	2m 1f	1K	Richard Johnson	78	4	9
	12-Mar-11	Chepstow	Hand. Hurdle	2m	2K	Jake Greenall	77	5	9
	28-Apr-11	Hereford	Hand. Hurdle	2m ½f	1K	Andrew Tinkler	73	5	12

RUNS	1ST	2ND	3RD	4TH
34	3	5	2	3

HORSE	DATE	COURSE	RACE	DISTANCE	PRIZE MONEY	JOCKEY	RATING	POSITION	RUNNERS
	9-Mar-06	Towcester	Nat. Hunt Flat	2m	2K	Mark Bradburne	–	2	11
	15-Apr-06	Haydock	Nat. Hunt Flat	2m	1K	Mark Bradburne	–	12	20
	26-Oct-06	Stratford	Nov. Hurdle	2m ½f	6K	Mark Bradburne	–	2	12
	15-Nov-06	Warwick	Nov. Hurdle	2m 5f	3K	Mark Bradburne	–	1	18
	30-Dec-06	Haydock	Nov. Hurdle	2m 4f	4K	Mark Bradburne	–	6	10
	3-Feb-07	Sandown	Nov. Hand. Hurdle	2m 4f	5K	Richard Johnson	110	10	17
Ordre de Bataille	22-Mar-07	Ludlow	Hand. Hurdle	2m 5f	4K	Mark Bradburne	108	1	17
	18-Apr-07	Cheltenham	Nov. Hand. Hurdle	3m	8K	Mark Bradburne	116	9	14
	2-Nov-07	Uttoxeter	Chase	3m	4K	Richard Johnson	–	3	10
	29-Dec-07	Bangor-on-Dee	Chase	2m 4½f	4K	Mark Bradburne	116	3	10
	24-Nov-08	Ludlow	Chase	2m 4f	5K	Richard Johnson	115	3	8
	26-Dec-08	Huntingdon	Nov. Chase	2m 4f	3K	Mark Bradburne	115	1	10
	27-Feb-09	Newbury	Nov. Hand. Chase	2m 6½f	6K	Christian Williams	121	4	9
	21-Mar-09	Bangor-on-Dee	Hand. Chase	2m 4½f	9K	Andrew Tinkler	121	1	9

(continued)

HORSE	DATE	COURSE	RACE	DISTANCE	PRIZE MONEY	JOCKEY	RATING	POSITION	RUNNERS
	16-Apr-09	Cheltenham	Nov. Hand. Chase	2m 5f	6K	Andrew Tinkler	126	4	9
	24-Oct-09	Stratford	Hand. Chase	2m 5f	11K	Andrew Tinkler	126	3	6
	23-Nov-09	Ludlow	Hand. Chase	2m 4f	7K	Andrew Tinkler	125	3	7
	12-Dec-09	Doncaster	Hand. Chase	2m 3f	13K	Mark Bradburne	123	5	15
Ordre de Bataille	27-Jan-10	Huntingdon	Hand. Chase	2m 7½f	5K	Richard Johnson	122	PU	10
	14-Mar-10	Towcester	Hand. Hurdle	2m	6K	Mr W. Biddick	117	13	15
	23-Oct-10	Stratford	Hand. Chase	2m 5f	7K	Timmy Murphy	122	PU	8
	11-Nov-10	Ludlow	Hand. Chase	3m	6K	Richard Johnson	113	PU	9
	28-Dec-10	Ffos Las	Hand. Chase	2m 5f	6K	Andrew Tinkler	107	PU	12
	9-Nov-11	Bangor-on-Dee	Hand. Chase	2m 4½f	3K	Andrew Tinkler	102	PU	7

RUNS	1ST	2ND	3RD	4TH
24	4	2	5	2

HORSE	DATE	COURSE	RACE	DISTANCE	PRIZE MONEY	JOCKEY	RATING	POSITION	RUNNERS
	3-Mar-07	Newbury	Nat. Hunt Flat	2m ½f	34K	Mark Bradburne	–	6	21
	21-Nov-07	Warwick	Nov. Hurdle	2m 5f	3K	Mark Bradburne	–	1	15
	5-Jan-08	Wincanton	Nov. Hurdle	2m 5½f	2K	Andrew Tinkler	111	4	11
	29-Feb-08	Newbury	Nov. Hurdle	2m 4½f	3K	Mark Bradburne	112	1	18
	18-Oct-08	Cheltenham	Hand. Hurdle	2m 5f	12K	Richard Johnson	114	11	16
	16-Nov-08	Cheltenham	Hand. Hurdle	2m 5f	15K	Mark Bradburne	113	11	19
	20-Dec-08	Haydock	Hand. Hurdle	2m 4½f	16K	Michael McAvoy	128	9	12
	26-Feb-09	Ludlow	Hand. Hurdle	3m	4K	Michael McAvoy	110	6	9
Timpo	25-Mar-09	Towcester	Nov. Chase	2m 4f	5K	Andrew Tinkler	105	3	7
	5-May-09	Exeter	Hand. Chase	2m 1½f	3K	Richard Johnson	105	9	11
	29-Apr-10	Hereford	Hand. Hurdle	2m 4f	2K	Richard Johnson	105	7	8
	6-Jun-10	Worcester	Hand. Hurdle	3m	2K	Richard Johnson	100	3	11
	6-Oct-10	Ludlow	Hand. Hurdle	2m 5½f	3K	Richard Johnson	100	6	17

(continued)

320

HORSE	DATE	COURSE	RACE	DISTANCE	PRIZE MONEY	JOCKEY	RATING	POSITION	RUNNERS
	29-Oct-10	Wetherby	Hand. Chase	3m 1f	2K	Andrew Tinkler	98	2	10
	22-Nov-10	Ludlow	Nov. Hand. Chase	3m	3K	Andrew Tinkler	96	2	9
	26-Jan-11	Huntingdon	Nov. Hand. Chase	2m 7½f	2K	Richard Johnson	98	2	6
	23-Feb-11	Ludlow	Hand. Chase	3m	3K	Jake Greenall	98	2	12
	23-Mar-11	Warwick	Hand. Chase	3m 5f	3K	Jake Greenall	98	PU	6
	20-Oct-11	Ludlow	Hand. Chase	3m	3K	Mr L R Payter	98	6	9
	2-Nov-11	Warwick	Hand. Chase	3m 2f	2K	Jake Greenall	96	2	5
	20-Nov-11	Towcester	Hand. Chase	3m ½f	2K	Andrew Tinkler	96	1	7
	26-Feb-12	Towcester	Nov. Hand. Chase	2m 5½f	2K	Andrew Tinkler	101	PU	11
Timpo	14-Apr-12	Chepstow	Hand. Chase	2m 7½f	2K	Jake Greenall	100	6	12
	20-Feb-13	Ludlow	Hand. Chase	3m	4K	Jake Greenall	97	F	13
	8-Mar-13	Leicester	Hand. Chase	2m 6½f	4K	Andrew Tinkler	97	3	10
	26-Apr-13	Chepstow	Hand. Chase	3m 2f	2K	Richard Johnson	95	2	8
	24-May-13	Towcester	Hand. Chase	3m ½f	2K	Richard Johnson	95	2	12

(continued)

HORSE	DATE	COURSE	RACE	DISTANCE	PRIZE MONEY	JOCKEY	RATING	POSITION	RUNNERS
Timpo	6-Nov-13	Warwick	Hand. Chase	3m 2f	3K	Jake Greenall	98	5	9
	15-Dec-13	Southwell	Hand. Chase	3m 1½f	2K	Jake Greenall	94	3	8
	13-Apr-14	Stratford	Hand. Chase	3m 3½f	3K	Tom O'Brien	91	PU	11

RUNS	1ST	2ND	3RD	4TH
30	3	7	4	1

HORSE	DATE	COURSE	RACE	DISTANCE	PRIZE MONEY	JOCKEY	RATING	POSITION	RUNNERS
	8-Mar-08	Sandown	Nat. Hunt Flat	2m	14K	Richard Johnson	–	7	19
	4-Apr-08	Aintree	Nat. Hunt Flat	2m 1f	19K	Mark Bradburne	100	13	20
	26-Oct-08	Towcester	Nov. Hurdle	2m	3K	Andrew Tinkler	–	8	15
	23-Nov-08	Towcester	Nov. Hurdle	2m 5f	3K	Andrew Tinkler	–	5	13
	11-Dec-08	Huntingdon	Nov. Hurdle	2m 3½f	5K	Dominic Elsworth	–	13	14
	28-Feb-09	Doncaster	Nov. Hand. Hurdle	2m ½f	3K	Andrew Tinkler	83	2	16
Cobbler's Queen	25-Mar-09	Towcester	Hand. Hurdle	2m 3f	3K	Jack Doyle	85	9	17
	6-May-09	Huntingdon	Hand. Hurdle	2m 4½f	3K	Richard Johnson	84	1	10
	30-Oct-09	Uttoxeter	Hand. Hurdle	2m 5½f	4K	Andrew Tinkler	92	4	15
	16-Nov-09	Leicester	Nov. Hand. Hurdle	2m 4½f	4K	Richard Johnson	92	1	12
	27-Jan-10	Huntingdon	Hand. Hurdle	2m 4½f	2K	Richard Johnson	99	1	13
	14-Feb-10	Hereford	Nov. Hurdle	2m 4f	3K	Mr W. Biddick	110	3	13
	27-Mar-10	Newbury	Nov. Hand. Hurdle	2m 4½f	22K	Richard Johnson	120	10	18
	5-Nov-10	Fontwell	Chase	2m 3f	3K	Richard Johnson	–	2	6

(continued)

UNDER ORDERS

HORSE	DATE	COURSE	RACE	DISTANCE	PRIZE MONEY	JOCKEY	RATING	POSITION	RUNNERS
Cobbler's Queen	16-Dec-10	Exeter	Nov. Chase	2m 3f	4K	Richard Johnson	118	5	7
	27-Jan-11	Ffos Las	Nov. Chase	3m	3K	Richard Johnson	113	2	4
	8-Mar-11	Exeter	Nov. Chase	3m	3K	Andrew Tinkler	111	3	12
	26-Mar-11	Newbury	Nov. Hand. Chase	2m 6½f	17K	Andrew Tinkler	115	UR	9
	30-Apr-11	Uttoxeter	Nov. Hand. Chase	3m	2K	Andrew Tinkler	110	1	5

RUNS	1ST	2ND	3RD	4TH
19	4	3	2	1

HORSE	DATE	COURSE	RACE	DISTANCE	PRIZE MONEY	JOCKEY	RATING	POSITION	RUNNERS
	18-Oct-08	Cheltenham	Nat. Hunt Flat	2m ½f	3K	Dominic Elsworth	–	11	17
	15-Nov-08	Uttoxeter	Hurdle	2m	6K	Will Kennedy	–	6	8
	20-Dec-08	Haydock	Nov. Hurdle	2m 4f	4K	Mark Bradburne	–	12	14
	28-Mar-09	Uttoxeter	Maiden Hurdle	2m 4f	2K	Mark Bradburne	–	1	12
	20-Apr-09	Kempton	Nov. Hand. Hurdle	2m 5f	4K	Mark Bradburne	108	8	18
	14-Nov-09	Uttoxeter	Hand. Hurdle	2m 4f	5K	Will Kennedy	108	6	9
	10-Dec-09	Huntingdon	Hand. Chase	2m 4½f	3K	Will Kennedy	105	2	16
Key Cutter	27-Jan-10	Huntingdon	Hand. Chase	2m 4½f	2K	Will Kennedy	110	2	13
	3-Mar-10	Bangor-on-Dee	Hand. Chase	2m 7f	6K	Will Kennedy	113	6	7
	25-Mar-10	Ludlow	Hand. Chase	2m 5½f	5K	Will Kennedy	113	2	13
	25-Apr-10	Ludlow	Hand. Chase	2m 5½f	6K	Will Kennedy	118	7	13
	6-Oct-10	Ludlow	Chase	2m 4f	3K	Will Kennedy	118	2	8
	11-Nov-10	Ludlow	Hand. Chase	3m	6K	Will Kennedy	118	2	9
	22-Nov-10	Kempton	Chase	3m	3k	Will Kennedy	119	1	5
	15-Dec-10	Newbury	Nov. Hand. Chase	2m 7½f	5K	Will Kennedy	122	12	16

(continued)

HORSE	DATE	COURSE	RACE	DISTANCE	PRIZE MONEY	JOCKEY	RATING	POSITION	RUNNERS
	25-Apr-11	Huntingdon	Hand. Chase	2m 7½f	4K	Dominic Elsworth	119	3	6
	12-May-11	Ludlow	Hand. Chase	3m 1½f	6K	Will Kennedy	118	7	11
	16-Oct-11	Kempton	Hand. Chase	3m	3K	Will Kennedy	115	2	7
	7-Dec-11	Leicester	Hand. Chase	2m 6½f	3K	Dominic Elsworth	115	1	5
	13-Jan-12	Musselburgh	Hand. Chase	2m 7f	6K	Dominic Elsworth	125	7	10
Key Cutter	17-Apr-12	Exeter	Hand. Chase	3m 6½f	6K	Dominic Elsworth	123	UR	9
	17-May-12	Ludlow	Hand. Chase	3m 1½f	6K	Dominic Elsworth	121	7	15
	25-Oct-12	Ludlow	Hand. Chase	3m	3K	Dominic Elsworth	117	PU	12
	2-Dec-12	Leicester	Hand. Chase	2m 6½f	3K	Denis O'Regan	115	2	6
	9-May-13	Wincanton	Hand. Chase	3m 1f	6K	Liam Treadwell	115	2	4
	26-May-13	Uttoxeter	Hand. Chase	3m	3K	Jake Greenall	113	PU	10

RUNS	1ST	2ND	3RD	4TH
26	3	8	1	0

HORSE	DATE	COURSE	RACE	DISTANCE	PRIZE MONEY	JOCKEY	RATING	POSITION	RUNNERS
	31-Oct-08	Uttoxeter	Maiden Hurdle	2m	2K	Mark Bradburne	–	5	16
	24-Nov-08	Ludlow	Nov. Hurdle	2m 5½f	5K	Mark Bradburne	–	8	9
	12-Jan-09	Fakenham	Maiden Hurdle	2m 4f	2K	Richard Johnson	–	5	13
	14-Mar-09	Uttoxeter	Nov. Hand. Hurdle	2m	6K	Richard Johnson	107	2	10
	11-Apr-09	Haydock	Hand. Hurdle	2m ½f	8K	Andrew Tinkler	112	7	10
	22-Oct-09	Ludlow	Hand. Hurdle	2m	4K	Richard Johnson	111	3	9
Arctic Ben	12-Feb-10	Kempton	Hand. Hurdle	2m	2K	Mr W. Biddick	112	4	16
	6-Mar-10	Newbury	Nov. Hand. Hurdle	2m ½f	6K	Mark Bradburne	112	3	11
	21-Apr-10	Southwell	Nov. Hurdle	1m 7½f	3K	Mr W. Biddick	115	4	8
	31-Oct-10	Huntingdon	Hand. Chase	2m ½f	6K	Richard Johnson	113	7	9
	25-Nov-10	Taunton	Nov. Chase	2m	4K	Andrew Tinkler	113	2	3
	27-Jan-11	Ffos Las	Nov. Hand. Chase	2m 5f	3K	Richard Johnson	113	4	6
	5-Mar-11	Kempton	Nov. Hand. Chase	2m	3K	Andrew Thornton	111	F	5
	3-Nov-11	Towcester	Maiden Chase	2m ½f	1K	Richard Johnson	111	3	5

(continued)

HORSE	DATE	COURSE	RACE	DISTANCE	PRIZE MONEY	JOCKEY	RATING	POSITION	RUNNERS
	25-Nov-11	Newbury	Nov. Hand. Chase	2m 2½f	7K	Richard Johnson	108	4	8
	14-Dec-11	Bangor-on-Dee	Hand. Chase	2m 4½f	2K	Jake Greenall	105	4	11
	31-Dec-11	Uttoxeter	Hand. Chase	2m	3K	Andrew Thornton	103	1	6
	26-Jan-12	Warwick	Hand. Chase	2m 4½f	4K	Richard Johnson	108	1	8
	25-Feb-12	Chepstow	Hand. Chase	2m	15K	Andrew Tinkler	118	3	9
	21-Mar-12	Haydock	Nov. Hand. Chase	2m	3K	Andrew Tinkler	118	1	3
	19-Apr-12	Cheltenham	Nov. Hand. Chase	2m 5f	6K	Andrew Tinkler	125	2	6
Arctic Ben	16-Nov-12	Cheltenham	Hand. Chase	2m	28K	Richard Johnson	125	11	14
	8-Dec-12	Chepstow	Hand. Chase	2m 3½f	7K	Andrew Tinkler	125	6	10
	27-Dec-12	Haydock	Hand. Chase	2m	9K	Jake Greenall	122	5	8
	11-Feb-13	Catterick	Hand. Chase	2m 3f	7K	Jake Greenall	119	4	9
	1-Mar-13	Newbury	Hand. Chase	2m 4f	3K	Jake Greenall	119	1	8
	5-Apr-13	Aintree	Hand. Chase Grade 3	2m 5f	67K	Jake Greenall	126	14	29
	31-Oct-13	Strattford	Hand. Chase	2m 3½f	6K	Jake Greenall	125	5	9
	29-Nov-13	Doncaster	Hand. Chase	2m 3f	6K	Nick Scholfield	124	8	11

(continued)

Statistics

HORSE	DATE	COURSE	RACE	DISTANCE	PRIZE MONEY	JOCKEY	RATING	POSITION	RUNNERS
	21-Dec-13	Haydock	Hand. Chase	2m	9K	Jake Greenall	122	4	6
	31-Jan-14	Catterick	Hand. Chase	2m 3f	7K	Richard Johnson	120	6	7
	22-Mar-14	Bangor-on-Dee	Hand. Chase	2m 4½f	3K	Jake Greenall	117	2	4
	23-Apr-14	Southwell	Hand. Chase	2m 4½f	3K	Jake Greenall	117	3	8
Arctic Ben									
	31-Oct-14	Uttoxeter	Hand. Chase	2m 4f	3K	Jake Greenall	115	2	10
	12-Dec-14	Doncaster	Hand. Chase	2m 3f	3K	Jake Greenall	119	F	7
	10-Jan-15	Wetherby	Hand. Chase	2m 4½f	3K	A.P. McCoy	119	1	8
	13-Feb-15	Fakenham	Hand. Chase	2m 5f	7K	Mr James Jeavons	125	5	8
	24-Apr-15	Chepstow	Hand. Chase	2m 3½f	6K	Tom O'Brien	125	4	5

RUNS	1ST	2ND	3RD	4TH
38	5	5	5	8

329

HORSE	DATE	COURSE	RACE	DISTANCE	PRIZE MONEY	JOCKEY	RATING	POSITION	RUNNERS
	26-Apr-09	Ludlow	Nat. Hunt Flat	2m	2K	Will Kennedy	–	7	13
	23-Nov-09	Ludlow	Nov. Hurdle	2m 5½f	4K	Andrew Tinkler	–	PU	9
	23-Jan-10	Haydock	Nov. Hurdle	2m 1f	3K	Andrew Tinkler	–	1	6
	20-Feb-10	Haydock	Nov. Hurdle Grade 2	3m 1f	17K	Andrew Tinkler	–	5	7
	3-Apr-10	Haydock	Nov. Hand. Hurdle	2m 4½f	11K	Andrew Tinkler	125	PU	13
Llama Farmer	26-Nov-10	Newbury	Nov. Hand. Chase	2m 2½f	7K	Dominic Elsworth	123	6	10
	29-Dec-10	Newbury	Nov. Hand. Chase	2m 6½f	5K	Dominic Elsworth	120	PU	15
	11-Jan-11	Leicester	Nov. Hand. Chase	2m	2K	Dominic Elsworth	115	7	9
	8-May-11	Uttoxeter	Hand. Chase	3m 2f	3K	Dominic Elsworth	110	4	6
	16-Nov-11	Warwick	Nov. Hand. Chase	2m 4½f	3K	Denis O'Regan	105	6	11
	8-Mar-13	Leicester	Hand. Chase	2m 6½f	4K	Liam Treadwell	100	PU	10

RUNS	1ST	2ND	3RD	4TH
11	1	0	0	1

HORSE	DATE	COURSE	RACE	DISTANCE	PRIZE MONEY	JOCKEY	RATING	POSITION	RUNNERS
	9-Feb-10	Market Rasen	Nat. Hunt Flat	2m ½f	1K	Jake Greenall	–	1	11
	3-Apr-10	Haydock	Nat. Hunt Flat	2m ½f	1K	Mr W. Biddick	–	1	5
	10-Nov-10	Bangor-on-Dee	Nov. Hurdle	2m ½f	3K	Richard Johnson	–	1	12
	1-Jan-11	Cheltenham	Nov. Hurdle	2m 4½f	6K	Richard Johnson	–	10	15
	15-Jan-11	Warwick	Nov. Hurdle Grade 2	2m 5f	14K	Leighton Aspell	–	3	8
	2-Feb-11	Leicester	Nov. Hurdle	2m 4½f	3K	Richard Johnson	120	6	12
Safran de Cotte									
	5-Nov-11	Sandown	Hand. Hurdle	2m	5K	Andrew Tinkler	120	4	12
	3-Dec-11	Sandown	Hand. Hurdle	2m 6f	9K	Richard Johnson	120	3	19
	17-Dec-11	Haydock	Hand. Hurdle	2m 4f	12K	Jake Greenall	119	1	13
	14-Jan-12	Warwick	Hand. Hurdle	3m 1f	10K	Andrew Tinkler	127	11	16
	18-Feb-12	Haydock	Hand. Hurdle	3m	11K	Andrew Tinkler	127	6	19
	19-Apr-12	Cheltenham	Hand. Hurdle	3m	7K	Richard Johnson	125	7	9
	1-Nov-12	Stratford	Chase	2m 6½f	5K	Richard Johnson	122	1	11
	23-Nov-12	Haydock	Nov. Chase	2m 6f	16K	Andrew Tinkler	128	3	6

(continued)

HORSE	DATE	COURSE	RACE	DISTANCE	PRIZE MONEY	JOCKEY	RATING	POSITION	RUNNERS
	29-Dec-12	Doncaster	Hand. Chase	3m	8K	Andrew Tinkler	126	4	11
	30-Jan-13	Leicester	Nov. Chase	2m 6½f	3K	Jake Greenall	124	1	6
	23-Feb-13	Chepstow	Nov. Chase	2m 7½f	3K	Jake Greenall	125	1	7
	20-Mar-13	Haydock	Hand. Chase	2m 4f	12K	Jake Greenall	130	PU	7
	1-Dec-13	Carlisle	Hand. Chase	3m 2f	8K	Jake Greenall	130	3	7
Safran de Cotte	21-Dec-13	Haydock	Hand. Chase	3m ½f	21K	Jake Greenall	129	PU	12
	11-Jan-14	Warwick	Hand. Chase Grade 3	3m 5f	34K	Jake Greenall	126	6	15
	22-Feb-14	Newcastle	Hand. Chase	4m ½f	37K	Jake Greenall	122	4	16
	15-Nov-14	Cheltenham	Hand. Chase	3m 3½f	28K	Andrew Tinkler	121	PU	14
	20-Dec-14	Haydock	Hand. Chase	3m	18K	Jake Greenall	121	6	8
	22-Jan-15	Warwick	Hand. Chase	3m 2f	4K	Richard Johnson	114	3	8
	3-Mar-15	Exeter	Hand. Chase	3m 6½f	11K	Jake Greenall	112	PU	13

RUNS	1ST	2ND	3RD	4TH
26	7	0	5	3

Statistics

HORSE	DATE	COURSE	RACE	DISTANCE	PRIZE MONEY	JOCKEY	RATING	POSITION	RUNNERS
	1-Dec-11	Leicester	3 YO Hurdle	2m	2K	Aidan Coleman	–	5	11
	4-Jan-12	Huntingdon	4 YO Hurdle	1m 7½f	2K	Aidan Coleman	–	6	15
	24-Feb-12	Warwick	4 YO Hurdle	2m	2K	Sam Thomas	–	2	12
	22-Mar-12	Chepstow	Nov. Hurdle	2m	2K	Aidan Coleman	108	1	13
Miss Tique									
	24-Jan-14	Huntingdon	Hand. Hurdle	2m 4½f	3K	Aidan Coleman	119	6	7
	19-Feb-14	Ludlow	Hand. Hurdle	2m	9K	Aidan Coleman	117	7	7
	10-Mar-14	Plumpton	Hand. Hurdle	2m 1½f	6K	Aidan Coleman	110	F	7
	10-Apr-14	Towcester	Nov. Hand. Chase	2m 4f	3K	Robert Dunne	105	8	12

RUNS	1ST	2ND	3RD	4TH
8	1	1	0	0

HORSE	DATE	COURSE	RACE	DISTANCE	PRIZE MONEY	JOCKEY	RATING	POSITION	RUNNERS
	1-Jan-11	Cheltenham	Nat. Hunt Flat	1m 6f	8K	Dominic Elsworth	–	15	16
	2-Mar-11	Bangor-on-Dee	Maiden Nat. Hunt Flat	2m ½f	1K	Jake Greenall	–	2	7
	23-Mar-11	Haydock	Nat. Hunt Flat	2m	1K	Dominic Elsworth	–	9	10
Sole Survivor	16-Nov-11	Warwick	Nov. Hurdle	2m	2K	Dominic Elsworth	–	1	15
	3-Dec-11	Sandown	Nov. Hurdle	2m	3K	Dominic Elsworth	–	11	12
	28-Dec-11	Leicester	Nov. Hurdle	2m 4½f	2K	Dominic Elsworth	–	12	15
	30-Dec-13	Haydock	Hand. Hurdle	2m 4f	3K	Jake Greenall	100	5	7
	24-Jan-14	Doncaster	Nov. Hand. Chase	2m 3f	2K	Denis O'Regan	100	PU	12

RUNS	1ST	2ND	3RD	4TH
8	1	1	0	0

HORSE	DATE	COURSE	RACE	DISTANCE	PRIZE MONEY	JOCKEY	RATING	POSITION	RUNNERS
	16-Nov-11	Warwick	Nov. Hurdle	2m 5f	2K	Denis O'Regan	–	9	17
	17-Dec-11	Haydock	Nov. Hurdle	2m 4f	4K	Sam Jones	–	6	9
	11-Jan-12	Doncaster	Nov. Hurdle	2m 3½f	2K	Dominic Elsworth	–	2	14
	31-Mar-12	Uttoxeter	Maiden Hurdle	2m 4f	2K	Dominic Elsworth	113	F	10
	18-Apr-12	Cheltenham	Nov. Hand. Hurdle	3m	6K	Dominic Elsworth	120	PU	17
	27-Oct-12	Aintree	Nov. Hand. Hurdle	3m ½f	3K	Dominic Elsworth	115	1	12
Sixty Something	23-Nov-12	Haydock	Nov. Hurdle	2m 4f	4K	Denis O'Regan	124	5	7
	14-Dec-12	Bangor-on-Dee	Hand. Hurdle	2m 7f	4K	Dominic Elsworth	124	1	8
	29-Dec-12	Doncaster	Hand. Hurdle	3m ½f	11K	Dominic Elsworth	129	5	8
	16-Feb-13	Haydock	Hand. Hurdle	3m	12K	Denis O'Regan	128	4	9
	10-Mar-13	Market Rasen	Hand. Hurdle	2m 7f	7K	Dominic Elsworth	127	1	9
	4-Apr-13	Aintree	Hand. Hurdle Grade 3	3m ½f	28K	Denis O'Regan	135	6	21
	2-Nov-13	Wetherby	Nov. Chase	3m 1f	4K	A.P. McCoy	135	F	6
	23-Nov-13	Haydock	Hand. Hurdle Grade 3	3m	45K	Jake Greenall	135	13	17
	10-Dec-13	Uttoxeter	Nov. Chase	3m	5K	Jake Greenall	132	2	8

(continued)

335

HORSE	DATE	COURSE	RACE	DISTANCE	PRIZE MONEY	JOCKEY	RATING	POSITION	RUNNERS
	27-Dec-13	Leicester	Nov. Chase	2m 6½f	6K	Jake Greenall	132	3	4
	15-Feb-14	Haydock	Nov. Hand. Chase	2m 5½f	8K	Jake Greenall	132	2	6
	22-Mar-14	Bangor-on-Dee	Nov. Chase	3m	3K	Jake Greenall	129	1	7
	17-Apr-14	Cheltenham	Nov. Hand. Chase	3m 1f	6K	Jake Greenall	129	2	10
Sixty Something	21-Oct-14	Exeter	Hand. Chase	3m	7K	Jake Greenall	129	F	10
	22-Nov-14	Haydock	Hand. Chase	3m 5f	16K	Jake Greenall	129	UR	8
	12-Dec-14	Doncaster	Hand. Chase	3m 2f	6K	Jake Greenall	129	1	5
	10-Jan-15	Warwick	Hand. Chase Grade 3	3m 5f	34K	Jake Greenall	132	4	14
	9-Feb-15	Catterick	Hand. Chase	3m 1f	7K	Jake Greenall	132	3	7
	12-Mar-15	Cheltenham	Hand. Chase	3m 2f	35K	Mr J.P. McKeown	131	F	24

RUNS	1ST	2ND	3RD	4TH
25	5	4	2	2

HORSE	DATE	COURSE	RACE	DISTANCE	PRIZE MONEY	JOCKEY	RATING	POSITION	RUNNERS
	6-Jan-12	Bangor-on-Dee	Nat. Hunt Flat	2m ½f	1K	Andrew Tinkler	–	4	7
	2-Mar-12	Newbury	Nat. Hunt Flat	2m ½f	1K	Andrew Tinkler	–	8	14
	8-Nov-12	Towcester	Maiden Hurdle	2m	1K	Jake Greenall	–	F	14
	31-Jan-13	Towcester	Maiden Hurdle	2m 3f	1K	Andrew Tinkler	–	3	13
	21-Feb-13	Huntingdon	Nov. Hurdle	2m 4½f	3K	Richard Johnson	–	3	13
	20-Mar-13	Warwick	Hand. Hurdle	2m 5f	3K	Paddy Brennan	98	2	4
	23-Apr-13	Ffos Las	Hand. Hurdle	2m 6f	3K	Richard Johnson	98	1	4
	1-Nov-13	Uttoxeter	Hand. Hurdle	3m	3K	Tom O'Brien	101	1	7
	23-Nov-13	Ascot	Hand. Hurdle	2m 5½f	5K	Richard Johnson	107	7	10
	30-Dec-13	Haydock	Hand. Hurdle	3m	3K	Jake Greenall	107	7	9
	27-Feb-14	Ludlow	Hand. Hurdle	3m	5K	Richard Johnson	105	6	10
Upbeat Cobbler	10-Apr-14	Towcester	Nov. Hand. Chase	2m 4f	3K	Jake Greenall	103	5	12
	23-Oct-14	Southwell	Nov. Hand. Chase	3m	3K	Tom O'Brien	101	2	7
	7-Dec-14	Huntingdon	Nov. Hand. Chase	2m 7½f	4K	Tom O'Brien	99	5	9

(continued)

HORSE	DATE	COURSE	RACE	DISTANCE	PRIZE MONEY	JOCKEY	RATING	POSITION	RUNNERS
Upbeat Cobbler	6-Jan-15	Bangor-on-Dee	Nov. Hand. Chase	3m	4K	Tom O'Brien	97	UR	7
	5-Feb-15	Taunton	Nov. Hand. Chase	3m 2½f	4K	Tom O'Brien	97	PU	12
	8-Mar-15	Market Rasen	Hand. Hurdle	2m 7f	3K	Andrew Tinkler	101	REF	5

RUNS	1ST	2ND	3RD	4TH
17	2	2	2	1

HORSE	DATE	COURSE	RACE	DISTANCE	PRIZE MONEY	JOCKEY	RATING	POSITION	RUNNERS
King Of Keys	29-Feb-12	Bangor-on-Dee	Nat. Hunt Flat	2m ½f	1K	Denis O'Regan	–	PU	8

HORSE	DATE	COURSE	RACE	DISTANCE	PRIZE MONEY	JOCKEY	RATING	POSITION	RUNNERS
	9-Feb-13	Warwick	Nat. Hunt Flat	1m 6f	1K	Aidan Coleman	–	3	8
	11-Mar-13	Taunton	Nat. Hunt Flat	2m ½f	2K	Aidan Coleman	–	4	7
	1-Nov-13	Uttoxeter	Nov. Hurdle	2m 4f	3K	Liam Treadwell	–	4	12
	16-Nov-13	Uttoxeter	Maiden Hurdle	2m 4f	2K	Liam Treadwell	–	5	11
	30-Nov-13	Bangor-on-Dee	Nov. Hurdle	2m 3½f	3K	Harry Challoner	–	4	7
	13-Dec-13	Bangor-on-Dee	Nov. Hurdle	2m ½f	3K	Robert Dunne	–	8	15
Royal Palladium	12-Mar-14	Huntingdon	Maiden Hurdle	3m 1f	3K	Liam Treadwell	104	2	7
	21-Mar-14	Newbury	Hand. Hurdle	3m ½f	3K	Aidan Coleman	104	7	17
	21-Oct-14	Exeter	Hand. Hurdle	2m 2½f	3K	Aidan Coleman	104	7	12
	11-Nov-14	Lincoln	Nov. Hand. Chase	2m 4f	4K	Aidan Coleman	100	1	4
	24-Nov-14	Ludlow	Nov. Hand. Chase	3m	6K	Liam Treadwell	105	1	8
	4-Dec-14	Market Rasen	Nov. Hand. Chase	3m	7K	Aidan Coleman	112	1	6
	15-Jan-15	Ludlow	Hand. Chase	3m	9K	Mr W. Biddick	124	F	7
	12-Feb-15	Leicester	Nov. Hand. Chase	2m 6½f	6K	Aidan Coleman	124	4	5
	10-Mar-15	Cheltenham	Nov. Chase	4m	50K	Mr T. Hamilton	122	UR	17

RUNS	1ST	2ND	3RD	4TH
15	3	1	1	4

UNDER ORDERS

HORSE	DATE	COURSE	RACE	DISTANCE	PRIZE MONEY	JOCKEY	RATING	POSITION	RUNNERS
	3-Mar-13	Huntingdon	Nat. Hunt Flat	1m 7½f	1K	Denis O'Regan	–	13	13
	24-Oct-13	Ludlow	Nov. Hurdle	2m	3K	Jake Greenall	–	6	14
	13-Nov-13	Bangor-on-Dee	Nov. Hurdle	2m ½f	3K	Denis O'Regan	–	5	7
	13-Dec-13	Bangor-on-Dee	Nov. Hurdle	2m ½f	3K	Liam Heard	–	5	15
Six One Away	29-Mar-14	Uttoxeter	Hand. Hurdle	2m 4f	3K	Denis O'Regan	106	PU	9
	25-May-14	Uttoxeter	Nov. Hand. Hurdle	2m 4f	2K	Denis O'Regan	100	7	8
	23-Oct-14	Southwell	Hand. Hurdle	1m 7½f	3K	Charlie Poste	95	PU	14
	3-Dec-14	Ludlow	Nov. Hand. Chase	2m 4f	5K	Jake Greenall	90	4	9
	21-Dec-14	Fakenham	Nov. Hand. Chase	2m ½f	3K	Jake Greenall	87	2	5
	12-Jan-15	Plumpton	Hand. Chase	2m 1f	2K	Jake Greenall	87	PU	6

RUNS	1ST	2ND	3RD	4TH
10	0	1	0	1

HORSE	DATE	COURSE	RACE	DISTANCE	PRIZE MONEY	JOCKEY	RATING	POSITION	RUNNERS
Pretty Mobile	3-Oct-14	Wolverhampton	Maiden Flat	2m ½f	1K	Denis O'Regan	–	PU	8
	2-Nov-14	Huntingdon	3 YO Hurdle	1m 7½f	3K	Jake Greenall	–	6	11
	7-Jan-15	Ludlow	Maiden Hurdle	2m	2K	Jake Greenall	–	10	14
	2-Apr-15	Ludlow	Nov. Hurdle	2m 5½f	4K	Jake Greenall	–	4	5

RUNS	1ST	2ND	3RD	4TH
4	0	0	0	1

HORSE	DATE	COURSE	RACE	DISTANCE	PRIZE MONEY	JOCKEY	RATING	POSITION	RUNNERS
Super Sam	5-Nov-14	Chepstow	Maiden Hurdle	2m 3½f	1K	Aidan Coleman	–	1	11
	29-Nov-14	Bangor-on-Dee	Nov. Hurdle	2m 3½f	3K	Liam Treadwell	–	3	5
	17-Jan-15	Taunton	Hand. Hurdle	3m	6K	Callum Whillans	111	3	9

RUNS	1ST	2ND	3RD	4TH
3	1	0	2	0

HORSE	DATE	COURSE	RACE	DISTANCE	PRIZE MONEY	JOCKEY	RATING	POSITION	RUNNERS
Another Cobbler	29-Nov-14	Bangor-on-Dee	Nat. Hunt Flat	2m ½f	2K	Jake Greenall	–	5	6
	12-Apr-15	Market Rasen	Maiden Nat. Hunt Flat	2m ½f	2K	Jake Greenall	–	9	12

RUNS	1ST	2ND	3RD	4TH
2	0	0	0	0

HORSE	DATE	COURSE	RACE	DISTANCE	PRIZE MONEY	JOCKEY	RATING	POSITION	RUNNERS
The Artful Cobbler	9-May-15	Warwick	Nat. Hunt Flat	2m	1K	Tom O'Brien	–	10	16

RUNS	1ST	2ND	3RD	4TH
1	0	0	0	0

RECORDS BY SEASON

	RUNS	1ST	2ND	3RD	4TH
2002–2003	4	0	0	0	0
2003–2004	3	0	1	0	0
2004–2005	4	0	1	0	0
2005–2006	7	0	1	0	0
2006–2007	14	2	2	0	0
2007–2008	12	3	1	4	2
2008–2009	34	6	3	2	3
2009–2010	31	5	4	5	3
2010–2011	43	3	10	4	3
2011–2012	41	8	5	3	4
2012–2013	35	8	4	5	4
2013–2014	43	2	6	4	4
2014–2015	41	6	3	4	5
	312	43	41	31	28

RECORDS BY HORSE

	RUNS	1ST	2ND	3RD	4TH
Transatlantic	10	0	1	0	0
Thievery	34	3	5	2	3
Ordre de Bataille	24	4	2	5	2
Timpo	30	3	7	4	1
Key Cutter	26	3	8	1	0
Cobbler's Queen	19	4	3	2	1
Llama Farmer	11	1	0	0	1
Safran de Cotte	26	7	0	5	3
Miss Tique	8	1	1	0	0
Arctic Ben	38	5	5	5	8
Sole Survivor	8	1	1	0	0
Sixty Something	25	5	4	2	2
King of Keys	1	0	0	0	0
Royal Palladium	15	3	1	1	4
Pretty Mobile	4	0	0	0	1
Upbeat Cobbler	17	2	2	2	1
Six One Away	10	0	1	0	1
Super Sam	3	1	0	2	0
The Artful Cobbler	1	0	0	0	0
Another Cobbler	2	0	0	0	0
	312	43	41	31	28

COST BY SEASON

	£	NO. HORSES IN TRAINING
2002–2003	6,209	1
2003–2004	7,472	1
2004–2005	21,576	2
2005–2006	30,987	3
2006–2007	27,205	3
2007–2008	60,990	4
2008–2009	80,382	7
2009–2010	109,996	11
2010–2011	137,064	12
2011–2012	138,859	12
2012–2013	101,599	10
2013–2014	161,349	11
2014–2015	149,480	14